EFFECTIVE TEACHING STRATEGIES WITH THE BEHAVIORAL OUTCOMES APPROACH

By MURIEL GERHARD

Here are 15 strategies you can use in your classroom immediately, to adapt conventional teaching methods in a new, more practical, more effective way than ever before!

These dynamic strategies are part of the new Behavioral Outcomes Approach (BOA) developed by Muriel Gerhard under a grant from The Fund For The Advancement of Education of The Ford Foundation.

Proven in actual classroom settings, BOA is the most practical modern way to motivate pupil self-direction . . . develop thinking skills . . . increase knowledge . . . and improve learning at all levels of ability.

Here's how this practical, easy-to-use guide will go to work in *your* classroom—

Self-Directed Behavior: BOA motivates pupils to learn, and to continue to learn *by themselves!* A learning climate called Responsive Environment motivates pupils to instruct themselves, set their own goals, and measure their own achievement with a minimum of teacher direction. What this means is:

- **Increased class participation!**
- **Improved self-discipline!**
- **More thorough learning in all subject areas!**

Develops Thinking Skills: You'll be particularly pleased with the BOA method that gives you a systematic way to develop thinking skills. The method enables you to develop pupils' thinking skills, while you teach subject matter quickly, easily! Your BOA thinking skills program comes with teaching aids that simplify the entire process:

- **Definitions and illustrations of the thinking processes**

- A Teacher's Periodic Table of the Thinking Processes
- Sample questions and activities you can take right from the book!

Accelerates Learning: Special BOA strategies enable you to easily determine realistic mastery levels for each student. This prevents pupil frustration . . . builds a positive attitude toward learning . . . eliminates the need for remedial instruction . . . accelerates the entire learning process!

Simplifies Planning: BOA Learning Units replace the lesson plans used in traditional approaches. These units enable you to teach tool skills, thinking skills, and content material at the same time. They also simplify the planning process and increase teaching efficiency while they save you time and effort!

The program comes complete with step-by-step directions for planning your own learning units, including a sample unit you can take right from the book!

Easy-to-use: Behavioral Outcomes requires no special equipment, plant facilities, grouping or scheduling procedures. You get complete details on how you can adapt conventional methods to the Behavioral Outcomes Approach without adding to your teaching duties or causing any frustration to your pupils.

If conventional methods have gone stale in your classroom, you'll want to begin using Behavioral Outcomes at once! The experienced teacher will admire its practicality. The beginning teacher will find its concrete guidelines and practices are indispensable tools.

When you see the difference in *your* classroom, you'll agree that Behavioral Outcomes is a whole new adventure in teaching!

egies

proach

PARKER PUBLISHING CO., INC.
West Nyack, New York 10994

Printed in U. S. of America

Effective Teaching Strategies
with the
Behavioral Outcomes Approach

Muriel Gerhard

Parker Publishing Company, Inc.   *West Nyack, N.Y.*

Printed in the United States of America
ISBN—0-13-246728-3
B&P

Dedication

To   Mark and Michelle
and
all our young people
who desire more than
procrustean schools

Acknowledgments

I owe the formulation of this book to the teachers and administrators of the Norwalk Public School System who were receptive to new ideas and were willing to give of their time and energy to bring this philosophy and approach to life. I am especially indebted to Dr. Esin Kaya, whose knowledge and guidance served as the impetus to this program and whose influence changed the course of my professional career. To Dr. Harry Becker, superintendent of the Norwalk Public School System, I extend my deep gratitude for his steadfast support in implementing and expanding this program. Nor for one moment can I forget the extensive efforts of Miss Helen Patterson and Dr. Milton Watenberg whose assistance and encouragement reinforced this total endeavor. To Mrs. Joan Gilbertie, I owe special thanks for her secretarial assistance.

My fullest measure of gratitude is to my family whose encouragement, support and understanding made this an adventure rather than a difficult task. As a parent and as an educator, I therefore dedicate this book to Mark and Michelle and all our young people who seek responsive schools in order to build a more responsive future.

The Purpose of This Book

The Behavioral Outcomes Approach, on the basis of actual experience and careful evaluation, has demonstrated great promise with all kinds of children. It has transformed the learning process into a stimulating, challenging, meaningful experience for all involved. Measured results have emphasized that education is a process involving far more than the passive transmission of knowledge. It has demonstrated that children can be taught to think for themselves, to learn how to acquire knowledge so they may continue to learn after their period of formal schooling. It has demonstrated that children who are provided with a responsive environment will experience an interest and intense satisfaction in learning that often exceeds the results from previous approaches.

In essence, the approach is characterized by three major factors: establishing the responsive conditions in which children become autonomous learners—using structured questions to promote the pupil's use of a variety of thinking processes—along with the initial and continuous use of diagnostic tools that help measure and insure increased effectiveness of results.

The total procedure transforms education into the dynamic, self-fulfilling interactive process that, in reality, it should be. How this is done is the purpose of this book.

The Behavioral Outcomes Approach focuses upon the development of the thinking processes in the learner and is described in detail as it was actually implemented with real children and real teachers. The exact procedures are spelled out in detail so you can apply the procedures to your own situation.

As most of us know, the day of "cork and funnel" teaching has passed. Johnny is not expected to come to school, remove the cork at the top of his head and expect the teacher to pour in the information and replace the cork. Nor is he expected to return the next day, remove the cork and regurgitate the information on the sacred test. There is more to education than merely transmitting knowledge and skills. Whether we listen to the scholarly wisdom of Dr. Marie Hughes or study the books of the late Dr. Hilda Taba, we have an increasing awareness that teaching is interaction and that children acquire information by processing (thinking) data.

If you are seeking an approach which stimulates children to *want* to learn, to become *actively* involved, to *enjoy* learning and value the time they spend with you, then the contents of this book provide the guidelines you need.

Your experiences will not be limited to passive reading. Ample opportunities are provided for you to interact with the materials. Exercises and self-quizzes enable you to become actively involved in employing a variety of thinking processes, to evaluate your own progress, to receive feedback and reinforcement, enabling you to put the materials to the most practical use.

Whatever your role in the educational community—experienced teacher, specialist or administrator, you will profit from the application of the Behavioral Outcomes Approach.

Muriel Gerhard

Table of Contents

Effective Teaching Strategies
with the
Behavioral Outcomes Approach

1

Analyzing the Teaching-Thinking-Learning Process

The Impact of Change on the Educational Scene

If there is one thing we can be sure of in education today, it is change. The educational ostrich is extinct! The educational ecology has been undergoing tremendous change, and the patterns of change are affecting all facets of the educational structure. School organizational plans, administrative practices, teaching methodologies, technological advances, knowledge of the nature of learning and human development are being carefully scrutinized and reexamined; a diversity of innovations is being implemented in an attempt to bridge the gap between theory and practice and to translate new knowledge into sound, constructive action.

As educators we have worked with the realities of the educational scene. We have operated under similar conditions, so aptly described by Belle Kaufman and John Holt. In educational research we have forged ahead in an attempt to arrive at empirical data to determine what is really known about the educative process, what are the conditions of learning and what constitutes effective teaching, in order to design better educational systems.

We have felt the impact of factors such as the knowledge explosion, the population and technological explosions, the dire need for improved curricular alternatives, for the application of new technologies, for the construction of new testing techniques, and for better ways to realistically provide for individual differences.

17

Building the Foundation for a Program
to Meet Pressing Educational Problems

In building a foundation for a program to meet these problems, we must face the hard facts and clearly specify our basic premises:[1]

- There is and never will be one panacea in education.
- Reality is characterized by change and therefore we must meet change with change.
- Our ability to predict precisely our children's future needs and problems is extremely limited.
- Individual differences exist among all of us whether we be pupils, teachers, or administrators.
- If educational practices are to be effective, they must be geared to these individual differences.
- If we are to provide children with the best education possible, we must operate with the foregoing premises in mind and transform our schools and all its components into flexible, modifiable instruments of education.

A Detailed Analysis of
the Behavioral Outcomes Approach

A program which is based on these premises and which achieves promising educational results is the Behavioral Outcomes Approach. This approach focuses upon the actions or behaviors of pupils which result from the teaching-learning process. The central concern is simply—what is the pupil able to do and what does he actually do as a result of our teaching?

Behaviors may be classified as *overt* or *covert* actions. Overt actions are those which are observable, as exemplified by a pupil being able to write a word; covert actions are those which are not observable, as exemplified by a pupil thinking or emoting about a given experience. A pupil's behavioral outcome may encompass both overt and covert components—and usually does.

Furthermore, both overt and covert behaviors occur within three domains. These domains are: the *cognitive* or knowing and thinking area, the *affective* or the feeling and emotional area, and the *psychomotor* or manipulative area. All behaviors fall into a combination of these three domains. For example, a child may read a short poem aloud and enthusiastically interpret its meaning to his classmates. The process of reading aloud involves both the psychomotor domain (speaking) and the cognitive domain (decoding); the act of interpreting falls into the cognitive domain, and enthusiasm is a factor of the affective or emotional domain. Here the child operates in all three domains. Therefore the pupil's behavioral outcomes may be totally observable or partially observable actions involving a combination of domains, and may result from a short period of instruction, such as a one-hour lesson, or a series of learning experiences extending over a period of a month or more.

In sum, by the terms behavioral outcomes we mean the overt and covert pupil behaviors or actions which result from a short or long-range period of instruction. These outcomes or results are *changes* in the pupil's behaviors which are the products of the educative process.

Defining the Educative Process

At this point we enter into the crux of the program by defining the educative process. Education is seen as a series of *teaching-thinking-learning experiences* which serve to change pupils' behaviors in specific, desirable directions. The thinking processes have been inserted between the acts of teaching and learning. All meaningful learning takes place via the thinking processes; we learn by *processing* information, by analyzing, by generalizing, and by classifying, etc. Learning is a search for meaning. To understand, one must think! Let us look backward. How much have we forgotten during our long period of formal schooling? How much information has gone down the drain simply because it was learned in a rote and meaningless context? What we have retained have been the products, the behavioral outcomes of thoughtful learning experiences, which have been applied and utilized.

This is not to say that rote learning has no place in education. It has, but it is a minimal place. Rote skills are retained only when they are in constant use. We are all too well aware of the fact that there are no rote solutions to new problems. Todays' world and tomorrows' world require thinking adults capable of creating and molding a better culture, of searching and discovering new solutions. Therefore our key goal of education must be the development of the child's thinking abilities

Our schools have a variety of educational objectives ranging from the development of the three R's to the promotion of self-direction, positive self-concepts, and human values and valuing. However, the goal serving as the organizing force is the development of the thinking processes. For in the process of achieving any of these goals—in acquiring knowledge, in the development of tool skills such as reading, writing, or computation, in learning to learn, in liking oneself, in valuing others, the child must apply his thinking processes. The basic unifying thread in the fabric of education is thought.

The Key Factors Operating in the Behavioral Outcomes Program

Viewing thought or process as the central goal, the behavioral approach is implemented by the combined utilization of three factors:

- the establishment of a responsive environment;
- the use of teaching strategies which promote the thinking processes;
- the use of diagnosis and continuous evaluation to measure pupil progress.

Establishing the Responsive Environment

Only within a responsive environment can the behavioral approach operate. This is a climate in which both pupils and teachers are free to interact, are free to attend to each other, to respond to each other, to be themselves and to become themselves. Pupils are not only given the opportunity to question, to make mistakes, to challenge each other intellectually, but they also take this freedom and use this freedom. Pupils become autonomous learners.

When we enter a responsive classroom, we immediately sense the difference: it is one of pupil involvement, wholesome interaction, the give and take of learning, and the realness of behaviors. The typical educational pingpong of "the teacher questions and the pupils respond correctly" is not in evidence. Within this setting the pupils ask their own questions, seek answers they need in order to fill their own conceptual voids or lacks, and strive to understand rather than arrive at the correct answer in response to the specific text-book questions.

In this setting pupils are not motivated by the grade, the gold star, and the need for the "perfect" paper to be displayed on the bulletin board, for they have begun to experience the satisfaction that can emerge from the active pursuit of real learning.

How we establish this environment will be dealt with in detail in Chapter 12. But what we must fully recognize at this time is that the responsive climate is an essential condition for behavioral change and growth.

Using Teaching Strategies Which Promote Thinking

Equipped with a responsive environment, we now incorporate the second major factor, the utilization of teaching strategies which *match* our objectives. Accepting the development of the thinking processes as the central operating goal which permeates all educational goals, we must then provide pupils with ample opportunities to *process* or "think through" information. Practice in process will promote and develop process. Therefore the teaching strategies as well as the materials, media, and texts we select must be adapted and geared to achieve this central purpose.

Traditionally, teaching strategies have been classified as a series of methods ranging from the lecture, discussion, and recitation to the multi-method, the project, the self-discovery, and the self-selection approach. Provided with these methods, how do we use them to promote process and how do they fit within the behavioral approach?

All of these methods serve a vital role and are an integral part of the approach. The essence of the approach lies in the kinds of questions the teacher structures to accompany each method.

- A lecture is presented—followed by a series of provocative questions centering on the contents of the lecture.
- An open-ended demonstration is presented—followed by pupil observations, explanations, theorization, and testing of the proposed theories.
- A discussion is initiated eliciting a variety of pupil viewpoints—followed by the requirement to substantiate these viewpoints with relevant data.
- A project is initiated to serve as a vehicle—followed by cooperative planning on the part of pupils and teachers in a systematic search to enlarge certain concepts.
- A problem is posed—followed by the self-discovery method in which relevant data is gathered, analyzed, and synthesized, resulting in testable hypotheses and possible solutions.
- A multi-method approach is employed involving a combination of a variety of methods and multisensory materials—followed by better pupil adaptation of individual learning styles to process data, acquisition of skills, and reinforcement both of the knowledge and skill development.

Whatever method or combination of methods is used, the thinking processes become an integral part of the process and product. The questioning techniques employed by the teacher and pupils are the basic factors. How to develop these questioning techniques and how to adapt them to the variety of teaching methods to achieve content, tool skills, and process goals will be dealt with extensively in Chapters 5 through 10.

Diagnosis and Continuous Evaluation of Pupil Progress

The use of diagnosis and continuous evaluation of pupil progress is the third operating factor in this approach. Diagnosis and evaluation are the most used and misused words in education today. There is no doubt that both of these processes are absolutely essential and that without them education becomes a blind, haphazard process. When we fail to use them we are operating in the same manner as the pilot whose directional equipment broke down and who reassured his passengers over the loudspeaker by announcing, "We are still lost, but do not be concerned, for we are making excellent time!"

The first step in the behavioral approach is diagnosis. We determine where the pupil is, what previous knowledge and skills he has acquired in a specific area, and what his weaknesses and lacks are. This data serves to assist us in determining the content, skills, methods, and resources to be used.

Let us assume that in terms of specific goals we have pre-tested or diagnosed our pupils to determine their present level of mastery. We then proceed to teach. However, this initial diagnosis has simply provided us with a profile of pupil progress at time X and nothing more. Continuous evaluation is now in order. We continuously assess the pupils' outcomes; pupils and teachers cooperatively review the progress in terms of their goals, and arrange and rearrange learning experiences.

The Behavioral Outcomes Approach makes extensive use of diagnosis and continuous evaluation initiated by the pretest and expanded by the use of written tests and performance tests as well as pupil-teacher conferences to determine whether the behavioral goals have been achieved. How these pre and post-tests are constructed and utilized will be dealt with in Chapter 11, providing the teacher with practical step-by-step procedures as well as sample items and tests which have been classroom tested.

Understanding the Effects on Pupils

Having identified the factors which operate in the behavioral approach, we now ask the crucial question: What are the effects of the program on pupils? Let us diverge for a moment and ask ourselves another question: Given optimal conditions, if this were humanly possible, what pupil effects do we as teachers and administrators strive for as a result of the educative process? A common reply would be: "We want our children to demonstrate increased achievement in the subject matter areas, mastery of the basic tool skills such as the three R's; we want them to be creative individuals, having a positive self-concept, capable of extending their own education and holding sound human values." These would be ideal end results.

Concerning the pupil's daily life in the classroom, as teachers we would make other educational "wishes." It would be *ideal* if pupils came to class self-motivated, not wasting a minute, getting right down to their tasks; if pupils attended and responded with great interest and were actively involved in an anxiety-free learning partnership with teachers and other pupils. This is *not* idealism, nor does it fall into the realm of an educator's vague "wishes," for let's take a look at the effects of the behavioral approach on pupils.

As a result of the pilot program involving 2,600 pupils and utilizing control and experimental groups, the following significant findings were established:[2]

- Pupils who had been taught by this approach demonstrated greater achievement on tests which called for the *processing* of information and the application of this information to new situations than did pupils who had been taught by conventional methods.
- Pupils who had been taught by this approach demonstrated greater growth in the development of their thinking abilities at the end of the year than comparable pupils in the control groups.
- There was no difference between the experimental and control pupil groups on the standard achievement tests. This is not suprising because the standard achievement tests measure one's recall of specific bits of information rather than one's ability to apply knowledge and understanding to unfamiliar situations.

In essence, these results, which were found significant at the .001 level, indicated that this approach produced growth in thinking skills and increased achievement in the meaningful acquisition and application of knowledge.

After a five-year period, the evaluation of the participating teachers in terms of pupils' day-to-day classroom behaviors yielded the following significant effects:

- All kinds of pupils, whether they were classified as low, average, or superior achievers, were highly motivated to learn.
- All kinds of pupils were more actively involved in classroom activities.
- Given time to adjust to the approach, pupils asked more questions and discussed problems with each other and the teacher more freely.
- Pupils viewed their teachers as warm, friendly human beings rather than evaluators or "grade givers."
- Pupils had more positive self-concepts. They not only liked themselves and others better, but also were willing to tackle new problems with greater self-confidence.
- Greater self-direction was evident. Pupils freely offered their own plans for specific activities and evaluated their own efforts.
- Pupils enjoyed thinking for themselves.
- Pupils were not flawed by the mistakes they made, but felt "It was just the way that everybody learns."

As for the long-range effects, teachers found that *more* children achieved mastery of tool skills and content and that the total learning climate was more vivid, alive, and satisfying. "You could easily tell if the teacher had used the approach during a certain class period. When the kids came out of the room, there was an exuberance, a sense of excitement that enveloped them," was heard again and again.

It was interesting to note that initially some of the superior achievers or accelerated youngsters in the junior high schools displayed an open hostility to the approach. "Mr. Jackson, as a teacher you are paid to tell us the answers!" But, after a few weeks, when these same pupils were asked if they would prefer to return to the conventional approach, the reply was a unanimous "No!"

A Listing of the Effects on Teachers

Had teachers not seen the value of this approach, had they not demonstrated enthusiasm and a commitment to continue, this book would not have been written. What the teachers experienced themselves and observed in their classrooms convinced them that they were moving in the right direction. The effects of the approach on teachers were dramatic. Those teachers involved in summer workshops seemed to live, breathe, and dream about the approach. The excitement generated in the summer workshops was contagious. Once the teachers returned to their classrooms and began to implement the approach, their feelings were characterized by a mixture of enthusiasm and frustration. They became aware that in spite of the fact that they had always felt they had taught the importance of *thinking,* they had not really utilized this approach to the extent that was possible. They became aware that the most difficult tasks were to refrain from giving information, to refrain from a large amount of teacher-talk, and to structure questions on the spot in terms of how the pupils responded. They were reluctant to return to conventional methods; some experienced guilt feelings when they did. Their initial frustrations and their analysis of their own teaching patterns served to strengthen their determination to continue.

The pilot study at the close of the first year clearly demonstrated that these teachers had changed in that their methods were more thought-oriented than during the pre-workshop period. As the program progressed, more and more teachers volunteered for the year-round workshops. Their decisions were based on what their colleagues had shared with them at lunch and other informal meetings as well as what they observed in terms of pupil reactions. Some teachers with 15 to 20 years of experience who had adopted the attitude of "I'll wait and see," soon joined the ranks and gave freely of their talents and experiences. The workshops were characterized by a realistic give and take; people were communicating, sharing problems, exchanging ideas and materials, and working together. Principals, department heads, and social workers as well as teachers were active members of the workshops. Communication was clearly evident when one principal remarked, "I have found these workshops invaluable. Now I really understand the extensive efforts that teachers make in implementing this approach."

The overall effects in terms of teacher interest, teacher satisfaction and professional growth have not been measured by objective, statistical means but they are clearly evident—the workshops continue, requests for advanced workshops are growing, new books on cognition and inquiry are circulating. Teachers are investigating means of promoting process via tape and television and through the adaptation of current materials to the approach. Many have become "intuitively" cognitive. It has become a more natural, effortless process. What is most important is that the program is becoming a teacher-propelled program characterized by realistic commitment rather than by administrative compliance.

The Reactions of Parents

The pupils' enthusiasm promoted parental interest. "What's happening in room 307? What is this behavioral approach?" These were questions which were answered in a variety of ways. PTA talks were devoted to the approach followed by question and answer sessions. Teachers invited parents to become students and gave lessons illustrating the approach. Newspaper articles described the basic philosophy and methodology. Requests such as, "May Paul have a behaviorally-oriented teacher?" were frequent. It appears that the proper use of the approach and its gradual implementation providing teachers, pupils, and parents with time to explore, adjust, and accept the new focus are the factors which are promoting its continual success. Parents are enthusiastic about the results of the approach; they are able to describe the changes they see in their youngsters.

Some parents have shared their own encounters with the approach at home: "I don't tell my daughter that she cannot go to the movies; I merely ask a few questions. Then I get the response of 'I don't think I'd better go because I won't have enough time for the things I have to complete.' We have fewer quarrels at home when I give my daughter a chance to make her own decisions rather than starting off with a dictatorial: 'No, you can't go because. . . .'"

In essence, based on the reactions of all involved—pupils, teachers, administrators, and parents—the program is proving to be a successful, satisfying educational venture and adventure. Our directional signals are operating, our course is clear, our time is good, and our results are extremely encouraging. We are all too aware that we are moving into the future at a rate unprecedented in history and that before we fully realize it, tomorrow will be here, but we are confident that we have an educational approach that will better equip our children for a more meaningful and realistic tomorrow.

FOOTNOTES

[1] Muriel Gerhard, "Behavioral Outcomes: What the child is able to do—and does—as a result of the teaching-learning experience." An excellent on-the-job report of the beginnings of this program has been presented in *Grade Teacher Magazine,* Teachers Publishing Corporation, Darien, Connecticut, April, 1967. This article is copyrighted ©1967 by CCM Professional Magazines, Inc. All rights reserved.

[2] Esin Kaya, "A Report on the Evaluation of the Behavioral Outcomes Pilot Program" (unpublished Mimeo 1965).

ABOUT THE AUTHOR

MURIEL GERHARD is Co-Director, in charge of Planning and Instruction for Project A.M.P., a regional program training teachers in the individualization of instruction. Preceding Project A.M.P., she served as Coordinator of the Behavioral Outcomes Program in a large Connecticut public school system. The productive results of this program led to a lengthy feature article in *Grade Teacher* magazine, and ultimately to the development of this book. Mrs. Gerhard received her B.A. from Brooklyn College, her Masters from New York University and is presently continuing her postgraduate studies. In 1965 she was instrumental in developing the Behavioral Outcomes Research Study and served as the Project Director of the program until its completion in 1967. The results of the research study served as the basic structure of Project A.M.P. which utilizes the Behavioral Outcomes Approach in an individualizing framework.

Mrs. Gerhard has served as a consultant to many school systems, has written articles on various aspects of BOA and has been a speaker at national, state and local conventions.

0-13-246728-3

2

Revitalizing Schools for
Meaningful and Relevant Learning

What is a school? How is a school facility transformed into a place where children not only are sent to learn, but also want to learn and do learn? How does it become an activating center generating enthusiasm, involvement, satisfaction—a place where each and every youngster searches for and finds meaning and relevancy?

Distinguishing Between Key and Facilitating Variables

What constitutes a school? What are the key factors operating within this setting? What are the facilitators which serve only as secondary roles or functions?

Let's stop and analyze "the school." We are faced with a variety of parts, all coming together like the pieces of a puzzle to make a vital whole. These parts can readily be identified.

First, we think of the school plant. We recall the little red schoolhouse and then our thoughts zoom ahead to the modern varieties of school plants. We find commonplace, conventional structures, unique structures, and most unique structures ranging from sectional schools, ameboid schools, snail-shaped schools, and schools in towering skyscrapers. We find egg-crate classrooms, flexible partitions, and the wide-open learning spaces lacking walls of any kind. Carpeting, lighting, varying floor heights, and sectional furniture serve as dividers in some of these plants. The architects' creative designs continue to amaze us as they modify the physical facilities. But physical facilities are precisely what they are: physical facilities which make possible a variety of school organizational patterns ranging from small group instruction to large group instruction, team-teaching, self-contained instruction, and numerous other patterns. But again, these are physical facilities to facilitate learning. Are these features of the school plant, the shape and the size of learning areas, of vital importance? Are they to be viewed as the major or key components of a school? The answer is quite apparent. No! Of course these features should not be underestimated, but neither should they be overestimated. But do we still regard them as key factors? Have we been conditioned?

I recall attending a conference of outstanding educators, researchers, and school architects who met to discuss the major factors operating in the teaching-learning process. The chairman set the stage by suggesting that we begin with a group of children in an open field. I was amazed at the difficulty we all experienced in generating ideas, for we were all stymied by the open field. We had been conditioned to think of education as taking place within a school plant. We had difficulty in taking off our traditional glasses. Only when we had enclosed that field and had a physical structure in our mind's eye could we move ahead.

As a result of a lengthy discussion, there was little doubt of the value of the physical facility, and that as the facility became more flexible it became more facilitative, but that it was by no means a key factor. It was clear that education can and does take place anywhere. Therefore the school plant was a secondary factor.

Another part of "the school" is the organizational pattern. There are few of us today who are not familiar with the variety of patterns being utilized, such as the self-contained classroom, cooperative teaching, team teaching, the dual progress plan, pupil teams, multi-age grouping, non-graded plans combining team-teaching with self-contained instruction, and other types of continuous progress procedures. These plans are serving to arrange and rearrange pupils and teachers into instructional groups to facilitate learning. They make possible a variety of groupings for specific instructional purposes, but the pattern of the grouping itself does not directly result in learning. The words used are "they make possible"—but these patterns do not insure anything! The organizational pattern is a secondary factor.

The administration is still another part of "the school." Key factor or facilitator? The principal and his assistants are individuals who are skilled in providing the educational leadership in the school. They are responsible for the smooth operation of the school. The administrator, as captain of the ship, commands, steers, and guides the ship and is accountable for the welfare of its crew and passengers.

How many times have we heard our colleagues and parents speak of principal X who runs a "tight ship"? Running that ship, tight or otherwise, is an essential function, but can we view it as a major factor? Let's hold our decision in abeyance and explore further.

Thus far we have looked at the physical plant, the organizational pattern, and the administration, and now we encounter another component, the curriculum. The specific bodies of knowledge and skills constitute a portion of the curriculum. We speak of the three *M*'s, namely Methods, Materials and Media. Important? Yes! Key factors? Let's continue our exploration.

Still another component of the school is the teaching staff. The teacher—a key factor or a facilitator? Entertain the notion of schools without teachers. Of course children can and do learn without teachers! They learn from books, films, television, a variety of teaching machines, computer-assisted instruction, and many other sources. But can these sources and resources diagnose a child's needs, guide a child, answer his specific questions, encourage him when he needs encouragement, assist him at the right time, help him develop healthy attitudes, interact with him, listen to his ideas and feelings and help him develop them, make him feel wanted and accepted as an individual who values himself and others? Can they promote the growth of a human being and provide him with a healthy self-concept, with a sense of human values as well as knowledge and skills? Is there a replacement for the human teacher?

At this point let us pause, for it is so simple to be simple, but let us not be simplistic. There is a need to take a hard look at "the school" and focus upon the most important, the more important, the important, and the least important components. For too long, we have been evading this question. As educators we do not doubt the essential functions and roles of school facilities, organizational plans, administrators, and curriculum, but we have not confronted the major factors. One key factor obviously is the teacher. A school is as effective as its teachers. But you may readily ask at this time, "What is an effective teacher?" We will analyze this "effectiveness" further on in this chapter, but let us go on to deal with the other major factor of the school, the pupil.

Schools for Children or Children for Schools?

At this point we should ask ourselves if we have "schools for children" or "children for schools." This question has been most clearly and vividly answered for me by a famous story told by an outstanding educator. He described the extensive efforts of a community, whose educators designed and built a beautiful school facility, carefully screened and employed the best administrators and most competent teachers available, selected a fine curriculum—and then it happened! On September 7th "the facility opened—and the wrong kids came to school!" The wrong kids? Are there wrong kids or are our lenses reversed? "Oh," we may reply, "it is quite obvious. Schools are designed for children. Children should not be designed for schools." But do we fully realize this? Of course every educator "knows" that children have individual differences. We do a beautiful job of verbalizing this. We do an excellent job of quoting each other. We "know" that schools should be tailored to meet individual differences, but are we still not in the era of Procrustean schools? Are we still attempting to remold children to fit our preconceived notion of education? Are we diagnosing children's needs and designing and redesigning our schools and all of their parts to meet and match those needs? "Wrong" is a word that is *not* applicable to children. There are *wrong* facilities, *wrong* administrative practices, *wrong* organizational patterns, *wrong* curricular offerings, and *wrong* teachers for specific children. The *match* is wrong; the match of school and all its components to the child! If this is the case, then let us begin where we should—with the diagnosis of children's needs. Let us begin to match and utilize, in terms of current knowledge, all of the components of the school to best serve these needs as realistically as we are able at time "now."

There is nothing new in the statement that there is no uniform prescription for all children. Teacher X may be the right teacher for child A, but the wrong one for child B; curriculum offering I may be great for child A, but inadequate for child B; team-teaching may be most effective for child C, but a self-contained classroom may be more supportive for insecure child D. We can go on and on. And we do! We persist! We pre-select, we plan, we design, we create, but we fail! We fail to start at the right point, and that right point is the child. Our paper plans are great, but they will only serve paper pupils—and they do not exist!

The Major Components—Pupils and Teachers

Our schools, then, have two major components, the pupils and the teachers. These are the most difficult components with which we deal. For here we interact with human variables, and yet are not these human variables the essence of education, the essence of living, of coping, of striving, of dreaming, and of becoming?

Too many educators grow fearful of human variables for they are not readily shaped, reshaped, or channeled. They are not readily controlled. It is a *relatively* simple task to design a school, to establish an organizational pattern, to select curriculum, and to control to a very large extent the physical, material, and monetary operations of a school. The results are highly predictable in these instances. But when we deal with changing human behavior, we are confronted with a tenuous hypothesis. Our movements are inhibited by the unpredictable, contaminating factors which suddenly emerge. But as educators we know that this is the case and will continue to be the case, and that we must modify all the components as each case warrants in terms of current knowledge. This is the only way to provide for human education, to discover better methods of transforming our schools into flexible, meaningful, relevant learning centers where children emerge and develop rather than become stifled and remolded into a robot cast. Our schools must be modifiable; they must not be bound by paper procedures, organizational patterns, schedules, and predetermined curricular guides. For these give only a semblance of ship-shape schools with crews and passengers who follow the "correct" procedures. In reality we are confronted with mutinous crews and passengers who are anxious to abandon ship at the earliest possible time.

Therefore let us focus our efforts on pupils and teachers and apply available diagnostic tools to determine the existing individual differences in them. Let us identify strengths and weaknesses and build on both these qualities in a realistic fashion. Let us set aside the old recipes, the old lenses, and take a good hard look at the key ingredients and work with them. Our purposes are to develop effective learners and teachers by utilizing and modifying all facilitating components to achieve this goal.

Up to this point, we have placed the components of the school in two key categories: (a) the pupils and teachers, and (b) the facilitating components, including the physical plant, the administration, the organization, the curriculum, and—we dare not forget—the budget and the community and its expectations. What we have said can be summarized in two statements and then reduced to one.

1. A school's effectiveness can be measured by the effectiveness of its

learners, by the learning outcomes in terms of growth and achievement along a variety of dimensions.

2. A school's effectiveness can be measured by the effectiveness of its teachers, the degree to which they promote the growth and achievement of pupil learning along a variety of dimensions.

In essence, how a school utilizes all of its components to obtain optimal conditions to promote pupil learning would constitute its degree of effectiveness.

How Teachers Perceive Pupils

Since our focal points should be pupils and teachers, let's begin by viewing pupils. The first day of school, we enter our classrooms and there they are, pupils with individual differences. This is our first "given," inescapable and real. But do we really observe them? What are our perceptions of these pupils based on our previous training and experience and our own experiences as pupils? What information do we use at the onset of the semester that immediately colors our perceptions and thereby establishes our expectations?

Have we been told that this group is the "accelerated," the "above average," the "average," the "low average," the "disadvantaged"? Has a perceptual set been established for us? What kinds of fallacious categories have been imposed?

Have we perused the records and noted the pupil's I. Q. and assumed that this is the complete measure of a child's intelligence as well as his potential? Have we read the comments of our colleagues and accepted them as gospel? Have we systematically or otherwise narrowed our vision and established "realistic" goals for the group? What kind of self-fulfilling prophecies have we generated? Have we reduced Johnny to a composite of an intelligence quotient, standard achievement scores, and the assessments of his previous teachers who had followed the same procedure? Have we quoted each other in terms of Johnny's potential until we all firmly believe it?

I cannot help but recall a remark made by a resourceful principal, "If you say it long enough, they finally get to believe it." In all probability, the myth of Johnny is perpetrated day after day and year after year. There is a need to stop quoting each other, to clear our lenses and open the shutter wide and let the whole of Johnny in as he is at time "now." We need to be wary of those halos we toss about and the hypothetical expectations we establish for our children, and observe what does indeed occur. Then we must modify these expectations.

The Effects of Teachers' Perceptions on Pupil Behavior

The results of the Rosenthal and Jacobson study merit our careful consideration.[1] The central concept behind their investigation was that of the "self-fulfilling prophecy." "The essence of this concept is that one person's prediction of another person's behavior somehow comes to be realized."

Rosenthal informed teachers that based on "obtained" results, specific pupils would demonstrate significant gains in academic achievement and could be viewed as potential academic "spurters." The data given to the teachers were false. The children who were designated as "spurters" were randomly selected. What was startling was that children from whom teachers expected greater intellectual gains did indeed demonstrate these gains.

In addition it was extremely interesting to note how the teachers perceived these "spurters." When asked to describe these children, the teachers stated that "they were more curious, more interesting, alive and more autonomous learners and had a better chance of experiencing happiness and success in later life than did their peers."

Essentially, Rosenthal had established rather glowing teacher expectations which obviously had some effects upon teacher behavior which in turn promoted pupil learning. Rosenthal had hypothesized that the teacher expectations may have been communicated by the teacher's tone of voice, facial expressions, or posture and this in effect somehow enhanced the child's self-concept, level of motivation, and cognitive skills. Further research will be needed to test this hypothesis. However, it appears that the "self-fulfilling prophecy" does operate, although we cannot offer a clear-cut explanation of the intervening variables functioning or specify the sequence of behaviors which are operating.

We began our exploration of the pupil by verbally accepting individual differences and by viewing the diverse ways, adequate or inadequate, by which we establish our pupil expectations, and we have touched lightly upon grouping procedures prevalent in many schools by which we label and group the "pupil specimens."

Examining Current Concepts of Pupil Models

A review of recent research provides us with a variety of extremely interesting pupil categories or models. The work of Heil, Powell, and Feifer[2] introduces a classification system based on pupil personality profiles. Utilizing the inventory "Assessing Children's Feelings," these researchers arrived at four pupil designations: the strivers, the conformers, the waverers and the opposers.

From our own experiences we can readily identify pupils who would fit these profiles. According to Heil and associates, children who are "strivers" may exhibit the following traits and behaviors:

- Set high goals of attainment for themselves.
- Demonstrate exhibitionistic needs by "show off" behavior.
- Withhold information regarding themselves.
- Anger readily in terms of scholastic achievement.
- Adhere firmly to the demands of society.

In describing the "conformers," the study yields the following traits:

- Accept and conform to adult standards.
- Are highly social-oriented.
- Manifest strict control of hostility and other impulses.
- Emphasize and attempt to demonstrate mature behaviors.

The "opposers," as we might anticipate, characteristically:

- Evidence disturbed authority relationships.
- Demonstrate feelings of inadequacy.
- Are usually pessimistic.
- See themselves as a selected target for hostility of others, peers as well as adults.
- Refrain from taking personal responsibilities for their actions.
- Demonstrate "show off" tendencies.
- Deny any push toward school achievement.

As for the "waverers," generally it is found that they:

- View adults as threatening, rejecting, and punitive.
- Become readily hostile toward adults, peers, and siblings.

- Are extremely fearful.
- Demonstrate high anxiety.
- Withdraw from emotionally-toned situations.
- Will not accept responsibility for themselves, place blame on others.
- Flounder and are indecisive.

The Heil study is indeed fascinating in terms of pupil personality profiles. Yet based on experience, additional profiles come to mind. The anxious pupil, who is fearful of all new experiences, who has to be eased into a situation and encouraged, and who does succeed after passing the anxiety barrier. The apathetic pupil who clearly displays the "I couldn't care less" attitude by lacking enthusiasm, rarely becoming involved, and demonstrating listlessness by making few, slow, and feeble movements. The creative child who generates novel ideas and approaches, asks the unexpected questions, verbalizes unique relationships, and engages in divergent thinking. The individualist who appears to have established his own patterns of behavior and who seems to be saying, "Here I am, accept me or reject me; the choice is yours."

All of us could probably go on and arrive at numerous other categories and specify the accompanying behaviors, but what are we really doing? How many children have we taught who were hybrids or mixtures of these traits; how many children have we known who were strivers in one context, opposers in another, creative in a third, and firm individualists in a fourth? What makes Johnny a conformist in one setting, a striver in another, and an opposer in still another? What causes a bright, creative youngster to abandon the school environment? We can readily answer the question with a global answer, "A variety of variables." Yet, based on our own day-to-day experiences, we have found that desirable behavioral patterns can be established and undersirable patterns can be reshaped. Of course, further research is needed to provide a more adequate empirical framework but as teachers, our educated and experiential intitution tells us this can be done. The kind of behaviors our children display in the classroom can be modified and shaped by us. Some of these profiles may serve as useful tools but we must ask ourselves, "In what context and under what conditions is pupil A displaying X behavior?" Only then can we begin to undertake the task.

In sum, if pupil models serve to narrow our perception, if we merely substitute one set of models for another, we will fail. Only as we use these models as partial tools, only as we try to view the total context, the total classroom interaction and transaction, will we make some progress. There is a deadly finality to the misuse of and total reliance upon pupil models which serves to restrict teaching practices. We categorize pupils and then sit back and explain the lack of progress by the fact that a child is "low average" or "apathetic." The process is ridiculously circular and the results are nil. If we are to extricate ourselves from this futile cycle and become effective teachers, we must become more cognizant of the variety of factors operating within our classrooms and we must attempt to view the total spectrum.

This brings us to the question of "What is an effective teacher?" The word *effective* is least effective here and must be expanded, for we are fully aware of the complexity of the question. An effective teacher for whom, for what, and under what set of conditions? As practicing teachers, let's take a look at the current status of teachership, and delve briefly into the research on teacher profiles in an attempt to arrive at some realistic data which we can apply here and now.

Identifying Characteristics and Roles of a Variety of Teacher Models

Within the past 20 years, the concept of the role of the teacher has undergone considerable change. The teacher is no longer viewed as the transmitter of knowledge, but as a diagnostician, a guide, an interactive participant in the the educative process. The objectives of education are no longer limited to the three *R*'s, reading, writing and arithmetic, but now encompass thinking skills, social skills, self-directive skills, and attitudinal changes. Therefore the teacher's role has taken on new dimensions.

In terms of these new roles and in terms of current research in the area of teacher characteristics and patterns of influence, can we construct a composite picture of a living teacher who will be effective for all kinds of pupils, for a diversity of purposes under a variety of conditions? Is this humanly possible or are there other solutions?

If we examine the research data in the area of "teacher," we find extensive investigations along four dimensions: dimension *one* encompasses the teacher's demographic traits and personal characteristics such as age, sex, marital status, intelligence, social-emotional adjustment, childhood and adolescent experiences, and socio-economic status; dimension *two* deals with the teacher's training, knowledge, skills, and experience; dimension *three* includes the teacher's attitudes toward pupils, teachers, administrators, education, and educational practices; and dimension *four* focuses upon the teacher's role and functions and classroom behaviors ranging from her classroom personality to her teaching strategies.

As we would expect, the largest number of research studies has been in the fourth dimension, the teacher's total pattern of behavior in the classroom. Of course it is anticipated that the teacher's demographic traits, training, knowledge, skills and attitudes affect her total pattern of classroom behavior and thereby indirectly affect pupils, but it is the total pattern of day-to-day behavior which has a direct impact on the pupils. Extensive data in terms of demographic traits, training, knowledge, skills, attitudes, and educational viewpoints have been gathered by D. Ryans in his ten-year study of teacher characteristics.[3] However, most of the data were correlates and the results could not be generalized. The most practical data were those which dealt with in-classroom behaviors or patterns of influence. By patterns of influence the researchers simply included all teacher actions from the moment of entrance into the school until dismissal time. This emphasis was upon not only what the teacher does, but also how she fulfills the role.

The earlier research studies viewed the teacher's pattern or style in terms of poles. The teacher was operating at one pole or at the other. She was either democratic or autocratic, integrative or dominative. The recent studies provided a more realistic view of teaching style, for the teacher was not seen as operating at the extremes, but along a continuum. Here the researchers were asking, what percentage of the time does the teacher demonstrate one kind of behavior and what percentage of the time does she demonstrate the opposite type of behavior? Here, the researchers were describing the living teacher in action.

One of the most realistic and significant series of studies on teacher behavior presents the I/D teacher profile.[4] The *I* simply stands for the percentage of the time the teacher displays indirect behavior and the *D*, the percentage of the time the teacher displays direct behavior. The result is a ratio depicting where the teacher is on this indirect-direct continuum.

But first we must have a clear-cut picture of indirect and direct teacher behavior. When you and I are indirect, we demonstrate the following behaviors:

1. Accept clarify and support pupils' feelings
2. Praise and encourage pupil behavior
3. Accept, clarify, and use pupils' ideas.
4. Ask questions to stimulate pupils' participation in decision-making.
5. Ask questions to orient pupils to school work.
6. Spend a greater percentage of class time listening to pupils rather than speaking.

When we are direct, on the other hand, we: (1) lecture, (2) give directions, and (3) criticize and justify our authority.

Naturally, if we were asked for an instinctive reply to the question, "Would you prefer a direct or indirect teacher?", most of us would choose the indirect teacher. But our experience clearly points out that there are times when direct teacher behavior is essential.

This I/D teacher profile is the work of N. Flanders and T. Amidon. The use of the interaction analysis scale and matrix which these researchers have produced has yielded some extremely significant findings. For example, it was found that when pupils were instructed by a teacher who had a high I/D ratio (utilizing the indirect pattern a large percentage of the time), the pupils demonstrated increased achievement in knowledge and tool skills.[5,6] It was found that the high I/D teacher was more effective with dependent-prone children and apathetic children in that the dependent-prone children became less dependent and the apathetic less apathetic. It was interesting to note that the high I/D teacher was more flexible and modifiable and could readily change her pattern from indirect to direct as needed.[6] However, the low I/D teacher, who was direct most of the time, had difficulty in becoming indirect.[6] Additional data, meriting our attention, indicate that the high I/D teacher engaged in a greater degree of teacher-pupil planning, obtained more information about her pupils, acquired increased knowledge of subject matter as a result of using the indirect pattern, and spent far less time disciplining the class.[5] What is of far greater importance is the practical value of this process of interaction analysis when used by the teacher to analyze her own behavior, to begin to see herself, and to work gradually to change her own pattern of behavior toward a more indirect mode.

Another teacher profile which emerges from a variety of research studies is what this writer calls the cognitive teacher. Whether we turn to the Behavioral Outcomes Research Study, the work of B. O. Smith and M. Meux on the "Logical Dimensions of Teaching," the work of R. Suchman on "Inquiry Training," the work of the late Hilda Taba, or the numerous studies on problem-solving, we are convinced of the value of teacher use of thought-provoking strategies.

"What precisely is a cognitive teacher?", you may ask. This is a teacher who structures the classroom activities by asking the kinds of questions which promote the pupil's use of a variety of thinking processes such as inductive and deductive reasoning, comparison, analysis, classification, categorization, divergent production, creative thinking, critical thinking, and many others. This is a teacher who serves as a "thinking" model, for it is not long before the pupils ask the *why* and *how* questions rather than the *what, who,* and *when* questions, which we have overemphasized in our conventional approaches. This is a teacher who promotes the "processing" of information rather than the mere recall of bits and pieces of data.

It is interesting to hypothesize what the impact of a high I/D teacher who utilizes the cognitive model would be on pupil achievement, thinking skills, self-concept, and attitudinal change, for the high I/D teacher creates the responsive environment so essential to cognitive growth.

Still another teacher profile, a personality profile, is found in the current literature. Again reference is made to the Heil, Powell, and Feifer study, *Characteristics of Teacher Behavior Related to the Achievement of Children in Several Elementary Grades.*[2] This study offers significant possibilities and might be classified as pupil-teacher personality matching. Determining the personality traits of pupils and teachers and placing specific types of pupils with specific types of teachers produced increments in academic achievement, as well as increased social effectiveness and self-direction and more positive attitudes toward schooling.

Heil's teacher personality profiles consisted of the self-controlling teacher, the turbulent teacher, and the fearful teacher. Based on the use of the Manifold Interest Schedule and Heil's Teacher Observation Scale, the self-controlling teacher may demonstrate the following traits and behaviors:

1. Is dominant, running the class with a firm hand.
2. Is orderly and prizes neatness, as demonstrated by having pupils do over papers that are not neat.
3. Is dependent and likes having a principal who takes a close interest in the things she does.
4. Exercises self-control by making sure that plans run smoothly and wants no "explosion" of any kind.

5. Plans in great detail all activities.
6. Is rigid in making "on the spot" changes.
7. Is very methodical and demonstrates an urge for compulsivity and ritualization.
8. Is self-severe in being a strict self-disciplinarian.
9. Is greatly concerned with cleanliness.

The turbulent teacher, as described by Heil, may demonstrate the following traits and behaviors:

1. States high likes and dislikes.
2. Deals with intellectual processes objectively.
3. Is outspoken.
4. Does not make any evaluative personal judgments about the children's interpersonal relations or their work.
5. Appears to lack any great need to be accepted by others.
6. Is spontaneous and appears unmethodical.
7. Enjoys dealing with ideas, enjoys abstract thinking.
8. Uses humor.

The fearful teacher is one most obvious to all of us. This teacher exhibits the following traits and behaviors:

1. Is most comfortable in work which is quite tightly prescribed by specific rules and procedures.
2. Appears to prefer work involving things and processes rather than people.
3. Responds more to her own needs than to those of the children.
4. Is low in leadership.
5. Is highly anxious, fearful and variable in her behavior towards children.

Most of us could probably identify colleagues of ours who would match these personality profiles. But if we focus on the results of pupil-teacher personality grouping, we find some intriguing results. The pupil personalities involved homogeneous groups of strivers, conformers, waverers, and opposers, each group being taught by a self-controlling teacher, a turbulent teacher, and a fearful one Some of us would probably like to stop our reading at this point, and make predictions as to how these children fared with these teachers in arithmetic, communication skills and science, and in self-attitudes and self-expression

The results of the study indicated that:[2]

1. Striving children showed increased achievement with all teachers.

2. The fearful teachers were uniformly ineffective with all kinds of pupils except the strivers, and had relatively clear-cut negative effects upon the children by inducing anxiety and arousing more primitive defensive reactions.

3. The self-controlling teachers obtained consistent achievement gains with all kinds of children. In direct contrast with the turbulent teachers, they obtained greatest achievement gains in reading and communication and least gains in arithmetic and science.

4. The turbulent teachers appeared to be most effective with conformers and strivers and quite ineffective with opposers and waverers. They obtained greatest gains in arithmetic and science and least gains in reading and communication skills. This pattern correlates directly with the interest patterns of this personality. These teachers appeared to promote more positive self-attitudes and freer expression of feelings in children.

5. It appeared that when opposers and waverers were taught by turbulent teachers, the children became less opposing and wavering and the teachers became less turbulent.

Although in our own classroom experience we have all been confronted with teacher-pupil personality clashes or mismatches, few of us have entertained the idea of personality groupings. From a practical point of view, a great deal of research is needed in this area prior to implementation. The study, however, raises a variety of questions, such as will this type of personality grouping in terms of content areas consistently promote greater pupil achievement? If so, at what age levels? Can we recruit new teachers more effectively if provided with personality profiles, and place them more appropriately in terms of pupil personality groups? Be it as it may (the much-used statement must be made); in this case further research is needed.

We have now dealt with but a few teacher models or styles: the high or low I/D teacher, the cognitive teacher, and the teacher as a personality profile. We can readily devote the next ten years to exploring the research on teacher effectiveness. This statement is based on a mere 15 months spent on full-time concentrated research in this area. Yet we are still confronted with, and cannot evade, the key question—*What is an effective teacher?* Can a conclusive answer be given? Can we reduce teachership to a formula? The answer is obviously *no*, although many have attempted to do just that. Are these teacher profiles of any practical value? Can we profit from research and abstract some working guidelines? The answer to both of these questions is obviously *yes*. We can readily see the value of high I/D pattern of influence, of a focus on thinking skills or the use of the cognitive model, of the awareness of personality interaction and transaction in terms of the effects which they promote and in terms of the pupils' behavioral outcomes.

Guidelines to Promote Teacher Effectiveness

Combining the work of all of these researchers, guidelines to promote teacher effectiveness can be stated as follows: A teacher moves toward greater effectiveness as she begins to—

1. Accept and develop pupils' ideas and feelings.[4]
2. Praise and encourage pupils.[4]
3. Stimulate pupil participation in decision making.
4. Listen to pupils[4]
5. Interact with pupils.
6. Promote process of thinking skills.
7. Establish a responsive environment where children are given the freedom to become autonomous learners.
8. Specify pupil objectives in behavioral and measurable terms.
9. Specify goals with clarity so that pupils understand precisely with their goals are.
10. Work cooperatively with pupils in specifying goals.
11. Use diagnostic tools.
12. Use a variety of methods, materials, and media.
13. Work cooperatively with pupils in evaluating achievement of goals.

These guidelines are working guidelines. Many of them will be expanded into concrete operations in this book. They are being utilized by classroom teachers and are demonstrating their practical value in terms of pupil outcomes. Teacher effectiveness has by no means been completely operationalized, but this does not mean that we, as teachers, cannot move ahead in terms of current data.

IN SUMMARY

We have taken a close look at "the school." We have identified the two major factors operating within "the school"—the pupils and the teachers. The facilitating factors such as the school plant, the organizational pattern, the administration, the curriculum, the community, and the budget have been viewed as secondary factors. A variety of pupil and teacher models were described as well as the factors which affect the way teachers perceive pupils. The concept of teacher effectiveness was analyzed and guidelines for practice were identified. The task of revitalizing schools for meaningful and relevant learning can be achieved only if we view these parts in their proper perspective and direct our energies and efforts toward the major factors of "the school"—the pupils it is designed to serve and the teachers who serve our pupils.

For success in revitalizing the schools we must utilize the proposed guidelines in our classrooms. Inputs that are merely informative, whether they stem from books, journals, inservice courses, or post-graduate work, are not inputs unless they are put into practice, carefully evaluated, modified in terms of the evaluative feedback— and demonstrate concrete results. Knowledge and the best of intentions are of little value unless they are functional. In essence, the educational process will become dynamic and realistic only to the extent that our inputs are transformed into actual efforts and practices in our classrooms. This is our task.

FOOTNOTES

[1] Robert Rosenthal and Lenore F. Jacobson, "Teacher Expectations for the Disadvantaged," *Scientific American,* Vol. 218, No. 4, April 1968, pp. 19-23.

[2] Louis M. Heil, Marion Powell and Irwin Feifer, *Characteristics of Teacher Behavior and Competency Related to the Achievement of Different Kinds of Children in Several Elementary Grades* (Washington, D.C.: Contract ∝SAE 7285, Cooperative Research, Office of Education, U. S. Department of Health, Education, and Welfare, May 1960).

[3] David G. Ryans, *Characteristics of Teachers—A Research Study,* [American Council on Education, Washington, D.C.] (Menasha, Wisconsin: George Banta Company, Inc., 1960).

[4] Ned A. Flanders, *Helping Teachers Change Their Behavior* (Ann Arbor, Michigan: The School of Education, University of Michigan, October 1965).

[5] Ned A. Flanders, "Some Relationships Among Teacher Influence, Pupil Attitudes and Achievement," *Contemporary Research on Teacher Effectiveness,* eds. B. J. Biddle and W. J. Ellena (New York: Holt Rinehart and Winston, 1964). pp. 196-231.

[6] Edmund J. Amidon and Ned A. Flanders, "The Role of the Teacher in the Classroom" (Ann Arbor, Michigan: The School of Education, University of Michigan, 1963 [Mimeo]).

3

New Educational Objectives—
A Blueprint for the Future

The Inadequacies of Current Educational Goals

In Chapter 2 we introduced the concept of "schools for children" as opposed to "children for schools." "Schools for children" reaffirmed the belief that if schools are to play a constructive role in these changing times and retain their relevancy and reality, they will have to be transformed into modifiable, flexible learning centers. They will have to be reshaped continuously to meet society's ever-changing needs and to translate these needs into educational goals and experiences to prepare our youth for the world that is, as well as for the world that is to be.

New goals will have to be established, for our current educational objectives are outdated. To most of us, this is not a new or startling statement. Despite our extensive and dedicated efforts, the schools have remained static; they do not reflect the times; they do not reflect the needs of life as it is lived outside the classroom walls. They are still caught in the quicksand of tradition; they still foster archaic standards, passivity, and conformity. They maintain a world divorced from the life forces that are struggling to be heard, to be channeled and to emerge as new constructive energizers.

Today's youth are activated by a multitude of stimuli; stimuli which many of us did not experience during our early years. They live in a vibrant, changing, and increasingly complex world—but are subjected to an education of obsolescence. They experience the impact of a multiplicity of explosions—knowledge, technological, ideological, sociological; they are keenly aware of the critical problems confronting us, but are held aloof and, more importantly, are not provided with the kinds of skills and structures of knowledge which will equip them to deal with the present and the future effectively, efficiently, or courageously.

As insiders, who work on a day-to-day basis with children, we can no longer cling to a naive faith in education. There is a need to reassess our objectives, our practices, and our procedures in an attempt to match reality. The new kind of education which is emerging must be characterized by a process which promotes knowledges, skills, attitudes, and values of changeability. Changeability is defined as the ability of an individual to cope with variation and diversity, to control and alter the forces about him, to mold and reshape them both in the internal and in the external world. Therefore, education for change constitutes our key objective. If we assign top priority to the process of changeability and operate within this framework, we will begin to close the gap between the current goals of the schools and the goals of life itself.

Fully accepting changeability as the overriding or central goal of education and moving beyond the valid criticism leveled at our schools and the eloquent phrases of our colleagues, we must address ourselves to a few very specific questions. What are the current educational objectives? To what degree do they foster the process of changeability? What should our new objectives be and how can we systematically and realistically move to implement them?

Let us begin by taking a realistic look at current educational objectives. To put it bluntly, the question of "Which ones?" confronts us vividly. The objectives which we view in the well-written, glossy brochures of X school system or the objectives actually implemented in the classrooms? The discrepancies between the written statements and the in-class implementations are decidedly great. Undoubtedly the "real" objectives are those actually implemented in the classrooms. These can readily be identified and classified, for they are as old as schooling itself: the acquisition of specific bodies of information and the development of basic, broad tool skills and specific tool skills. In practice, these two objectives are given the major emphasis. They are indeed important objectives, but they are by no means the only objectives, nor will they in total promote the needed skills of changeability.

However, in keeping with the most current literature, numerous school systems throughout the country have "tacked on" other objectives—the development of problem-solving, the promotion of self-concept, and the fostering of independent study, to mention but a few. But in practice few of these "tacked on" objectives have been systematically implemented in the majority of the classrooms. For the most part, they receive verbal homage, but they clearly indicate a significant trend—and they raise a few crucial questions. Are not these "tacked on" objectives of equal or greater importance than those which are being implemented? Should we not be taking a hard, critical look at all of these objectives, whether we call them old or new, traditional or most current, and attempt to produce a viable blueprint for education?

Today, more than ever before, there appears to be general agreement among educational leaders as to the new goals to be established as well as the old goals to be discarded. The voices of recognized authorities such as Jerome Bruner, Robert Hutchins, Bruno Bettelheim, Donald MacKinnon, and Herbert Thelen are being heard. Many of our old goals require redefinition and revision if they are to become relevant. Many of our practices are outdated; many of our innovations have not been clearly understood by the innovators and are being implemented with negative results.

For the most part, few of us as experienced educators would disagree with the following statements as to what our educational objectives should not be:

- They should not serve to maintain the status quo or "status past." This is not adequate.
- They should not merely serve to transmit our cultural heritage by providing children with increased masses of factual data.
- They should not merely train our children in the broad tool skills. Broad tool skills are basic, but there is a need to incorporate new skills as well.
- They should not promote "problem-solvers" who solve pre-packaged problems devoid of personal meaning and personal inquiry.
- They should not stultify and stifle creativity in favor of thoughtless conformity to trivial practices and procedures.
- They should not reduce the child to a mass mold in order to produce common patterns of behavior.
- They should not inhibit the development of a sense of personal identity, inner freedom, and personal autonomy.
- They should not promote competitive attitudes at the expense of cooperation, compassion, and the spirit of humanness.
- They should not foster verbal values that are preached by all and practiced by few.

We can continue to add to the list of "they should not," but in truth, are not some of the above statements actual descriptions of current educational practice? Our schools continue to stress the "coverage" of subject matter and the training of broad tool skills. Manufactured problems are solved correctly; large masses of data are memorized in the "proper" sequence for recitation. Creative kindergartners become seventh-grade conformers. Children are still encased in bell jars and plotted on bell-shaped curves. The development of self-concept is left to happenstance. Competition, rather than cooperation, reaches its peak at the high school level. The teaching for values is reduced to platitudinous verbalizations. Need we go on?

"Education for Change," "Skills of Changeability," "Education for What Is Real" remain the titles of books or chapter headings, but this need not be the case for we are adequately equipped to take constructive action.

Proposed: New Goals for Educational Practice

What, then, may we propose as an educational blueprint for change? In view of all that has been stated and without belaboring the obvious any further, the following seven generic goal areas are proposed for thought and action:

1. Knowledge and "Knowing"
2. Tool Skills—Broad and Specific
3. Cognitive Processes
4. Self-Concept
5. Self-Direction
6. Social Effectiveness
7. Positive Attitudes and Interests

Knowledge—A Search for Personal Meaning

When we speak of *knowledge,* what precisely do we mean? Do I understand the term as you understand it? Does the term *knowledge* retain the same definition when it is used in the context of language arts, science, mathematics, social studies? Is knowledge simply a collection or a body of information classified into a variety of disciplines, or are we being shallow in our definition? As .erome Bruner[1] has so clearly indicated, does not each discipline have its own underlying structure, its own organizing threads, its own propositions, its own perspective, its own methods of investigation or "knowing," its own attitudinal sets and its own expectancies?

But we have not viewed knowledge as such nor have we taught for knowledge as such. In all probability, based on our own educational experiences, knowledge has indeed been viewed as a collection of data. We have been taught and still teach for subject matter—for bodies of facts. We continue to confuse knowledge with factual data. The "pipe line" education of data transmission continues.

Knowledge is not synonymous with information. Information becomes knowledge when it is processed, when it is transformed into meaning, when it is viewed in a specific contextual sense. For information to become knowledge it must be "accommodated," "assimilated," and "internalized."

By accommodation we mean preparing the child to receive information by giving him a conceptual framework into which the information can be "fitted." By assimilation, we are referring to the process by which the child acts on the information and transforms it by making it a meaningful part of his existing conceptual framework, thereby enlarging the framework. Internalization is the resultant of both processes. The child who has internalized information now "knows" and "understands." The fit has been completed and the knowledge *is* knowledge, for it is part and parcel of the child. We are in error when we view knowledge as a noun; it should be a verb, for all of us, children and adults, are engaged in "knowing."

In this process of "knowing" we sift, examine, and analyze information that impinges on all of our senses. More than ever before this process of "knowing" is crucial. Our children must be able to interpret information, differentiate between false and valid assumptions, identify deceptive propaganda, and view the truth as it relates to differing situations.

Therefore one of our major objectives is to provide our children with adequate opportunities to acquire (accommodate, assimilate, and internalize) knowledge or more accurately to be actively involved in the process of "knowing." This is a new objective for we are not striving merely to impart facts or information; what we are striving to do is to provide for increased concept formation. We may argue, and rightfully so, that facts or information are the building blocks of concepts. They are indeed. However, what we have been doing to date has been to stop short, by merely reducing "knowing" to a game of memorizing information rather than providing the proper climate, time, and conditions to allow the child to build concepts from this data.

In essence, "knowing" a discipline involves understanding the key concepts, generalizations, and principles; it means understanding the methods of exploration in that discipline. For example, a child's "knowing" in science is not merely the acquisition of specific facts or principles but, far more, it is the feel for the "sciencing" of the scientist. It is the understanding of how the scientist operates, feels, thinks; what attitudes he holds when he questions his environment and the environment responds or fails to respond. This is the essence of science. Having taught science as a fact-oriented teacher in the late forties and a structure-oriented teacher in the early sixties, I have seen the differences in my pupils. I question whether I really taught anything of any lasting value in 1947.

What is proposed here as the objective of knowledge or "knowing" is applicable to every discipline. If we view this objective in this context, we will provide our children not only with knowledge but also with the means for self-knowing. And this indeed is a major objective.

Tool Skills—Broad and Specific

The need for broad tool skills such as the three *R*'s is well documented. We have only to look at the way we live to determine the skills which are essential. No disagreement arises over the need for communication skills such as reading, writing, speaking, listening, or computational skills. Nor do we differ in proposing the need for specific skills such as the use of the ruler, protractor, slide-rule, microscope, or typewriter, to mention but a few. As long as we, both teachers and pupils, view these skills in terms of what they really are—means to an end; arbitrary skills; ways, procedures, or systems which we have established to perform a specific task, to achieve a given end effectively and efficiently—all is well.

But here is precisely where we fail. The objective of tool skill development is basic, is essential, is practical—but our methodology in providing instruction in this area is grossly inadequate. Too often we teach these skills as if they were the ends in themselves. We are so intent on developing these skills that we lose sight of their true purpose. We inform, we drill, we reinforce, and we hammer the skill to death. A large percentage of our children learn to read well, communicate well, and compute well—but how many of our children, in the process of skill development, learn to dislike and possibly hate to read and to write and to compute? In these cases, what, if anything, are we achieving?

Teaching a skill for skill's sake is a mistake. Let's get down to the practical level. Those of us who have worked with "difficult" children have learned that when we identify children's interests and use those interests which then become meaningful purposes for these youngsters, they want to read, they want to listen, they want to communicate, they want to develop skills. This is not a new idea. We have read about it in the texts of the twenties and thirties. But the point is—it works.

I have taught seventh graders to read, to compute, to learn by using interests such as hot rods, photography, and radios. These basic skills become operationally basic when they serve children's purposes. Skill development taught in a vacuum only develops in strivers and conformers. Those children who are not developing these skills must be taught them in a purposeful context. More of the same outdated methodology and the use of more practice results only in negative outcomes. Routine practice devoid of meaning is utterly useless. Practice must be viewed as a means of achieving a larger goal, not merely the goal of skill development. When a child is practicing because he is told to practice, he is going through a practice exercise, a series of motions and nothing more. This is not skill development.

In sum, our objective is to develop the essential skills in a purposeful context. The purposes will vary with different groups of children, but the skills will be developed because they meet a personal need for each child.

Learning is a natural process, as natural as breathing. One neither wants nor does not want to breathe—one merely does. The same is applicable to learning. The child's learning is a natural process. The factor of "wanting to" can be guided by each of us, by the context we search for, identify, and provide in terms of the youngsters' interests, expectations, goals, and emerging needs. The concept of the *match* is a practical approach in skill development. The need is to match the specific skills to the child's interests, purposes, and goals. We may be greatly surprised at the rapid and extensive skill development which children will demonstrate.

These basic tool skills, broad or specific, are by no means the only skills we seek to develop. New groups of skills are dramatically evident—cognitive or thinking skills, personal skills, social skills and humanistic skills are critically needed. This leads us logically to the next proposed objective, cognitive skills.

Cognitive Skills—The Thinking Processes

The development and widespread application of the thinking processes or cognitive skills should be the central and pervasive goal of education. In theory and in the literature of the field this is not a new objective. Recognized authorities in education have emphasized and re-emphasized this objective. John Dewey, prior to being "out-Deweyed," stressed the significance of the thinking processes in *How We Think;* Max Wertheimer aptly described this need in *Productive Thinking;* Hilda Taba, Jerome Bruner, Richard Suchman, Richard Crutchfield, James Gallagher, Benjamin Bloom, and numerous others have written extensively and taken constructive action to promote this goal.

In its 1961 report entitled *The Central Purpose of American Education,* the NEA Educational Policies Commission stated, "The purpose which runs through and strengthens all other educational purposes—the common thread of education—is the development of the ability to think. This is the central purpose to which the school must be oriented if it is to accomplish either its traditional tasks or those newly accentuated by recent changes in the world. To say that it is central is not to say that it is the sole purpose or in all circumstances the most important purpose, but that it must be a pervasive concern in the work of the school. Many agencies contribute to achieving educational objectives, but this particular objective will not be generally attained unless the school focuses upon it. In this context, therefore, the development of every student's rational powers must be recognized as centrally important."[2]

But in practice have we made substantial progress in implementing this goal by providing children with cognitive climates, cognitive opportunities, cognitive curriculums, cognitive instruction, and cognitive skills? As educators we have often told both lay people and our colleagues that it is an easy task to be critical. However, to be critical is not necessarily bad when one couples this critical set with realistic and constructive action.

The majority of our schools have made little progress in promoting thinking or cognitive skills. Traditional instruction is still the pervasive force, content-coverage is stressed and practiced, the college-bound students are being "prepared"; but the major skills of the educated individual, the cognitive skills, are being left to chance. Most schools are schools of content, schools of tool skills; rarely do they become schools of thought.

However, a rather large number of school systems have expounded the process approach, the discovery method, inquiry strategies, and the Behavioral Outcomes Approach. Innovative educators have engaged in stimulating and enthusiastic sessions involving demonstrations and lively discussions, but the stage of actual implementation has been reached by but few.

The educators' cognitive talk brings to mind a cartoon depicting two young children standing in a classroom and looking intently at a large sign which in bold letters has one word—*Think*. And one child is saying to the other, "I know what it says, but how is it done?"[3]

Those of us who have devoted extensive time and energy to promote and further develop children's thinking skills are able to provide realistic guidelines and strategies to enable others to achieve this goal. How this is done will be dealt with in Chapters 5 through 10. But prior to the "how," we as educators must be firmly convinced of the value of this goal. Even more, we must have substantial evidence that this is indeed a realistic goal—namely that when children are provided with ample opportunities to process information by applying a variety of thinking skills in numerous disciplines they do demonstrate significant gains in these cognitive skills.

Evidence of this sort is available. To cite but one example, the research conducted by Covington, Crutchfield, Goodwin, Klausmeier and others has yielded significant findings.[4] In school studies, utilizing many hundreds of fifth and sixth grade children over a period of years, these researchers have found that children who were provided with cognitive opportunities significantly surpassed their matched controls in practically all of the variables of productive thinking performance.

As these researchers point out: "The trained children (trained in thinking skills) excel in being sensitive to puzzling facts, in asking relevant information-seeking questions, in generating ideas of high quality, in seeing problems in new ways, in planning a systematic attack on problems, in evaluating ideas and in achieving actual solutions to problems."

What was extremely significant in these research studies was that this type of training in thinking skills produced significant gains in children of average and below average IQ as well as for higher IQ children.

Again to quote Dr. Crutchfield: "Indeed, despite the substantial initial correlation found between productive thinking performance and IQ, the effect of the training is such that trained children of average intelligence (mean IQ of 99) come to score virtually as high on the productive thinking tests as do the untrained children of high intelligence (mean IQ of 124)."

For a long period of time, many of us have searched for evidence of this type–evidence which in effect would say to the classroom teacher: Your average and low average children have thinking skills other than recall which can be further developed and strengthened. Children can and should be made aware of these thinking skills which they possess. Their minds are not merely memory banks, but sharp tools which can be honed and refined still further.

Children are capable of utilizing these skills to a far greater extent than they or we are cognizant of. We have not developed these skills in terms of the children's potential simply because we have not given them ample opportunities to practice the skills in a diverse and large number of contexts. Teaching for thinking is a key goal of education. It is a critical goal today. Education should be the teaching-thinking-learning process.

If we mirror society's needs and read the message, it is clearly apparent that in all phases of life we are seeking "thinking" individuals, individuals who are able to be creative, analytical, and critical; individuals who can identify and specify problems, provide divergent possibilities as solutions; individuals who can synthesize new solutions; individuals who are able to see new, unique relationships which few of us have ever dreamed of.

Industry has seen the value of Osborn's brainstorming techniques, of attribute listing, of Gordon's Synectics and many other strategies to release man's creative and cognitive potential. Our schools must do the same. The process of "knowing," of "becoming," of "coping" is a complex of interrelated cognitive, affective, and psychomotor components. The educational system cannot continue to pursue the traditional approach characterized by rote learning and content coverage. Education involves much more than this. If we are to move education off dead center, our course must be a highly cognitive course.

Self-Concept–A Search for a Positive Self

A major and critical goal area which has received extensive literary emphasis and which has been clearly demonstrated as vital to human functioning is the development of a positive, healthy, and productive self-concept. Self-concept has been described in a variety of ways. Social scientists have written and spoken about personal identity, finding oneself, becoming oneself, the feeling of individual uniqueness, the master skill of being, the knowing of "who I am," the ability to remain an individual in a mass society, and the freedom to be oneself and "win."

At times, the most dramatic way of defining or communicating the meaning of a term is by utilizing the back door approach and specifying what the term is not or what occurs when it is lacking. For example, the lack of self-concept has been best expressed for me by Emily Dickinson in her poem where she writes: "I am nobody! Who are you? Are you nobody too?"[5]

Were we to use the front door approach, we could readily accept the description by Jersild—the self-concept as a "composite of thoughts and feelings which constitute a person's awareness of his individual existence, his conception of who and what he is."[6]

As educators, we are familiar with many of the social scientists such as Erikson, Freud, James, Horney, Rogers, Maslow, Bettelheim, MacKinnon and others who have dealt analytically and systematically with the complex phenomenon of self-concept. We have read the descriptive data relative to the functioning of the self in the dynamics of how people behave and how the self-concept affects behavioral patterns. A beginning has been made and intensified efforts affording greater study of self-concept are in process. But the schools, the schools for children, have not utilized this data and converted it into practice.

There is not one sliver of doubt that self-concept is a prerequisite to learning; that it is a prerequisite to all of our actions. Each of us continuously confronts questions such as *Who am I?* and *What am I?* And our responses determine our actions, positive or negative. How we view ourselves and how others view us are communicated and determine our behaviors. If we view ourselves positively, we will act positively; if we view ourselves negatively or are viewed negatively, in many cases the results are self-defeating or destructive behaviors.

There is no lack of evidence to substantiate the "cruciality" of the development of a positive self-concept. Studies of school dropouts indicate the dire need. Those of us who have "taught" the dropout know the symptoms:—The student demonstrates a strong feeling of failure which appears to come from school experiences. The child fails to meet the school's expectations; he learns to fear disapproval, criticism of any ort, and ridicule He attempts to defend himself—he withdraws from the educational game for he is in the process of becoming a nobody. He becomes alienated from his peers, from adults. He has a feeling of overwhelming helplessness. He can see no purpose, no goal, no future. He lacks dignity and self-respect. He tries to stop the world; he has no alternative but to get off.

Of course the school is not the only factor operating here—but it can become a key factor in bringing about positive changes in how our children view themselves and can thereby alter and modify the behavioral outcomes.

Schools for children can promote a responsive climate for the development of self-concept. Many of us might place ourselves in the situation of the youngsters viewing the sign "Think" and merely substitute the word "Self-Concept" and ask, *How is it done?*

The guidelines and practices incorporated in the Behavioral Outcomes Approach will serve as a systematic beginning. The details will be provided in Chapter 12 but some general guidelines should be provided at this point.

To promote a positive self-concept, the pupil must become an active partner in the educational process; he should be involved in establishing his own goals working cooperatively with the teacher; he should be involved in personal inquiry, in discovery, and in realistic problem-solving. The school curriculum should be experience-based rather than primarily symbol-based. It should provide for direct, purposeful, concrete experiences, and insure a large measure of success for each pupil. Pupils who experience success will derive satisfaction from learning, which in turn will keep the cycle moving. The learning environment should be open and threat-free. Pupils should not be fearful of making mistakes, for most of us have learned far more from our mistakes than from our successes. Evaluation should be a shared process involving pupil self-evaluation as well as constructive teacher evaluation. Excessive use of praise or criticism promotes negative or meaningless results. Therefore, teachers should exercise care in evaluating pupils. Marie Hughes, in her writings, has provided useful guidelines for evaluating pupils with public and private criteria.[7] As teachers, when we provide public criteria we simply communicate the general rule and the reasons for the rule in terms of our behavior. When we provide personal criteria, we are communicating our suggestions for improvement in terms of the individual pupil's performance; his strengths, weaknesses, and needs. This is entirely different from the cold criticism so frequently leveled at pupils.

In sum, the development of self-concept should not be left to chance. The active partnership of pupils and teachers, the use of personal inquiry and realistic problem-solving, the introduction of an experience-based curriculum, the insurance of a large degree of pupil success, the cautious use of criticism and praise, and the use of pupil self-evaluation will serve to promote a more positive self-concept.

In addition the school can actively enlist the assistance of parents to achieve this goal. Numerous action programs indicate that parents can play a vital role in helping their children to improve their self-concepts. These parents are trained in methods to achieve this goal and the parental influence proves to be far greater than the conventional methods of group counseling or discussion with the pupils themselves.

In essence, self-concept will be promoted in our schools if we face up to the reality that we must modify our schools and operate on the premise that "Schools for Children" rather than "Children for Schools" is what is most desirable to meet current needs. We will have accomplished this goal when a child can say, "I count; my thoughts, my feelings are welcome here. I have something worthwhile to contribute. I can change things. I can help to make decisions. I can assist in guiding my education. I am somebody; are you somebody too?"

Self-Direction

The goal of self-direction has received its share of verbal and literary reinforcement. This concept of self-direction, encompassing learning to instruct oneself and then evaluating one's own behavior or progress along specific desired dimensions, is by no means new. The cruciality of this goal has become forcefully apparent.

We firmly believe in the pupil's freedom to initiate self-learning experiences, to establish goals which are relevant and meaningful to him, to select activities to achieve these goals, and to self-evaluate the degree to which these goals have been attained. We are firmly convinced that these self-directive skills are essential not only during the years of formal schooling but more importantly at the time that the educational umbilical cord is cut, for learning is a continuous process in the individual's life span.

Yet, this belief, however firm or strong, has not been translated into action. How many times have we as teachers and administrators been confronted with the pupil's question, "Mr. Z, what do I do now?" And how many times have we been tempted to reply, "Johnny, what do you think you should do now?"

But that question is an indicator of the kind of dependent-prone children we are molding. The message is there. The remedy is ours to prescribe. The question mirrors our teaching practices, the attitudes and the expectations we have so clearly communicated to our children. "Do it my way. Follow my directions!"

Of course we have made initial attempts at fostering self-learning. We have established pupil contracts, we have constructed individualizing learning packets, we have instituted independent study programs at the secondary level, we have provided specific pupils with a variety of choices in some learning activities. But the point is that we have not allowed the attitude of self-directiveness to permeate all of our teaching. We have not begun at the beginning—at the kindergarten level—and consistently reinforced self-directive behaviors. That children are self-directive from birth on is old hat to all of us but this is precisely the point—we have not worn that old hat!

We have only to visit classrooms or video tape ourselves in action to demonstrate the degree of directive teaching behaviors we exhibit and the degree to which we realistically provide for self-direction. In truth, many of us are fearful of letting it happen. We are fully capable of reciting the psychological data—but reciting the data and having the courage to promote self-direction are two different ball games.

We are all aware that we do not give a course in self-direction or initiate specific lessons in self-direction. This would not only border on the ridiculous, but would constitute sheer and utter nonsense. Nor is the remedy as simple as providing ample opportunities for self-learning.

All of us have taken numerous "courses," attended workshops, study groups, and conventions and learned the basics of self-initiated learning. First and foremost we are aware that although children may be given the responsibility for their own learning, they will not zoom into orbit and accept this responsibility. They will resist the initial opportunity. Providing them with additional opportunities will do little unless we as teachers and administrators establish the proper climate for this freedom.

Establishing this climate is by no means an easy task—for the climate is far more than the conventional curricular climate of a variety of available alternatives. It is a "person" climate. It is an atmosphere in which we as educators clearly communicate our trust in pupils as human beings. It is one in which we demonstrate our belief in the pupil's capacity to develop his own potential. It is one in which we display our sincerity, our realness, our honesty in our relations with our children. What we are communicating by our be haviors is that we care; we value our children; we accept their ideas, opinions, feelings; we have empathy and we are willing to give of ourselves, but we are not imposing ourselves on our children.

When we have succeeded in communicating all of these "person" messages we will clearly see the differences. When self-direction becomes truly behavioral, we will find that our children will have no need to utilize and adapt to our idiosyncrasies to achieve their goals. They will have no need to watch and carefully plan their "moves." Freedom will become a reality in that spontaneity of thought and action will be demonstrated. Children will exhibit flexible, creative behaviors; self-responsibility will increase, and the number of self-initiated tasks will grow. Adaptiveness and change-ability will confront us and we will be able to do more than speak of self-direction—we will see it, hear it and feel it. It will have happened.

In essence, by first creating an authentic climate for self-direction, by communicating our belief in the child's ability to be self-directive, by providing opportunities for these behaviors to take place, and finally by encouraging, supporting and guiding these initial steps, we will enable our children to become self-directive in-dividuals.

Social Effectiveness—Skills of Human Relatedness

Social effectiveness is proposed as another major goal of our schools. We do not lack high sounding statements to describe this goal. In essence, social effectiveness is human effectiveness. It is the application of the "skills of being human" to our total environment. These "skills" have been described as traits such as honesty, in-tegrity, responsibility, respect for others, cooperation, sympathy, empathy, compassion, authenticity and others. These "skills" are based upon what John Seeley[8] has so aptly described as "people knowledge," knowledge of the self, knowledge of others, and know-ledge of what I would call "us." As individuals we become more socially effective as we acquire increased people knowledge of the self, of others, and of us and apply these skills of relating in realistic day-to-day situations. In general, we are socially effective when we are able to achieve a balance between our individual needs and those of society.

Psychological data clearly indicates that children naturally seek activities involving other persons. In the primary grades, the children begin to develop skill in serving both their own interests and those of the group.

As educators we do not question the need for or the worth of these skills. Many of us firmly believe that these traits permeate our school environment and do develop in our children.

However, within the past five years, it has become increasingly apparent that these less tangible or intangible skills have not been adequately developed.

We are aware that we cannot develop these traits per se in isolation. We have confronted questions such as: how does one teach for integrity; how does one teach a child to reach out to others, to care for others, to share, to try to understand another's feelings, dilemmas; how does one convey the need to be real, to be sensitive to others, to value others although they differ from you; how does one develop a sense of humanity; how does one experience a sense of human purpose and human meaning?

Based on classroom experiences, we know children learn these "intangible" traits. We may recall the words of a famous song: "You have to be carefully taught to hate all the people your relatives hate, you have to be carefully taught."[9] We do not doubt that love, a sense of humanity, a sense of wholeness, and a sense of cooperative purpose can be taught. But how this is to be accomplished requires some specification.

The answer is partially found in the quest for "people knowledge"—knowledge of self, of others, and of us; of providing opportunities to know oneself and others; of entering into interactions and transactions; of being involved with authentic individuals; of discarding the game of playing school and of role-playing the stereotype of pupil and teacher, and of developing a free and open climate for the growth of humanness. These skills of relating will develop in an open climate provided that appropriate human models are available. In essence, we are addressing ourselves to the question of how we as educators, who serve as human models, demonstrate our authenticity.

Each of us is a product of our perceptions, our beliefs about ourselves and others, our values, and our attitudinal sets. To begin to reexamine ourselves and to move toward increased knowledge of self and others in order to become more authentic, is a difficult step. But it appears that this is the first step. Only as we move toward a greater knowledge of ourselves—only as we attempt to reach out and expand our people knowledge—will we serve to promote these traits in our pupils. Only when we serve as *living* models will we produce pupil behavioral change.

We can go back to the data provided by the Anderson and Brewer studies[10] which indicated that integrative teachers produced integrative behaviors in their pupils and that dominative teachers produced dominative behaviors in their pupils. We cannot lose sight of the power of the teacher as a model. The growth of social or human effectiveness in the pupil will be determined by the degree of human effectiveness demonstrated by the teacher. Texts on educational practices offer a variety of suggestions for promoting human effectiveness. These suggestions include: providing children with opportunities to work cooperatively in small groups; encouraging youngsters to critically analyze data and identify biases or unwarranted assumptions; utilizing role-playing and involving pupils in realistic encounters with diverse groups of people to acquaint them with cultural diversity. These are indeed useful methods, but their application, or the realization that diversity is not a weakness but a means of providing strength and growth, is not sufficient. Unless the teacher and the climate she provides are authentic, the process and the results will be the outcomes of the game and nothing more.

Social or human effectiveness must begin with the educator. A new type of inservice education is needed—one to promote the goal of developing authenticity. This training should assist each of us, teachers and administrators, in examining our perceptions of ourselves, of others, of our beliefs and our values; it should assist us in acquiring greater sensitivity to our students and in developing methods which fit our perceptions and beliefs. Once we as educators become actively involved in this type of assessment, we will be on the road to humanizing children rather than solely intellectualizing them. Only as we, the educators, gain greater insights in the skills of relating, can we anticipate increments in the human effectiveness of our children.

Positive Attitudes Toward and Interest in Learning

The proposed educational blueprint providing a statement of goals urgently needed to restore relevancy to education concludes with the goal of promoting positive attitudes towards and interest in learning. We can readily cite numerous instances to substantiate our limited success in achieving this goal.

We are all too familiar with the increased rate of student dropouts, of student rebellion, of the increased number of underground student publications and of the physical damage to educational resources and plants. These are indeed tangible proofs of the so-called intangible, negative attitudinal sets and lack of interest in schooling which an ever-increasing number of our children are experiencing. Need we go on?

It is of little practical value whether we label attitudes and interests as intangibles or less tangibles. The fact is simply that they are in operation; they are demonstrated by specific behavioral indicators. We can measure them and we can take constructive action to promote their growth along a more positive dimension.

It is common knowledge that when we speak of attitudes we are simply speaking of an individual's predisposition to act in a specific way in regard to objects, content, people, events, etc. The specific predisposition is a result of many factors. We may be global and state that any predisposition to act stems from an individual's total experiential background. Each of us tends to respond or interact with something or someone when we feel positive or favorable toward the stimulus; conversely, we tend to withdraw or refrain from any action when we feel negative, doubtful, or fearful in regard to the stimulus.

All of us, whether we are teachers, administrators, or students, bring our attitudinal sets into the classroom. Essentially, we have three major concerns. First, we are faced with the need to develop a continual awareness of our own set of attitudes toward the educational milieu. Second, we need to further develop our ability to sense and identify the behavioral indicators which reflect our pupils' attitudes towards learning. And third, once having pinpointed their attitudes, we must utilize our resources to move the pupils gradually and indirectly, along the positive side of the continuum.

How many times have we heard a teacher or administrator in desperation confront a pupil with, "I don't like your attitude!" How many times have we heard the response, "What are you going to do about it?" Do we lack instances such as "I'm learning my math, but I sure hate it!" "I hope I can sit through language arts today!" All of these statements are obvious indicators—indicators of negative attitudes as well as indicators of lack of pupil interest.

In regard to the factor of interest we have a variety of available definitions. For example, we may state that an individual displays interest when he chooses to attend to something and indicates that this something is of concern to him. Or we may enlarge this definition and state that the pupil displays increased attention to learning tasks and exhibits self-initiated participation by asking many questions, volunteering information, and bringing a variety of related materials to class. On the other hand, we may utilize the back door approach and arrive at a definition of interest by defining a pupil's lack of interest. For example, a pupil demonstrates lack of interest or involvement when he displays no desire to continue the class activity. Whenever the teacher stops "shepherding" the group, the pupil stops his work.

The point being emphasized is that as educators we are able to identify these "intangibles" such as pupils' attitudes and interests and therefore should be able to move toward their increased development.

It would indeed be naive to assume that we are solely responsible for these negative attitudes or for the lack of interest in learning, but we do have the responsibility of attempting to alter them. Sufficient data is available to enable us to establish the kind of psychological climate, to utilize effective educational procedures and resources, which would serve to promote this goal. Chapter 12, "Developing Responsive Pupils and Responsive Environments," will deal with these practices. This goal of promoting positive attitudes toward and greater interest in learning is by no means a simple one, but the urgency to take constructive action is dramatically apparent.

Understanding the Interactive Nature of These Goals

In sum, the proposed new goals for educational practice may be synthesized into the following statement: Each child will be provided with ample opportunities to acquire knowledge and tool skills, to develop and apply a variety of cognitive processes, to demonstrate growth in self-concept, self-direction, social effectiveness, and positive attitudes towards and interests in learning.

In essence the proposed blueprint provides for seven interrelated educational goals; each of the goals has an effect on all the others. The central or pivotal goal is the development of the thinking or cognitive processes. Sample interrelationships may be expressed as follows: The pupil's application of the thinking skills in acquiring knowledge and tool skills results in greater understanding and increased retention of these knowledges and skills. This increased achievement serves to enhance the child's self-concept, self-direction, social effectiveness, positive attitudes and interests, which in turn promote further achievement. Any one of these goals once achieved serves to enhance a series of others. One obtains a chain reaction. Increased knowledge, for example, provides the child with a larger information base enabling him to apply his cognitive skills in depth. Increased cognitive skills enable the child to become more successful in his self-directive behaviors. And this cycle continues in a variety of ways based on the individual pupil. The cognitive and affective domains are continuously interacting. The child makes his progress by moving along the rungs of two ladders, the cognitive ladder whose rungs include thinking skills, knowledge, and tool skills, and the affective ladder whose rungs include the feeling components of self-concept, self-direction, social effectiveness, and positive attitudes and interests.

All goal areas become intertwined and serve to promote the growth of the total child. Whether the term *total child* brings to mind associations of the "whole" child or shades of progressivism is of little matter, for our concern is with the total child. However, the goal which has served as our central focus has been the promotion of cognitive or thinking processes.

Why the Central Focus on the Thinking Processes?

The rationale for the focus on the development of the child's thinking skills was based on the following premises:

A. The key "constant" in today's world is change.
B. Since numerous problems of tomorrow's world defy prediction, children must be equipped with skills of "changeability."
C. Skills of "changeability" would best be developed if children were provided with ample opportunities to utilize their thinking processes in acquiring knowledge and tool skills; and children would thereby be far better equipped to deal with novel situations than would children who merely store information.

The above rationale provided the initial impetus for the program. But the factors that were of far greater significance and provided the thrust to continue and to expand the program were the observed results in terms of the pupils' behavioral outcomes. Pupils in cognitive classrooms demonstrated increased skill in thinking, acquired knowledge in depth, exhibited more positive self-concepts, were more self-directive and more socially-effective, and displayed more positive attitudes towards and interests in learning. In essence, the pivot of cognition set in motion all of the behavioral goals, and the results were clearly evident in our pupils. "Changeability" required no stronger rationale; it was happening. The blueprint of new educational goals was no longer a blueprint for us, but a behavioral reality for our children. There is little doubt that in years to come this blueprint will require revision but, equipped with "skills of changeability," our new teachers should be well equipped to continue the task. At the present time this blueprint serves us well, as you will observe when you appraise "classrooms for thinking" in the following chapter.

FOOTNOTES

[1] Jerome S. Bruner, *The Process of Education,* Cambridge, Massachusetts; Harvard University Press, 1965).

[2] Educational Policies Commission, *The Central Purpose of American Education,* Washington, D.C., The National Education Association, 1961, p.12.

[3] Larry Zanco, "Think" Cartoon, NEA Journal, September 1963.

[4] Richard S. Crutchfield, "Nuturing the Cognitive Skills of Productive Thinking," in *Life Skills in School and Society,* ed. Louis J. Rubin, Association for Supervision and Curriculum Development, NEA, Washington, D.C., 1969, pp. 66-71.

[5] Emily Dickinson, "I'm Nobody," in *The Poems of Emily Dickinson,* (Boston: Little, Brown & Company, 1939).

[6] Reprinted with the permission of the publisher from Arthur T. Jersild *In Search of Self (New York, Teachers College Press), 1960.*

[7] Marie M. Hughes, "Patterns of Effective Teaching" Provo, Utha: Second Progress Report of the Merit Study of the Provo City Schools, June 1961.

[8] John R. Seely, "Some Skills of Being For Those in Service in Education," in *Life Skills in School and Society,* ed. Louis J. Rubin, Association for Supervision and Curriculum Development, NEA, Washington, D.C., 1969, pp. 116-119, pp. 128-129.

[9] Richard Rogers and Oscar Hammerstein 2nd, Lyrics from "Carefully Taught" in *South Pacific,* Williamson Music Inc., New York, 1949.

[10] John Withall and W. W. Lewis, "Social Interaction in the Classroom," N. L. Gage, ed., *Handbook of Research on Teaching,* A project of the American Educational Research Association, © Rand McNally & Company, Chicago, p. 693.

4

Appraising "Classrooms for Thinking"

The most effective strategy for demonstrating the worth of the Behavioral Outcomes Approach is the live demonstration. When teachers and administrators observe the approach in a classroom setting, little else is needed to convince them of its merits. The results speak for themselves. However, since it is not possible to provide the live demonstration within the format of a book, the next best alternative will be used, that of providing a written transcript of the teacher-pupil interactions in a "classroom for thinking." We will "observe" a lesson taught via the Behavioral Outcomes Approach and then one taught by a conventional approach. This will enable us to analyze and compare the lessons, pinpointing the outcomes of each to determine the superiority of one to the other.

Prior to appraising the approaches, it is essential that we establish the criteria to be used. A careful analysis of the major premises and key factors of the Behavioral Outcomes Approach should yield these useful yardsticks.

The Major Premises

1. Education is interaction. This interaction involves the pupils, the teachers, and the subject matter.
2. Education is a process of behavioral change and growth. Behavioral change is transformed into behavioral growth when learners are given ample opportunities to internalize these changes, sustain them, and make them a permanent part of day-to-day behavioral patterns.
3. Schools are real-life learning centers functioning to promote the development of knowledge, tool skills, thinking processes, self-instruction, social effectiveness, and positive educational attitudes and interests in pupils.

The Key Factors

1. *Establishing a Responsive Environment*

   The teacher creates a responsive environment by clearly communicating by action as well as words that the pupils are free to think for themselves; that their thoughts, ideas, and feelings are welcome; and that mistakes are normal occurrences in the learning process from which one profits. Pupils are given freedom and are provided with ample opportunity to take this freedom and to become autonomous individuals.

2. *Focusing on Process*

   Learning activities are designed and structured to promote growth in process (the thinking processes). Learning is viewed as a *processing* of information rather than the absorption or sponging up of data. The pupil processes by reasoning inductively or deductively; by becoming an inquirer, a problem-solver, a decision-maker, a creator of ideas rather than by functioning as a memory bank.

3. *Employing Continuous Diagnosis*

   Initial and ongoing diagnosis is used to measure and insure increased effectiveness of learning. Pupils are pre-tested to determine where they are prior to instruction. During the learning sequence, pupils are evaluated in terms of their performance. At the close of a sequence pupils are post-tested to determine if they can *apply* and *process* their newly acquired knowledge and skills to *new* situations.

Provided with the major premises and key factors of the approach, namely, education as an interactive process serving to promote behavioral change and growth in terms of the six educational objectives and the need to establish a responsive environment, to focus on process, and to use continuous diagnosis, we can readily establish the criteria which will serve as yardsticks.

The Yardsticks

A. Is there interaction? What kind? To what degree?
B. Is there evidence of behavioral change in terms of:
   Knowledge
   Tool Skill Development
   Thinking Processes
   Self-Instruction
   Social Effectiveness
   Positive Educational Attitudes and Interests
C. Has the teacher established a responsive environment?
D. Is the focus on the thinking processes?
E. Is there diagnosis? What kind? To what extent?

Visiting a Classroom for Thinking

Equipped with our criteria, we now enter a "classroom for thinking." We are in a science classroom in a junior high school. Fifteen large tables are arranged in three rows. At each table there are two chairs. At the front of the room is a large laboratory table and along one side of the room is a series of laboratory stations. The front wall and side wall consist of blackboards. The back wall houses a reference library and a large bulletin board. The teacher's desk is located in one corner at the front of the room. Chairs along the back of the room accommodate visitors. The bell has just rung and 30 eighth-grade pupils enter. It is the first day of school.

As the students take their seats the teacher announces, "Kindly refrain from handling the shoe boxes on your tables." Students are seated, attendance is taken, and the lesson begins.

Mrs. X, the teacher, stands in front of the laboratory table. "Based on your facial expressions, I have a feeling that many of you are rather curious about the shoe boxes on your tables. Are there any questions you would like to ask?"

There is a massive showing of hands.

"What's in the box?" asks one pupil.

"Why are the boxes sealed?" asks another.

"What are we going to do with the boxes?" inquires a third pupil.

"I'm so glad you asked," replies Mrs. X, smiling. "The answers to all of your questions constitute your task for today. You are to attempt to discover what's in the box and describe the contents as precisely as you can."

Everyone exchanges glances and one student remarks, "Are you kidding? That will be easy!"

"Not quite so easy," the teacher replies. "You are not to open the box!"

"Oh no!" groans one student.

"How are we going to do that?" blurts out another.

"That is your problem! Think about it," responds Mrs. X. "After you have made your observations, you are to make three guesses as to what the object might be. You may construct any type of data sheet that you wish to record your findings. List your three guesses and state the reasons for your answers. You may do anything you wish with the box except open it. You may exchange boxes with your neighbors for purposes of comparison and you may discuss your observations with your classmates. You are free to ask me any questions you wish except 'What's in the box?' "

The room is filled with an uncertain silence. The students appear to be slightly frustrated. Then the silence is broken. Some frantically begin to shake the sealed boxes. Some move the boxes cautiously close to their ears. Some appear to be weighing the boxes. Each student, like a blind man examining a cold snowflake in his warm hand, is attempting to "see."

Mrs. X is circulating about the room replying to the students' questions.

"I don't think my box has anything in it. Are any of the boxes empty?" asks one student.

"No" replies the teacher. "Why do you assume it's empty?"

"It's so light!"

"Well, if the object is so light, can this bit of data lead you anywhere?"

"Maybe, if the object is light, it might be a piece of tissue paper, a Kleenex, a piece of absorbent cotton, or just plain air! Say, I'm beginning to get somewhere!"

Mrs. X pauses to observe another student who is cautiously moving the box in all directions.

"Why are you doing that?" she asks.

"Well, if the object is symmetrically round, it will roll smoothly in all directions, producing the same sound of motion. I think I have a symmetrically round object. Listen."

Mrs. X listens and remarks, "Possibly."

She continues to move about the room guiding the pupils. At no time does she give a definitive answer. The students are conferring with each other, exchanging boxes, collecting and recording their observations. The period is drawing to a close and the teacher calls the class to attention.

"I believe most of you have gathered and recorded some observations. The first part of your homework assignment is to review the data, list three guesses as to the contents of the box, and state the reasons for your guesses. The second part of your assignment is to think about the 'What's in the Box' problem and describe the purpose of the activity and how it is related to the scientist's quest for knowledge. Tomorrow many of you will present your results to the class, give the reasons for your guesses, explain how you arrived at them, and then you will be permitted to open your box and confirm your analysis. Any questions?"

"Yes," one student replies. "A few of us, in discussing our observations, had an idea we would like to try. We would like to return after school to borrow our boxes and take them home. We plan to put certain objects into our own shoe boxes at home and compare what we sense with the shoe box we have in class. We think we know what this box contains, but we would like to set up the same conditions in another box and compare. We will not open the box."

Mrs. X smiles. "An interesting idea. Be my guest." The bell rings. Period one students begin to file out of the room and period two students are arriving.

"Shoe boxes! What gives?" a voice calls out.

"You wouldn't believe it! You might call it 'Shoe-Box Science!' " a voice replies.

The Lesson Continues

The next day we are back in our visitors' chairs. The students are grouped around the tables discussing their results. Enthusiasm is high and everyone seems to have something to say. Mrs. X leaves her desk and stands in front of the large laboratory table. Silence envelops the room.

"I think you are all anxious to open your boxes and confirm your results. Many of you are interested in how your classmates arrived at their guesses. Therefore may I suggest that as you volunteer to share your information with us you use some systematic procedure. For example, you might state your observations, then your guesses, then ask for our comments, and finally open the box. However, feel free to use any procedure which you wish."

Bill, one of the students who had borrowed a box for home use, volunteers. "I guess I did what most of us did yesterday. I started out frantically shaking the box. Unlike most of my friends, I didn't hear anything. At first I thought Mrs. X had forgotten to put something in the box and I asked her. She said that there was something in the box. My observations were the following: (1) The box was not empty. (2) The object was very light in weight. (3) When I shook the box, I couldn't tell if the object was moving. I guessed that the box contained tissue paper, absorbent cotton, or air. When I took the box home, I compared it with another shoe box in which I placed a small piece of tissue paper, cotton, and then just air at different times. It didn't work. I do not have enough information. However, I will stick to my three guesses: tissue paper, absorbent cotton, and air. Any comments or ideas?"

Another student replies. "If I had your box I don't think I could do any better. I like your idea of using another shoe box for comparison."

Bill opens the box. Each student appears to hang from the edge of his seat. A piece of absorbent cotton faces the class. "It was just luck!" Bill smiles and takes his seat.

Sandy volunteers. "I think I have a pretty good idea of what's in this box. My observations are the following: (1) There is more than one object in this box. (2) In fact, shaking the box and listening to the sounds leads me to believe that there are about three small objects which are made of glass. (3) They roll and therefore they should be round. I 'guesstimate' that there are either three marbles or three glass beads in the box. I can't think of anything else made of glass that is small and rolls. Anyone have any ideas or suggestions?"

"Would you shake the box?" calls a boy at the back of the room.

Sandy complies.

The class agrees that marbles or beads are a distinct possibility. Sandy opens the box and displays three marbles.

Janet follows Sandy. "My observations seem to lead me nowhere. The object is heavy and it rolls. I can sense that it is long. My guess is that it is a heavy, long cylinder of some kind. Any comments?"

"How about a piece of pipe?" one student volunteers.

"No, it feels and rolls more like a solid cylinder." Janet replies.

Janet opens the box and displays a solid cylindrical magnet.

Mrs. X walks to the center of the room. "It would be ideal if we had time to continue to share our observations. At this time I suggest that each of you open your boxes and confirm your results." Covers are removed and exclamations are exchanged.

"Now that we have all worked in a box, we should explore the purpose of this activity. Why were you asked to find out what was in the box? All ideas are welcome."

Janet volunteered. "I think you wanted to get us to think. That sounds funny, but I really think that was it. You didn't let us open the box and therefore we had to start thinking about other ways of finding out. I don't think you wanted us to know that Bill's box contained cotton or that Sandy's box had marbles or mine had a magnet. I don't think it mattered if we were right or wrong. I think what mattered was that we were *thinking.*"

As Janet spoke a great many heads nodded in agreement. Bill raised his hand. "I think Janet is right. We all did a lot of thinking and a lot of good talking. We sort of searched together, exchanged ideas, and listened hard to the other guy's ideas. But I think there were other purposes. The homework assignment had a question about how this activity was related to the scientist's quest for knowledge. Well, last night when I was playing around with the shoe box, it sort of dawned on me that scientists work in shoe boxes. What I mean is that many times a scientist can't really use his eyes or all of his senses in exploring."

Tony chimes in, "Bill has something there. Last year we studied astronomy. Well, the astronomer works in a shoe box. He can't pull a star out of the sky and examine it in the lab. He finds other ways of studying the stars. He invents telescopes and spectroscopes."

Dolores volunteers. "We studied biology last year. I guess studying tiny cells is similar to working in a box. Unless the scientist has a microscope to help him, he can't get very far. I think, Mrs. X, your main goal was to get us to think for ourselves, but I think you wanted us to discover other things. I think that now we all understand that scientists don't have easy jobs in exploring nature. Their senses can't give them all the answers. Therefore, they invent instruments to extend their senses. I also think you gave us a chance to work the way scientists do. We had a problem. We tried out our ideas; some of us succeeded and most of us failed in solving our problem. Scientists probably have the same kinds of experiences."

Sue waves her hand enthusiastically. "I agree with Dolores, but I think that all of us work in closed boxes. What I mean is that it isn't only the scientist. What I mean is that every day in getting along with people, we are sort of guessing what's in the box. I guess what I'm really saying is that people are human shoe boxes, closed boxes. You don't really know all the time how people think and feel. You 'guesstimate' with people too."

"Yes, Sue," Mrs. X wound up the discussion, "I would certainly agree with you. In fact there are social scientists who study human behavior. Since the period is drawing to a close, I would like to make some comments about what you people have accomplished yesterday and today. I think you have succeeded admirably in identifying the major goal of this year's work which is to *think* in the process of learning. You have experienced some of the realities of scientific exploration. You are aware of the limitations of our senses, of the value of instrumentation, and of some of the systematic steps employed by the scientist. I am very impressed with your relating the shoe-box approach to the area of human relations as well as to the physical and biological sciences. Since all of you did not have the opportunity to state your reactions to this lesson, I am requesting that you prepare a written appraisal of this lesson by the end of this week. Feel free to express your reactions. Don't hand me what you think I would like to hear. Any questions?"

The bell signals the close of the period. The students start filing out of the room.

The Same Teacher with a Conventional Approach

We have just observed a teacher using the Behavioral Outcomes Approach. Now we will view the same lesson as it is taught by the same teacher employing a conventional approach. It should be noted that the conventional teacher, unlike the behavioral teacher, is not primarily concerned with the thinking processes. Her concern is with the content objectives.

We are again seated in the same science classroom. The bell has just rung ushering in a group of 30 eighth-grade students. The students take their seats, the teacher checks the attendance roll, and the lesson begins.

Mrs. X stands in front ot the lab table. "Today we are going to examine the role of the scientist, how he conducts his explorations, what his limitations are, and how he attempts to overcome these limitations. Let's start with the role of the scientist. What is the scientist trying to do?"

"He is searching for facts," John volunteers.

"Correct!" replies Mrs. X.

"He is searching for the truth," Jane replies.

"Correct!"

"He is trying to explain why things happen," Tom adds.

"He is trying to explain how things happen," Kim replies.

"Right! Now I would like you to open your notebooks and record what we are discussing. It is essential that you have a record of what is covered in class so that you may refer to your notes as needed. Let us begin by noting that the scientist searches for the truth and for explanations as to why and how things occur in our environment."

Mrs. X circulates about the room as the students record the information.

"How does the scientist discover the truth?" she asks.

"He experiments, tries things out, and tests things," Tim replies.

"Good! How many of you have heard of the scientific method?"

There is a large showing of hands.

"What is the scientific method?"

"We talked about it last year," Tim replies. "The scientist has a problem to solve, he thinks about methods of solving his problem, he tests his methods by experimenting, he records his observations, and he uses them to reach conclusions."

"Sometimes his conclusions are not conclusive," Jane adds. "What I mean is that his conclusions do not give us definite answers, but lead to other problems so that he has to continue to experiment."

"Very good! Let us record our information in our notebooks. Using what Tim has said, I will list the steps of the scientific method on the board."

Mrs. X speaks as she writes on the blackboard.

Step 1. The scientist states the problem.
Step 2. He formulates methods of solving the problem.
Step 3. He experiments and observes.
Step 4. He interprets the information.
Step 5. He reaches conclusions.
Step 6. He may uncover new problems.

"Has everyone recorded the steps? Fine. If we were to interview a group of scientists we would find that they do not always use these steps in the order we have listed. Many scientists use this method to check their work when it is completed. However, these steps present a systematic plan for problem-solving and problem-checking. Let's take a closer look at Step 3. The scientist experiments and observes. Let us suppose that his problem deals with the composition of Saturn's rings. How does he observe these rings? Of what value are his eyes?"

"He can't use his eyes alone. He uses a telescope," Bill volunteers.

"He may also use a telescope and a camera," Tim offers.

"How about a spectroscope?" Jane asks.

"Yes, he may use a telescope, a combination of a specific kind of telescope and a camera, and a spectroscope to analyze the light rays. What you are all saying is that the scientist, because of the limitations of his sense organs, constructs a variety of instruments which serve to assist him in his explorations. Let us make a note of the value of instrumentation."

Mrs. X dictates: "The scientist constructs instruments to supplement his senses. These instruments aid him in exploring his environment."

Mrs. X directs the students' attention to the laboratory stations at the side of the room where she has displayed a variety of instruments.

"How many of these instruments can you identify?"

John volunteers and identifies a microscope, stroboscope, spectroscope and radiometer.

Janet's hand is raised and then quickly lowered.

"What were you going to say, Janet?" Mrs. X asks.

Janet hesitates. "I thought I knew what that instrument is, but I'm not sure that I'm right."

"That is a Geiger counter," Mrs. X offers. "It is used to measure radioactivity. At this time we are going to see a film strip dealing with scientific instrumentation. I would like you to turn to a new page in your notebooks and divide the page into two columns. Label the first colum *Name of Instruments* and the second column *Use of Instrument.* As you view the film strip, you are to record the information in your notebooks."

The film strip is shown and the pupils note the data. Mrs. X glances at her watch. "I find we have about two minutes before the bell will ring. Therefore, I will give you your assignment for tomorrow. Using your textbook or any other resource material, I would like you to expand the list of instruments you have. See if you can add five other instruments which the scientist uses to analyze, examine, weigh, or measure the phenomena around him. Are there any questions?"

The bell signals the close of the period. The students start filing out of the room and so do we.

Pinpointing the Behavioral Outcomes of Each Approach

Having "observed" both a behavioral and a conventional approach, we are now prepared to apply the criteria which we have previously established to each approach. Our purpose is to pinpoint the behavioral outcomes of each in order to determine which is the superior methodology. Our criteria are the following:

A. Was there interaction? What kind? To what degree?
B. Was there evidence of behavioral change in terms of:
   Knowledge
   Tool Skill Development
   Thinking Processes
   Self-Instruction
   Social Effectiveness
   Positive Educational Attitudes and Interests
C. Did the teacher establish a responsive environment?
D. Was the focus on the thinking processes?
E. Was there diagnosis? What kind? To what extent?

At this time, you may wish to conduct your own analysis of the approaches and then compare your responses with the ones which follow, or you may prefer to continue reading. The choice is yours.

Criterion A—
Interaction. What Kind? To What Degree?

In the behaviorally-oriented approach there was a high degree of pupil-pupil interaction with the teacher serving as a guide and diagnostician. Pupils were free to confer with each other and to consult with the teacher as the need arose. The second half of this lesson exemplified the same pattern— a high degree of pupil-pupil interaction. The pupils presented their results and asked their peers for comments and suggestions. Teacher-talk was minimal, and occurred at the close of the lesson, providing the pupils with feedback in terms of the teacher's assessment of their performance. The assignment given at the close of the lesson served as a vehicle for pupil feedback involving every member of the class. Pupil-subject matter interaction was extremely high. Pupils were actively and enthusiastically involved in the problem. In sum, the interaction of pupils with each other and with content was extremely high. The teacher- pupil interaction was essentially a function of the individual pupil's need.

In the conventional approach a high degree of teacher-pupil interaction was demonstrated, while pupil-pupil interaction was minimized. The teacher asked the questions and the pupils responded. It was analogous to a game of ping-pong. The teacher was the director and programmer of instruction. Her lesson was well-sequenced; her questions were carefully structured. She gave information, directed the pupils with clarity, and corrected pupil responses. The content was "covered" by the teacher and recorded both on blackboard and in notebooks. Pupil interaction with subject matter was limited and controlled. There was little opportunity for exploratory or search behavior. The prescribed dosage was administered. Feedback or knowledge of results occurred after each question, when the pupil was told if the response was right or wrong. Pupils like Janet were afraid to make mistakes. She raised her hand and then quickly lowered it because she wasn't sure. Pupil-pupil interaction occurred naturally. However, not enough opportunity was provided to foster it. In essence the interactive process in this approach was highly limited. It was controlled and structured so that closure was attained at the end of the period.

Criterion B—
Pupil Behavioral Change in Terms of Objectives

In order to evaluate the kind and degree of pupil behavioral change which occurred in each setting, we must first identify the specific objectives of each lesson. It is not realistic to assume that *every* lesson will foster all six objectives. However, the greater the number of opportunities we provide to promote most of these objectives, the greater will be the probability of developing the pupil's total growth pattern.

Objectives of the Lessons

It was quite clear that the behaviorally-oriented lesson had one major goal, that of communicating to the pupil that his key function in the science classroom was to use his thinking processes in the acquisition of knowledge. The secondary goals dealt with the content. The content objectives were explicit. The pupils were to demonstrate verbally or by other actions that man's senses were inadequate for the exploration of environmental phenomena, that man constructed instruments to extend his senses, and that he employed a systematic, problem-solving methodology in his efforts to extend the frontiers of knowledge.

The conventional lesson dealt primarily with the content objectives. The teacher was not concerned with building up an awareness in the pupils of their central role as thinking or problem-solving individuals. The content objectives were well defined. The pupils were to demonstrate verbally their knowledge of the role of the scientist in his search for truth and explanations of natural phenomena, the scientific method employed and the specific steps constituting the method, the limitations of the sense organs and the value of instrumentation.

The content objectives for both lessons were identical. The basic differences were the focus upon the thinking processes and the active involvement of the pupils as problem-solvers in the behavioral lesson.

Knowledge

From our one "observation" of each approach, we cannot validly determine the degree to which the pupils acquired and assimilated the content. What we can say is that in the conventional lesson, the pupils attended and responded to the teacher's questions by recalling previously learned material; their involvement was decidedly limited to response by recall, notebook record-keeping, and viewing a film strip from which they extracted and recorded data. This was the extent of the content involvement in contrast to the dynamic, pupil-content interaction in the behavioral setting.

Continuous observation of the program has demonstrated that *retention* of knowledge is far greater as a result of active involvement as opposed to passive attending. Pupils who have been taught by the behavioral approach demonstrate this retention. This is readily understandable, for as educators we have clearly established that the learning process is essentially a function of the pupil. The teacher's role is that of providing the pupil with a learning environment. Some teachers will interpret this as providing information in a didactic, expository manner; others will view it as providing pupil opportunities for active discovery and inquiry. In either case it is the pupil who does the learning. But—the temporary acquisition of knowledge is of little worth! We are vitally concerned with long-range retention of knowledge and skills. The Behavioral Outcomes Approach promotes this retention.

Tool Skills

Assessing both lessons in relation to the second objective, the development of tool skills would be of little value. Since neither lesson dealt with this objective, we may simply state that this goal is not applicable to our sample lessons

Thinking Processes

In terms of the program's third objective, the pupil's use of a large variety of thinking processes, we find that this objective is applicable to both lessons. Although the teacher in the conventional classroom did not primarily concern herself with this objective, the pupils did think. At this point we might ask, what kind or kinds of thinking would we assume the pupils were using in the conventional classroom? An analysis of the kinds of questions the teacher asked indicates that the pupils were limited to the process of recall. In order to reply to the specific questions asked, the pupil had to search his mental storage bank and retrieve the correct data. Pupils operated merely on a *memory level.*

In the behaviorally-oriented lesson, the pupils used a large variety of thinking processes. They were presented with a problem which was obviously new to them. They were required to *devise* methods to solve the problem. As evidenced in the lesson, they arrived at many ways of attacking the problem: shaking the box and listening to the movement of the contents to determine the "heard" properties, holding the box to determine the weight, and simulating the conditions with another object in a second box and *making a comparison.* The pupils gathered, *analyzed,* and *synthesized* the data to arrive at three possible answers. In searching for the three "quess-timates" they *associated* the observed properties of the objects with objects already known to them. At this point, their memory bank was used. The thinking processes such as *divergent production* (arriving at many solutions to a problem), *analysis, comparison, synthesis* and *association,* were employed. These processes will be developed in detail for practical application in Chapters 4, 5, 6, and 7. At this time it is essential that we fully realize what was required of the pupils in each lesson. In the conventional lesson pupils were required to give the correct responses. We might ask: does the act of providing the correct answer indicate that the pupil "really understands"? Practical experience has shown that verbalization is not synonymous with understanding. Many of our pupils have memorized data to parrot on the sacred test. Many have understood a concept but have been unable to communicate it verbally.

In the behavioral lesson, the pupils were presented with a problem and were given the opportunity to explore, think, examine, and interact with the content. The pupil's mind was viewed and used as a sharp instrument capable of manipulating data rather than as a memory bank storing and retrieving information. The right or wrong answer was not a crucial factor. The emphasis was on the pupil's use of process in the acquisition of knowledge. In sum, the Behavioral Outcomes Approach is markedly superior to the conventional approach in that extensive opportunities are provided for thinking rather than restricting pupils to mere rote recall. Only if we focus on thinking will we succeed in transforming today's children into tomorrow's thinking adults.

Self-Instruction

Evaluating both lessons on the basis of self-instruction (self-direction and self-evaluation), we encounter basic differences. In the behavioral lesson the pupils were provided with ample opportunity to determine their own course of action, to evaluate their performance, and to change course as they deemed necessary. The teacher served as a guide, a motivator, and a reinforcer. At no time was she strongly directive. On the other hand, the conventional lesson was firmly directed by the teacher. There was little opportunity for the students to determine their own course of action or to evaluate their performance. In this case the teacher firmly established the parameters of instruction and served as the sole director and sole evaluator of instruction. Self-instruction consisting of self-direction and self-evaluation was a major component of the behavioral lesson. The conventional lesson was entirely lacking in this respect. Again it is quite clear that pupils will not become self-learners unless opportunities are provided to achieve this goal!

Social-Effectiveness

Opportunities for working with one's peers, interacting cooperatively, exchanging information, listening with respect to another's ideas, suggestions and viewpoints constitute social-effectiveness. We may ask: in which classroom was there greater opportunity for social effectiveness? There is little doubt that the behavioral classroom provided the situational context, the time, and the freedom for greater social interaction. Pupils did exchange ideas freely, did interact and work cooperatively toward a solution.

Socially effective behaviors were prevalent. The conventional approach did not provide for social interaction. The social behaviors which did occur in this setting just happened. No provision was made to encourage or foster them.

Positive Attitudes and Interests

The attitude of the pupil is a key factor operating in the classroom. How the pupil perceives the task, how he feels about it, will determine the degree of involvement and of learning which results. This goal appears to be difficult to measure on the basis of observation. How do we know that the pupils hold a positive attitude toward this specific learning situation or that they are really interested in the science lesson? Were we not limited to merely observation, we might employ a series of inventories. However, here we are faced with the less tangible objectives of instruction and the need to evaluate them. Any teacher will tell us that she does evaluate attitudes and interests. Pupils demonstrate positive attitudes toward and interest in subject matter by (1) asking numerous questions; (2) volunteering to engage in tasks which are not required; (3) bringing additional resource materials to class; (4) becoming actively involved in the classroom by attending to the tasks for a long period of time; (5) requesting to borrow materials for home use; and (6) returning after school to pursue their interests. These constitute sample behaviors which may be employed to measure the pupil's attitudes and interests.

From the responses made in the conventional classroom we may say that the pupils held positive attitudes and displayed some interest. They did attend to the teacher's presentation and did respond to the required tasks. There were no instances observed where the pupils refused to attend or respond or actively withdrew. Neither were there instances which would lead us to believe that they were highly stimulated and motivated to move beyond the assigned task.

In the behavioral classroom we found an entirely different situation. There were instances which clearly pointed to a high degree of interest on the part of the students. The pupils who requested to borrow the shoe box for the purpose of simulation and the pupil who described that he had listened "hard" to his classmates demonstrated high interest. The fact that on their return the following day the pupils could not wait to open their shoe boxes and exchange information indicates that they had been highly motivated. On the whole, we may state that the interest level in the behavioral classroom was considerably higher than in the conventional one. Were we to continue to observe the behavioral class over a long period of time, we would find that the high interest level would be maintained. This is precisely what our experiences have shown.

Reviewing the outcomes of both lessons as they relate to the six objectives, we can readily conclude that the behavioral approach has demonstrated its superiority. The pupils are given greater opportunities to acquire and retain knowledge, to think, to use self-instruction, to develop social-effectiveness, and to increase positive attitudes toward and interest in schooling—and they utilize these opportunities and demonstrate the outcomes.

Criterion C—
The Responsive Environment

As we examine the two classroom settings, we find that each teacher provided a specific kind of climate for learning but that the climates differed tremendously.

The conventional teacher provided a highly directive, controlled climate as opposed to a creative, flexible, meet-the-individual pupil-needs climate. She was the director and programmer as evidenced by her well-planned lesson, her firm sequence, her carefully structured questions to elicit the correct responses, her precise information-giving, and her emphasis on note-taking. She achieved "her" goals efficiently. Closure was attained at the close of the period. The instructional package was neatly wrapped and the bow was tied on top.

The behavioral teacher, rather than being a director of learning, was a creator of conditions for learning. Her lesson was well-planned but her plans were open-structured. She provided the pupils with a task, made herself available for consultation, guided the pupils for self-discovery, listened and accepted pupils' ideas, and encouraged them in their explorations. She attained closure at the end of two class periods. She was concerned with providing a responsive environment, an environment where children were given freedom, where time and space for thought and exploration were available. Her questions were open-structured, not requiring the response. She did not seek immediate closure. She responded to her pupils' questions with other questions permitting them to solve their own problems. She was not right-answer oriented. She responded with "Possibly." Her lesson did not consist of neat packages of information for storage and retrieval. Her lesson consisted of providing pupils with actual experiences. Pupils were in active contact with a task, with subject matter, with each other, and with the teacher. Learning was inter- action. Were the process of education a simple one of information- giving, record-keeping, and memory-retrieval, our present efforts would indeed be superfluous and the products of our schools would not be what they are. Responsive schools produce responsive in- dividuals. If we as educators are deeply concerned with the development of flexible, responsive pupils, then methods such as the Behavioral Outcomes Approach should be used to the fullest extent to attain this goal.

Criterion D—
The Focus on Process

Essentially we have dealt with the focus on process or thinking. It is central to the behavioral approach and non-operative in the conventional one. If we accept the premise that all learning is a result of processing information, accommodating data within a conceptual framework, assimilating data, and applying it in a situational context, then the behavioral approach is an essential vehicle.

Criterion E—
Diagnosis

Operating within the framework of our "observations," we can identify very little diagnosis in the conventional approach. "Did the pupils offer the correct response?" was the extent of it. It was apparent that the pupils already had extensive knowledge of the scientific method. The review and note-taking were not needed. Had the teacher administered a diagnostic pre-test, in all probability she would have found that the content objectives of this lesson had been previously attained. At this point, a word of explanation in regard to the pre-test is in order. The first step of the Behavioral Outcomes Approach is the use of the pre-test. This is a test which is given prior to instruction for the purpose of diagnosing where the pupils are in terms of content and skills. The results of the pre-test enables the teacher to tailor the lessons to meet the pupil's needs. Chapter 11 deals with the testing procedures and provides useful and practical guidelines and materials for classroom application.

Now to return to our assessment relative to diagnosis. In the conventional classroom, other than the one-shot verbal response to specific questions diagnosis of any type was completely lacking. In the behavioral classroom ongoing diagnosis was in progress, as exemplified by the teacher circulating among the pupils, observing and questioning their actions. Pupils in need of assistance freely requested it and made their needs known. The climate was totally open to diagnosis. The fact that the teacher did not occupy the center stage throughout the lesson but was free to circulate and diagnose was a significant factor. Diagnostically speaking, the behavioral approach is markedly superior. There is no need to teach in a closed box when the box can be opened!

How Pupils React to Thinking Classrooms

Pupils' reactions to this approach are quite apparent in the following written products:

THE JOURNEY INTO NOWHERE

This title started off our first science lesson.

When we started we were given a box and Mrs. Gerhard very calmly said, "All you have to do is find out what is in the box." Everyone looked at each other and said, "Is she kidding? That will be easy." Then after a few minutes she included, with a smile, the fact that you couldn't take the lid off the box. Suddenly everyone began to groan and with sick faces said, "How are we going to do that?"

Mrs. Gerhard then told us that this was *our* problem. "Think," she said.

In this lesson I began thinking for myself and using all methods possible to discover what was in the box.

My guesses were wrong, but it didn't really matter because I had gotten the idea of the lesson. That was to think for yourself because no one will do it for you.

This title no longer holds true because even since that first lesson, I have been going somewhere.

Dorothy S.

IN MY OPINION

I think this year's science program is the best I have ever been enrolled in. This year I have learned more in two months than I did in almost all of last year. This year we do more experiments than in the past. This gives us a better opportunity to see the changes ourselves and to think out why they occur. This year we're learning to think for ourselves, we're learning to solve our own problems. And I think this is important, to think for yourself.

Diana D.

Last year I had Mrs. Gerhard for Science for half the year, and I have her again this year. There is a great difference between the two years. Last year, she did many experiments, but she explained them to us and give us the conclusions. This year we have to think for yourselves in all we do. It may be much harder than last year, but we get more interesting results.

Catherine W.

In my science class this year I have done more learning than I have in the past two years.

My science teacher teaches in a way that gives you a chance to find out solutions for yourself. We don't do much book work in class which in my opinion, is boring anyway, but we do lab work which is interesting to me because this way I get to learn with my eyes and brains.

For the sake of next year's science classes, I hope our school uses the same teachnique in teaching science to students because now we are really learning.

Mildred T.

I think this year is more interesting because we do experiments ourselves and we don't just listen to the teacher talk. I think I will learn more this year because I have to think how and why things happened.

I had chemistry last year, but I seem to be understanding it better and learning more about it this year.

Pat A.

I like the way the science class is being taught. It is more interesting and I'm learning more. We have done a lot of experiments on our own. Watching experiments and doing them yourself is more interesting than reading about them in a book. You can see for yourself what really happens, something that the best book in the world might not be able to describe.

Georgia R.

I think I will learn more this year in science than last year, because the class is very interesting. Some teachers talk all through a class and the pupils get bored, but in this class, when the teacher talks she makes it sound very interesting. When we come to class, there is always something different for us to do. She has a very interesting method of teaching her classes.

Grace F.

The Teacher Speaks

As evidenced from the written products, it is apparent that the pupils enjoyed and profited from this approach. When this program began, many years ago, I was the teacher of each of these classes. The conventional lesson was the one which I had taught prior to my training in the program. The behavioral lesson depicted the "after" stage.

The differences which I experienced were quite dramatic. The students in the process-oriented classes demonstrated a more meaningful acquisition of knowledge. They experienced, they understood; they were not merely verbalizing. They used the thinking processes. They did not readily accept ideas but challenged and interacted. Enthusiasm was high and a readiness to participate was prevalent. They enjoyed and valued the class. When working alone, each demonstrated initiative in setting up his own plans of operation. The total environment had changed. Learning had become a dynamic, living process, not only for the pupils, but for the teacher as well. My experiences in the thinking classroom could not be compared to those in the numerous years I had previously taught. The contrast was so great that it was like moving from one pole of a continuum to the other. My pupils and I were now on the road to "Thinking, Behaving, and Becoming."

Selecting the Approach

When we get down to basics we will find that our view of the school and its functions will determine the kind of approach we will select. If we are to view the school as merely an agency whose prime function is the transmission of bodies of knowledge and the development of tool skills and nothing more, we may screech to a halt at this time. The conventional mode is adequate. If, on the other hand, we are firmly convinced that the school's function is to promote the growth of the total pupil, then the behavioral methodology is vitally needed. We have a new role and a new task. We will direct our efforts toward setting up a responsive environment, structuring activities for thinking, providing opportunities for self-instruction, social effectiveness, and attitudinal change. The task is not an easy one. It requires knowledgeable effort, but it will yield immeasurable satisfaction.

The chapters which follow contain detailed descriptions, specific methods, practical exercises and illustrations, and teacher-useful materials to provide you with a base from which to begin.

5

The Thinking Processes as
Conceptual Tools
for Pupils and Teachers

In the previous chapter we "visited" two classrooms and observed and compared the conventional with the behaviorally-oriented or cognitive approach. We noted the similarities and more importantly the significant differences between these approaches. We are now at the stage similar to the one depicted in the "Think" cartoon in which one youngster reading the word "Think" clearly states his problem: "I know what it says—but how is it done?"

How it is done—and here we are referring to the Behavioral Outcomes Approach—is the subject of this and the following chapters. We will be dealing with the cognitive tools, procedures, and strategies which will provide you with the know-how for implementing this approach in your own classrooms.

Acquiring Essential Terminology

We will begin by defining the essential terminology so that we speak the same language and convey precise meanings. In education it is a relatively easy task to drown in words and to convey a multiplicity of meanings using the "same" terms. Many of us, to save ourselves from the deluge of "educationese," have resorted to operational definitions. By describing our terms as a series of operations and restricting their use to these operations, we give our terms more specific meanings. In those cases where operational definitions were difficult to arrive at, we simply defined our terms and stated that we assigned but one meaning to a given term and that it was not to be used interchangeably with any other.

Therefore, we will proceed by defining the key terms used in this approach: behavior; outcome; behavioral outcomes; overt and covert behaviors; the cognitive, affective and psychomotor domains; and each of the cognitive processes.

Behavior is defined as any action on the part of an individual. Speaking, reading, writing, listening, thinking, feeling, emoting are all examples of behaviors.

Outcome is defined as a result. In this approach we constantly use the term behavioral outcome. By this we mean the specific *action* a pupil demonstrates as a *result* of the teaching-learning process. For example—if a pupil, as a result of specific instruction in his math class, is able to use the slide rule—this is a behavioral outcome: namely, the pupil does use the slide rule. Or if the pupil, as a result of reading the poems of Frost, develops an appreciation of this poet's works—this is a behavioral outcome: namely, the pupil does appreciate Frost's literary products.

We differentiate between a behavior and a behavioral outcome in that a behavior is any action an individual displays, but a behavioral outcome is a result of the teaching-thinking-learning process. A child may come to school for the first time fearful about the requirements. This is an entry behavior; it is not one he has acquired in the school setting. When we refer to behavioral outcomes, we limit ourselves to those we assume have been learned or modified in the school environment.

Behaviors may be classified as overt or covert actions. Overt actions are observable actions. Writing, speaking, laughing, crying, executing somersaults are samples of overt behaviors. Covert behaviors are those that are not observable, as exemplified by processes of knowing, understanding, thinking, appreciating, and valuing. We have no way of directly observing when a child is thinking or what particular thinking process he is using, unless we ask him to think aloud. I recall a session in which a group of psychologists, in an attempt to learn more about children's thinking, had youngsters think aloud. The children had adjusted beautifully to the task and were completely at ease. One youngster, in tackling his problem, stopped suddenly and uttered a series of "uh's." I turned to one of the investigators, who was busily taking notes, and asked, "What kind of behavior is that?" He stared at me, paused, and then with a smile replied, "Search behavior!" Until the time when "search behavior" has been adequately researched and yields significant results and adequate procedures we will continue to classify the thinking processes as covert behaviors.

For purposes of convenience, both overt and covert behaviors are further classified into three behavioral domains: the cognitive, the affective, and the psychomotor domains. The cognitive domain includes all behaviors which place primary emphasis on the thinking and intellectual skills of the pupil. Processes such as association, analysis, inductive and deductive reasoning are samples of cognitive behaviors. The affective domain encompasses behaviors which are essentially feelings, emotions, attitudes, appreciations, interests, and values. Our acts of liking, of disliking, of experiencing anxiety or hostility are samples of affective behaviors. The psychomotor domain places primary emphasis on physical skills and neuromuscular skills. Swimming, executing push-ups, hitting a target, manipulating a typewriter, holding a pencil are sample behaviors in this domain.

In working with behavioral outcomes, we are concerned with all three of these intertwining domains. A specific behavior usually involves components of two or more domains. To illustrate, you are reading the words on this page—meaning is communicated—this is primarily a cognitive act. Certain neuromuscular skills are involved in the physical act of reading; here we have the psychomotor components. You may be interested, bored or harbor a wait-and-see attitude; this is the affective component. The behavior of reading, although primarily cognitive, had psychomotor and affective components. This concept will be further developed in Chapter 9.

Let us pause, review, and sum up what we have discussed up to this point.

- Behavior is defined as any action on the part of the pupil.
- An outcome is a result.
- A behavioral outcome is the action a pupil demonstrates as a result of the teaching-thinking-learning process.
- Behaviors are classified as overt or observable actions and covert or non-observable actions.
- Behaviors are further classified into three domains: the cognitive, knowing and thinking domain; the affective, feeling or emotional domain; and the psychomotor, physical skills or neuromuscular domain.
- Behaviors usually involve components of two or more domains.

If we synthesize all of this, we may conclude that when we use the term behavioral outcomes, we are referring to the overt and covert actions which pupils demonstrate as a result of the teaching-thinking-learning process and that these behavioral outcomes may be primarily cognitive or affective or psychomotor, but usually contain components of two or more domains.

The Four Levels of the Teaching-Learning Process

Our prime emphasis in the Behavioral Outcomes Approach is on the cognitive domain. Our major objective is to promote the development of cognitive processes in pupils, to move away from low level cognitive processes such as recall and toward higher cognitive functions such as analysis, synthesis, and critical thinking, to mention but a few. Too much of current learning is restricted to the first level—the *memory level.* Our concern should center on the teaching-learning levels so aptly described by J. Cecil Parker in The Oregon Plan,[1] namely, the *meaning level* dealing with the *"whys,"* the "operations" that make things work, the *significance level* involving implications and consequences, and the *action level* or "doing something" stage in which knowledge is applied to new situations. On this highest level, "knowledge becomes a vehicle rather than a destination. On level one, the memory level, the child wears a ready-made mind which is directed toward the sponging up of bookishness."

To move our pupils up the cognitive ladder and thereby achieve our goal, we should be equipped with:

- Clear-cut definitions of the specific cognitive processes we are to develop in pupils.
- Practice with these processes so that we experience and therefore "understand" what is involved when we utilize each process.
- Strategies to promote pupil's use of process.
- Process-centered activities.

Defining the Cognitive Processes

We will begin by defining the specific cognitive processes which we wish to develop in our pupils. For this purpose, a list of cognitive functions is presented. This list is by no means exhaustive. It contains those processes which have become an integral part of the behavioral outcomes program. The definitions are working definitions serving to provide a common language. It is not expected that you memorize these definitions. As you work with these processes you will "learn" them. Imagine how ridiculous the following situation would appear to be:

> *Teacher:* "This semester, we are going to make greater use of many thinking processes. We will begin with inductive reasoning. On the board are the steps involved in this type of reasoning. Please note them and *memorize* these steps so that you will be able to apply them in class tomorrow."

The list of definitions is to serve as a *reference.* A large number of these definitions were provided to our staff by Dr. Esin Kaya, the principal consultant to the project. Some were obtained from Bloom's *Taxonomy of Educational Objectives.* Many of the original definitions were modified and expanded upon as our work progressed.

Following a review of these definitions, exercises will be provided to enable you to experience process and to understand what is involved as you work with each one.

A LISTING OF A VARIETY OF COGNITIVE PROCESSES

Process	Working Definition
1. Associating	—Relating of objects or thoughts as they come to mind; usually there is found to be a tie between the related items.
a. Free Association	—Relating of objects or thoughts as they come to mind with no restrictions imposed.
b. Controlled Association	—Relating of objects or thoughts as they come to mind, but restricted to a given context or area.
c. Linked Association	—Relating of objects or thoughts as they come to mind, in which each association becomes the stimulus word for the next association, resulting in a train of associations; i.e., red→ light→ sun→ Florida→vacation.
2. Comparing	—Determining similarities and differences on the basis of some criteria.
3. Convergent Thinking	—Arriving at one pattern or one solution out of diverse elements using some criterion. ("The right answer" or "the correct solution" is required).

Process	*Working Definition*
4. Divergent Thinking	—Offering *various* patterns or solutions to the same problem.
5. Synthesis	—Putting together parts and pieces to form a whole; arranging, rearranging and combining parts to establish a pattern or product not clearly present before.[2]
6. Analysis	—Breaking down a concept, problem or pattern into its component parts so that the relative hierarchy of ideas or procedures is made clear and/or the relations between ideas or procedures expressed are made explicit.[2]
7. Inductive Reasoning	—Using specific situations, objects, and ideas and arriving at generalizations, principles, or rules.
8. Deductive Reasoning	—Starting with generalizations or universal propositions and arriving at a specific. This process is the reverse of inductive reasoning in that one arrives at a specific statement or conclusion which is *not* applicable to a class of objects, ideas or phenomena.
9. Classifying	—Establishing an arbitrary system of groupings and sub-groupings on the basis of the *common* characteristics of elements.
10. Categorizing	—Placing objects, ideas, and phenomena into a *given* classification system. One does not establish one's own grouping system.
11. Critical Thinking (Evaluating and Judging)	—A complex process which involves analysis, a weighing of the components either qualitatively or quantitatively, and making a selection or decision on the basis of evaluation.
12. Creative Thinking	—Developing or reorganizing ideas, objects, words, etc., and arriving at a product, (or products) which is novel, original, unexpected, and imaginative in its new form.
13. Concept Formation	—Arriving at a broad understanding. Concept formation involves many of the processes above and results in the enlargement of an understanding

In addition to the list of cognitive terminology, a few terms are defined below because they are related closely to the cognitive processes.

Process	Working Definition
Variables	—Isolated factors that can be manipulated, measured, or observed.
Hypotheses	—Tentative statements of relationship between variables. These statements are subject to evaluation before conclusions may be drawn.
Control	—A set of restrictions imposed on the manipulation of a variable. Sometimes it refers to a standard against which another variable is compared.

Developing Skill in Utilizing the Thinking Processes

Only when we as teachers experience process are we able to teach for process. It's that old, old story of "no one understood." I taught the lesson the first day, but *no one understood.* I taught the lesson the second day, but *no one understood.* I taught the lesson the third day, and *I understood.* Therefore we will involve ourselves with each of the processes so that we reach that third day of "I understood."

Associating

Beginning with the process of association, we will deal briefly with all three kinds. First—free association. Using the word *round* as the stimulus word, list all the objects or ideas that come to mind as you focus on *round.* Jot down anything that occurs to you. Free-wheel! There are no right answers. All of your associations are acceptable.

Now let us use controlled association. In this case the stimulus word is *light,* but think of it *only in a scientific sense.* List all the objects and ideas that come to mind. In this case your thinking is restricted to a scientific context. Your lists will vary based on your scientific background. Sample lists have included *light, wave length, Laser, coherent, incoherent, Edison, electric, beam, speed of, weight, sun, atoms,* etc. The complexity of the terms you elicit reflects, somewhat crudely, the extensiveness of your knowledge pertaining to the scientific concept of light.

The third kind of association is linked association. We start with one word which serves as the initial stimulus word which leads to another which now serves as the new stimulus word. For example, the word *red* may lead to *light* which in turn reminds one of *sun* which is associated with *Florida* and so on. The chain of association therefore looks something like this: red→light→sun→Florida. Now *red* has nothing to do with *Florida,* but this is not our concern. We achieved our objective—that of using linked association.

In experiencing this process, what did we actually do? We related objects or thoughts as they came to mind. Based on our knowledge and experience, there was a tie between the related elements.

This process is more than an amusing game; it is a useful tool to both pupils and teachers and is applicable to every content area at every age level.

Classroom Applications of Association

The process of association serves two major functions in the classroom. One is highly cognitive, and the other highly affective. The use of association results in stimulating creativity and in activating pupils to become more attentive and responsive learners.

Association has opened the door to creativity. Many times pupils are unable to generate ideas, words, or thoughts. Providing them with association as a *tool* will do much to promote creativity, to make them aware of the store of ideas they do have but of which they are not cognizant. Too often, both teachers and pupils view the creative process as a special and rare talent possessed by a few individuals and are suprised at the originality and inventiveness displayed by pupils. All children possess creative abilities; we have only to release them. Association is an invaluable tool to trigger this process.

What was startling to most teachers was the effect of the use of association on pupils' affective behavior. When given the freedom to associate, when told that their ideas were welcomed and valued, pupils who normally retreated from classroom activities became actively involved. Youngsters who thought they "couldn't," *could!* Passive pupils became active learners. The climate required for association produced these results. There were no "wrong answers," therefore, each response was positively received and each child received positive feedback. For many youngsters, association "created" a new beginning, a willingness to attend, to respond, to free-wheel and to create. A responsive-creative cycle was generated.

For many teachers, the process served as a motivating device. For example, when the teacher asked, "What words or ideas come to your mind when I say *poetry*?", every pupil had some response to offer. There was no "right answer" blocking the pupils. Involvement was initiated.

For some teachers, association, when used in specific contexts, provided increased knowledge of their pupils. The pupils' responses provided them with a general map of what their pupils were acquainted with in terms of knowledge and experience. In some cases, it served to identify pupils' interests which provided the teachers with another vehicle to promote learning.

Structuring Questions and Content for Association

The process of structuring questions to promote association requires little effort. Questions such as the following are used and applied to the samples given below:

- What words or ideas come to mind when I say------------------?
- What do you think of when you hear the word------------------?

  a) *Mathematics*—Set, number, numeral, fraction, rational number, number line, etc.

  b) *Language Arts*—story, poem, noun, verb, adjective, metaphor, simile, analogy, etc.

  c) *Social Studies*—democracy, nationalism, common market, industrial revolution, bureaucracy, etc.

  d) *Science*—mass, weight, density, sound, light, energy, living, non-living, chemical change, etc.

  e) *Art*—form, color, perspective, balance, etc.

  f) *Music*—sound, noise, clef, note, measure, etc.

Association is an excellent tool to establish a responsive learning environment and to initiate the creative process. Need we say more?

Comparing

This process requires brief treatment. Comparison is used extensively in most of our classrooms. We learn far more by comparing than we do from merely describing. For a practice exercise, we might compare a blackboard and an overhead screen. What kinds of statements would result?

The responses will vary, based on observations of the two objects and on the relationships one has to the other. We might state that they differ in color, size, position, material. We might add that they have similar as well as different uses. In essence, we would identify the differences and the similarities which exist.

Practical Classroom Uses of Comparison

In our classrooms, it is essential that pupils are provided with sufficient opportunities to note likenesses and differences. The common practice is to focus on differences initially. It *appears* that what makes the difference is what really matters. Few of us observe the numerous similarities which exist. When we ask children to compare, we are asking them to describe *both* the similarities and the differences. When we ask them to contrast, we are asking for differences. The kinds of comparisons we attempt to elicit will depend on a variety of factors, namely, the age, grade level, and maturity of the child as well as the nature of the task at hand. Too often comparisions are limited to similar phenomena which have obvious and definite relationships. In these cases the bases or criteria for comparison are not difficult to determine. This is exemplified by the usual class activities such as: compare two numbers, compare two maps, compare two sentences, compare two songs, compare two poems, etc. This type of comparison is fine for elementary school children but we should extend the process to a higher level of complexity for older pupils involving bases or criteria which are not so readily discernible.

In the early grades, comparison may involve concrete objects; in the later grades, abstractions.

Structuring Questions and Selecting Content

The process of structuring questions to promote this process is almost effortless. Questions such as the following are used:

- Compare two or more_____.
- Contrast_____with_____.
- What are the significant similarities between_____and _____?
- What are the significant differences between_____and _____?
- Differentiate between_____ and _____.

The content for comparison is huge. The following are provided as common sample items:

- Compare two or more number systems.
- Compare two or more geometric forms.
- Compare two measurement systems (English and Metric).
- Compare two or more historical events.
- Compare two or more methods of transportation.
- Compare two or more forms of government.
- Compare a variety of physical phenomena.
- Compare a variety of plant forms.
- Compare a variety of animals.
- Compare literary products such as poems, plays, stories, essays, newspaper and magazine articles, etc.
- Compare a variety of art forms.
- Compare a variety of musical compositions.

In sum, the opportunities for using comparison are tremendous. Children enjoy comparing and as their experience with this process grows, they acquire not only more meaningful knowledge, but also a skill which is an essential component of other thinking processes. The processes of inductive reasoning, classification, critical thinking, and creative thinking are complex functions which require comparison.

Convergent Thinking

Convergent thinking has been defined as the process of arriving at one pattern or one solution out of diverse elements, using some criterion. The result of this process is a correct or right answer. This process requires little treatment.

As teachers and as pupils, we have been reared and geared in convergent thinking. It is the most extensively used process in our schools. The types of questions structured to promote this process can readily be illustrated by such familiar samples as: What is the answer? Can you fill in the missing blank correctly? Is this statement true or false? Can you select the correct item in this multiple choice question? Are you able to match these columns? This total and overwhelming stress on convergent production has served to reduce education to a training program.

We have taught extensively for convergent behaviors and have focused primarily on two processes, namely, recall and convergent thinking.

There is no doubt that there are indeed right or correct answers as of time now. There is no doubt that we have relevant and meaningful knowledge to "transmit" to our pupils. The key problem is *how* we as teachers *expose* youngsters to this knowledge, what kinds of opportunities we provide to enable them to *process* this knowledge. The basic problem has not been with convergent production as a process, but with the overuse and abuse of this function. To provide opportunities for a child to arrive at one pattern or one solution is fine, but a variety of thinking skills should be promoted rather than one process—convergent thinking—if our schools are to develop all aspects of the child's intellect.

IN SUMMARY

In this chapter we have defined the essential terminology used in the Behavioral Outcomes Approach. The four levels of the teaching-learning process were described; the definitions of each of the thinking processes used in this approach were provided. The processes of association, comparison, and convergent thinking were dealt with in detail by providing practice samples, practical classroom uses, structured questions, and sample content items for each. In the following chapter we will expand our conceptual tool kit by focusing on additional cognitive functions and their practical applications to promote the teaching-thinking-learning process.

FOOTNOTES

[1] J. Cecil Parker et al, "Four Levels of Teaching-Learning" in The Oregon Program, *The Structure of Knowledge and The Nature of Inquiry,* issued by The Division of Education Development, State Department of Education, Salem, Oregon, 1965, p. 19.

[2] Benjamin S. Bloom, ed. *Taxonomy of Educational Objectives, Handbook I: Cognitive Domain,* New York· David McKay Company, Inc., 1956, pp. 205-206.

6

Expanding the Conceptual Tool Kit

In this and the following chapter, we will be working with a variety of processes which serve to promote the "meaning," "significance," and "action" levels of the educative process. Our format will consist of definitions, practice with process, practical uses, structuring questions, and selecting appropriate content.

DIVERGENT THINKING

Divergent thinking might be viewed as the reverse of convergent thinking, for in diverging we are offering various patterns or solutions to the same problem. Our thinking is not geared to a single track or path; our thoughts branch out in many directions.

To obtain some practical experience with divergent thinking, let us use the following sample: *List at least five different uses for a pencil.*

Compare your lists with the following items: write a letter; write a poem; write a play; write a memo; write a story. Responses such as these can be reduced to one use for a pencil—that of writing. This is not divergent thinking. However, if you have listed responses such as: use it as a dowel stick, as a wedge, as a pointer, as a baton, as a drumstick, as a lever, as a skewer, as a corrector (the eraser), as a measuring instrument, or as a back scratcher, you have diverged. You have not merely recalled the usual use of the pencil. When we use divergent thinking, we allow our thoughts to move from the usual to the unusual; we do not seek one instant correct response; we search for and explore a variety of patterns or solutions to a given problem; we offer more than one response; and we apply our total knowledge and experience to the problem.

Many teachers are under the impression that they are promoting divergent thinking when they present the class with a problem and each child presents one different solution. Each child, if he is involved in divergent production, should present at least two or more solutions. A class does not think! No doubt children profit from each other's thoughts and hitchhike on each other's ideas, but *only an individual thinks.* Brainstorming sessions may have divergent thinkers, each one providing a variety of alternatives, but we must be careful not to equate a pooling of ideas with divergent production.

Understanding the Mind Set

Before we can attempt to promote divergent thinking, we must be wary of establishing in our classrooms fixed or rigid mind sets, or what the late Dr. Max Wertheimer referred to as "functional fixation." For example, few teachers realize how simple it is to establish a specific mental set in a classroom. This can be demonstrated by the following workshop exercise: I assume the role of instructor and the teachers are the pupils. I state that I will read aloud a list of words which end in *oke* or *olk*. As I read each word, the teachers spell each one aloud. The list reads as follows: *coke, broke, poke, stroke, polk,* and *the white of an egg.* All goes well until we get to the white of an egg. The responses are either *y-o-l-k* or *y-o-k-e.* "The white of an egg," I repeat. *Y-o-l-k* is the usual repeated response. "The WHITE of an egg", I repeat again. Then someone finally replies, "That's *albumen!*"

Everyone had fixed their attention on *o-l-k* and *o-k-e.* No one bothered to think. A rigid mind set had been established, therefore—why think?

Avoiding Functional Fixation

In his book, *Productive Thinking,*[1] Dr. Max Wertheimer provides us with an excellent illustration of a mind set. He describes a visit to a mathematics class, in which the teacher presents a problem and its solution in such a way that the relationships become fixed. The teacher is demonstrating to the class how one finds the area of a parallelogram. On the previous day, the class had obviously been exposed to the rectangle and had been told that the area of a rectangle is equal to the product of the two sides. The teacher draws on the board a parallelogram such as this  and explains that a parallelogram is a plane quadrilateral, the opposite sides of which are equal and parallel. He then goes through the usual procedure of dropping perpendiculars and extending baselines and finally provides the usual proof that the area of a parallelogram is equal to the product of the base by the altitude. The pupils are then assigned a number of problems in their text which involve finding the area of the parallelogram. Everyone is busy dropping perpendiculars and extending baselines.

The next day, Dr. Wertheimer asks the teacher for permission to put a question to the class. Given permission, the good doctor draws the figure at right and asks the pupils to find the area. The pupils are obviously taken aback. One pupil simply states: "Teacher, we haven't had that yet." Others look unhappy and perplexed and simply write: "The area is equal to the base times the altitude"—a statement they have memorized but are unable to apply in this context.

After reading this account, one questions as did Dr. Wertheimer: "What have they learned? Have they done any thinking at all? Have they grasped the issue? Maybe all they have done is little more than blind repetition."

There is no need to belabor the point. It is obvious that functional fixation or the establishment of rigid mind sets has no place in a realistic learning environment.

Behavioral Outcomes of Divergent Thinking

By encouraging pupils to provide various patterns or solutions to a given problem, two objectives are achieved, namely:

1. The pupils no longer view a problem in one specific context. The realization that there is not always one correct solution to a given problem is reached. The pupils begin to flex their mental muscles and explore problem situations in new and different ways.

2. The pupils demonstrate increased creative thinking. Divergent thinking is a contributing function in the creative process for it serves to promote ideational fluency, flexibility, complexity, and spontaneity. Objects, words, ideas, facts are utilized in many new

ways; no one prescribed procedure is followed. The results clearly demonstrate the uniqueness and individuality which pupils possess. The individual differences glow bright and clear, and are welcomed and rewarded.

Structuring Questions for Divergent Thinking

By now, it is quite apparent that the way we structure a question will, to a large extent, determine the kind of process the pupil will use. The definition of divergent thinking dictates the structure or kinds of questions to be used. Provided with the definition, we find the task simple, as illustrated by the following:

- What different ways are there to solve problem X?
- How many kinds of problems could have arisen from situation X?
- In this role-playing situation, how many other ways could Y have responded to the problem?
- How many different ways can object Z be used?
- Provide two or more endings to this story.
- Provide two or more beginnings to this story.
- How many different ways can you group these objects, words, ideas, etc?
- List at least two alternative responses to the following questions:

  a. What would have happened if America had not been discovered until the 19th century?

  b. What would have happened if Lincoln had not been assassinated?

(The "what would have happened if" structure has wide application to all content areas at all grade levels).

- How many different ways can we compare the following items?
- How many different patterns do you observe in this picture, song, etc.?
- How many different views can we anticipate in terms of this issue?
- How many different predictions can we make relative to X occurrence?
- How many different conclusions can we draw from this data?
- How many different errors can we make in the process of _____(measuring the school yard)?

A perusal of the types of questions and the activities they suggest demonstrates that this process provides diverse, stimulating, and creative possibilities for meaningful learning.

SYNTHESIS

Synthesis involves putting together parts and pieces to form a whole. The process entails arranging and combining parts to establish a pattern or product not clearly present before.[2]

As a practice exercise, let us use the following words to synthesize a sentence: train, orange, horse, and window. Add any other words that you may need.

The sentences which are constructed will vary. Samples from teacher workshops read as follows:

- As I sat in the orange train, I saw a horse through the window.
- Looking through the train window, I saw a horse wearing an orange hat.
- As I sat in the train enjoying an orange, I caught sight of a beautiful horse through the window.
- I tried to train my horse to dance on an orange.
- I never horse around in an orange train because I might break a window.

In the above process, teachers combine their concepts of horse, train, orange, and window and constructed sentences—patterns—each of which conveyed a different meaning. Although the words were the same, the patterns which emerged were not clearly present before. This is analogous to the process of baking. Given specific ingredients such as flour, eggs, sugar, milk, etc., the synthesized products could vary from cakes to biscuits, waffles, muffins, cookies, puddings, etc. The ingredients or parts were combined to establish a product clearly not present before. In synthesizing we may be creative in that we not only produce a product clearly not present before, but an original product. On the other hand, the result may be of a commonplace nature.

In our day-to-day activities we synthesize continuously. In communicating with others we synthesize our thoughts, feelings, and experiences; in planning our work, we synthesize our schedules; and in enjoying our leisure time, we synthesize our activities. This process is like a thread patterning our entire life.

Behavioral Outcomes of Synthesis

In providing opportunities for and practice in synthesizing, we serve to:

1. Develop the child's ability to communicate—to organize ideas, thoughts, experiences, feelings, and data of all kinds.

2. Develop the child's ability to plan—to devise and create methods and procedures for doing things.

3. Develop the child's ability to integrate a variety of ideas and concepts into larger concepts so that he can perceive the interrelationships among these ideas and concepts and view the larger whole. Too many times we are compelled to teach courses, units, or segments and have little opportunity to unite and relate these segments. As a result of our piecemeal plans, our children have failed to see the interrelationships which do in fact exist.

4. Provide the child with an essential thinking skill which contributes to the development of other cognitive functions. In the process of inductive reasoning, the child uses synthesis, for in order to arrive at a generalization, the child must first combine and organize his data. In the process of creative thinking, the child organizes, arranges, and patterns an idea or product; he synthesizes creatively.

In sum, this process should be viewed in terms of its practical value. If we are preparing our children for the future, we should provide them with the tools to *synthesize* a better one than we have wrought.

Structuring Questions
Combining Synthesis and Content

The definition of synthesis provides the structure for the questions we will use. The key words in our definition serve our purpose: namely, *Putting together parts* and pieces to *form* a *whole; arranging, rearranging* and *combining parts* to *establish* a *pattern* or *product* not clearly present before.[2]

The following sample questions emerge:

- Combine the following unrelated words into a meaningful sentence.
- Combine the following characters from X, Y, and Z books or stories and construct your own story.
- Given the following purpose and data, develop a plan to achieve this purpose.
- Organize the following information into a meaningful report.
- Using your personal experience, write a short story or poem conveying what happened, how you felt, etc.
- Combine the following lines, shapes, etc., into a pattern.

- Given the following items, construct a mobile, a collage, a picture, a diorama, etc.
- Combine the following simple machines into a complex one.
- Given the following arithmetic operations, construct a problem using all of them.
- Given the following figures and data, construct a graph.
- Combine the following geographical data into a map.
- Combine the following data and state the interrelationships which you perceive.

ANALYSIS

A brief review of our list of definitions indicates that the process of analysis is the reverse of synthesis. In analysis, we are breaking down a concept, problem, or pattern into its component parts—systematically—so "that the relative hierarchy or sequence of ideas or procedures is made clear or the relations between ideas expressed are made explicit."[2]

To understand the process, we should experience it. Let us assume that you have undertaken the task of teaching your son to drive a car. The task then is to be able to describe and demonstrate how one drives a car. What mental gymnastics do you go through to describe this procedure? Essentially, you are analyzing. You are breaking down the procedure into a series of steps—sequential steps. Or we might deal with a different task. Let us assume that you are watching a TV commercial and your purpose is to identify the techniques and gimmicks used to persuade you that the purchase of product X will cure all of your ills. The process you are using is the same. You are analyzing the commercial and identifying the specific persuasive stimuli impinging on your thoughts, dreams, desires and feelings.

In sum, when we analyze we are asking ourselves—how is something done; what is the pattern in operation; what are facts and fallacies which are being presented; how are the elements arranged or related?

Behavioral Outcomes of Analysis

The statement which follows will probably appear circular but the results obtained in the terms of pupils' behaviors are not. Providing pupils with ample opportunities for analysis resulted in increased ability in analysis. Specifically—greater use of this process enabled the pupils to:

1. "See" order in their world.
2. Search for logical structure.
3. Search for sequence—"What do I do first, what do I do next?"
4. Identify patterns and sequences.
5. Recognize patterns in mathematical and scientific systems as well as in literary and artistic forms.
6. Differentiate among facts, fallacies and fantasies.
7. Recognize persuasive techniques in advertising and a variety of forms of propaganda.
8. Focus on details after breaking down a whole.
9. Break down a problem into the factors involved.
10. Focus on essentials.
11. Separate the relevant from the irrelevant.
12. Identify parts and describe "how they come together."
13. Use other thinking processes such as classification, categorizing and critical thinking more effectively since analysis is an essential function in each of these processes.

Teachers who made greater use of analysis in their mathematics classes were surprised at the results. It appeared that a number of "poor" math students suddenly blossomed and became "above average" students. Again it appeared that students learned more math by analysis than by rote memorization!

Visual analysis proved to be invaluable with elementary school children as well as with secondary school pupils. The analysis of drawings, photographs, diagrams, scale models and graphs were used extensively.

Questions to Promote Analysis

The following sample questions serve to promote analysis:

- What are the parts of a sentence, paragraph, story, poem, machine, compound, etc.
- Describe the steps or procedures needed to_____.
- Break the following code to interpret directions_____.
- What are the essential factors involved in this problem, experiment?
- List the parts of X and describe how they are related.
- In solving X problem, list the steps you would take.

- Describe the pattern you discovered in X musical composition, Y design, Z poem, etc.
- Analyze the given data and identify the facts and fallacies.

Sample Classroom Activities

- Pupils view a film *without sound* and analyze film by providing their own dialogue. Pupils then reply film with sound to confirm analysis.
- Tape a lesson. Pupils listen and analyze their contributions and evaluate them to arrive at suggestions for improvement.
- Pupils observe and analyze artifacts.
- Pupils view a film and analyze film to arrive at the sequence of events shown in the film.
- Pupils view a silent science demonstration and analyze to determine what they have observed.
- Pupils read a variety of humorous stories and analyze these stories to determine what factors operate to make something funny.

INDUCTIVE REASONING

Inductive reasoning is the process of generalizing. When we carefully observe specific situations and phenomena and formulate a rule, a principle or a general statement which is applicable to a class or group of objects or situations, we are reasoning inductively. The end products of sound inductive reasoning are always generalizations. The statement you have just read is a generalization! Essentially, most of us are generalizers as well as collectors of generalizations. (This statement is a proportional generalization.) We tend to collect and retain generalizations, principles and rules which are in operation and we readily forget specifics and details. We learn most effectively and efficiently via generalizing.

To experience the process, let us begin with a test item which has been modeled after L. L. Thurstone's *Letter Grouping.* Examine the following five groups of letters. Four of the groups are alike in some way, one group does not belong. State the *rule* that makes four of these groups alike; cross out the one that does not belong.

1. ABC   CDE   EFG   GHI   JKL Which group of letters does not belong? What rule have you induced from your observations in case number one?

2. ZYX   VUT   RQP   NML   IHG In this case, which group does not belong? Based on your observations, what rule applies in this case?

In case number one, you crossed out the last group JKL. The rule in operation is—the letters, grouped in threes, are arranged in alphabetical progression where the first letter of each succeeding group is the last letter of the preceding group.

In case number two, you crossed out IHG. The rule in this case is—the letters, grouped in threes, are alphabetically reversed, with every fourth letter omitted.

Now let us examine the actual processes we used in arriving at these rules. First, we *compared* each of the five groups of letters, we sought similarities and differences. Based on what we hypothesized to be the similarities, we *formulated a pattern or rule* which we applied to each of the similar groups. When the rule withstood the test and one group was eliminated, we assumed that our rule was correct.

In the process of inducing the rules, we used additional cognitive processes—namely, comparison and analysis. We compared each of the groups; in the process of comparing we centered our attention on each whole (a group) and broke it down into its components. Based on this analysis, we formulated a pattern or rule. As we work with the cognitive processes, we realize that a variety of thinking skills are intertwined. In many cases there appears to be a sequence of cognitive processes involved in what we initially viewed as one process.

Let us explore another sample of inductive reasoning. In this case, instead of formulating a rule, we will establish a generalization in the area of mathematics. Assume that you were given the following information:

The sum of the angles of isosceles triangle ABC is 180 degrees.
The sum of the angles of right triangle DEF is 180 degrees.
The sum of the angles of equilateral triangle GHI is 180 degrees.
The sum of the angles of a scalene triangle JKL is 180 degrees.
Based on this data, what generalization would you make? Within the confines of the given data we would state: In all triangles the sum of the angles is always 180 degrees.

You will note *within the confines of the given data* in the above statement. This is an essential qualifier.

One of the best illustrations of a child's use of inductive reasoning within the confines of the given data was presented in a

Chem Study unit a number of years ago.[3] The story recounted was that of a young child who was lost in the woods and had given up hope of being found that night. Being practical, he decided that he would build a fire and stay warm. Fortunately he came across some tree limbs, broom handles, chair legs, pencils, berries, rocks, marbles and paper weights. As he sat by the fire, he decided to list the objects that had "flammability." His list consisted of tree limbs, broom handles, chair legs and pencils. Looking over his list carefully he induced a generalization—one which—few, if any of us, would have arrived at. They all burn. They are all cylindrical. *Therefore, all cylindrical objects burn!* The next day, unfortunately he forgot his list, but—he did recall the generalization. This time he collected a tree limb, three baseball bats and an old cane and discarded a large wooden door, a chain and an automobile radiator. He was warm that night. The third day, keeping his generalization in mind, he located two pieces of pipe, a ginger ale bottle and an axle from an old car and disregarded a large box of newspapers. During the cold night that followed, he reviewed his generalization. Obviously the cylindrical property was not related to flammability. Perhaps, he thought, wooden objects burn. What's interesting about this child's first generalization—cylindrical objects burn—was that within the bounds of the data he had *initially* collected, the generalization was correct. Only when he continued to sample his environment, did he realize that he lacked an adequate sample and that his generalization was false.

In our classrooms, when we initially use the inductive approach we have many "lost children." However, our pupils soon learn to search for adequate samples or they qualify their statements with "as far as I have gone, it seems that" or "from the books we read or experiments we did, we think that."

Behavioral Outcomes of Inductive Reasoning

Provided with the tool of inductive reasoning the following results were evident:

1. Pupils not only acquired generalizations, but retained these generalizations for a long period of time. They were no longer swamped with details. The essential details seemed to adhere to the generalization and were recalled readily.

2. Pupils applied the process to all content areas; it seemed like the natural thing to do.

3. Pupils became "predictors." Based on their generalizations, they tended to take "inductive leaps." "If this is true, couldn't we say that"—was a common question.

4. Pupils became more analytical and critical about materials they read. They were CAUTIOUS. (This brings to mind that old anecdote about the cautious shepherd whose neighbor, glancing at a flock of sheep stated, "Those sheep were sheared recently." "Yes," said the cautious shepherd, "at least on this side.")

Sample Questions to Promote Inductive Reasoning

The basic structure of the questions to promote induction is exemplified by the following:

- Given the following specific situations, objects, data, etc., what *big statement can you make that applies to all?*
- Given the following words, sentences, mathematical operations, what *rule can you formulate?*
- Given the following geometric forms, state what is *common to all of these?*

The possibilities of utilizing content in all subject areas is tremendous. To cite but a few examples:

In the language arts area, children may be provided with lists of words to elicit spelling rules, paragraphs to elicit rules of punctuation, poem forms to elicit literary structures, a variety of stories, essays, books to formulate generalizations relative to human behavior. There are few limits to the possibilities which exist.

In social studies, children may be provided with a variety of maps, original documents, paper backs, films, tape recordings of speeches to elicit generalizations.

Science is a "natural" for the inductive approach. A series of experiments, demonstratons, films, filmstrips with masked word headings and the real phenomena serve to provide the resources for induction.

Mathematics is another gold mine. Specific samples of operations, concrete objects, pictures, graphs of all kinds and cuisinaire rods serve this purpose.

In sum, we have ample opportunities to convert our classrooms to classrooms of EXPERIENCES for we learn from our experiences, we generalize from particular cases and we retain these generalizations for future use!

DEDUCTIVE REASONING

In the process of deduction, we start with a generalization and arrive at a specific statement or conclusion namely, one which is not applicable to a class of objects, situations or phenomena. The syllogism, a deductive scheme of a formal argument consisting of a major and a minor premise and a conclusion, is familiar to all of us. Since deductive involvement is our purpose, let's try a few sample exercises. We are to supply a specific concluding statement in each case below:

Major premise: 90% of all teachers are warm, friendly and understanding.
Minor premise: Mary Brown is a teacher
Conclusion: Therefore, _____.

Major premise: Pupils with I Q's below 100 are not capable of employing higher cognitive functions (False, of course).
Minor premise: Mary's I Q is 98.
Conclusion: Therefore_____.

In each case, given a generalization, true or false, and some specific data pertaining to an individual instance, we are required to reduce a specific conclusion. In the first syllogism, our response may read: There is a 90% probability that Mary Brown is a warm, friendly and understanding teacher. In the second syllogism our conclusion may read: Mary is not capable of employing higher cognitive functions. The fallacies in deduction are readily discernable from the above samples. The validity of our *conclusions* rests upon the validity of our major premise.

In addition to the use of formal syllogisms, we employ the deductive process when we search for logical explanations using generalizations which are not explicitly stated but are "in mind."

For example, we may test our ability in the common case of the archeologist who reported finding two gold coins dated 46 B.C. Later at a dinner in his honor, he was thoroughly and openly discredited by a disgruntled fellow archeologist. Why? Obviously, how does one mark a coin 46 B.C., when Christ is yet to be born?

Another example utilized in our workshops is the case of The Man in the Elevator. This man exhibited unusual behavior. He lived on the twelfth floor of an apartment house. Each morning he entered the elevator and descended to the ground floor but—each evening he took the elevator to the sixth floor and then proceded to walk up six flights of stairs. He consistently exhibited this pattern. What caused his unusual behavior? Our workshop participants, when presented with this problem, may ask for additional information. Questions in regard to the height of the push button panel in the elevator and the size of the man usually serve to elicit the specific explanation. In this unusual case, we had an unusual man, a midget.

Commonplace examples of deductive reasoning may be readily cited. A lawyer is trying a case in court. He is using the laws of the state and applying them to particular cases. The process he is using is deduction. A chemist, engineer or mathematician who uses a general formula to solve a particular problem is using deductive reasoning. The skill of deductive reasoning has widespread application.

Behavioral Outcomes of Deduction

The use of deductive reasoning serves to:

1. Stimulate pupils to become critical listeners and critical readers.
2. Provide pupils with a tool for logical sequencing and detection of fallacious conclusions.

Sample Questions to Promote Deduction

- *If* this generalization or principle or rule is given and X information is known *then* what is concluded?
- Apply Z rule or Y formula to the following cases.
- Given the following major and minor premises, state your conclusion.

Math

Major Premise: In all right triangles, $c^2 = a^2 + b^2$

Minor Premise: Triangle ABC is a right triangle

Conclusion: Therefore in triangle ABC, $c^2 = a^2 + b^2$

Science

Major Premise: All objects in motion will remain in motion unless acted upon by some outside force.

Minor Premise: This ball is in motion.

Conclusion: Therefore, this ball will continue to move unless acted upon by some outside force.

The above may be a demonstration in which pupils are given the major premise, observe the minor premise and conclude on their own. Filmstrips may be used to generate deduction. Simply arrange the filmstrip in the projector so that all of the written data is *not visible*

Social Studies
  Major Premise: All American citizens, 21 years of age or more, have the right to vote.
  Minor Premise: John is an American citizen and is thirty years old.
  Conclusion: Therefore John has the right to vote.

The process of deduction is the reverse of induction or generalizing. We use a generalization or rule or principle to arrive at a specific. In a broad sense, when the pupil thinks in a logical sequence and arrives at a specific item of data, he is deducing. Equipped with both inductive and deductive reasoning our pupils have a "two-sided" tool for they are able to generalize from specifics as well as "draw out" the logical consequences of what they already know.

TO SUMMARIZE

In this chapter we have expanded our conceptual tool kit to include divergent thinking, synthesis, analysis, inductive and deductive reasoning. We have "experienced" the mind set and "observed" its effects on children's learning. In terms of the thinking skills dealt with, the behavioral outcomes of each were clearly delineated, specimen structures were provided to enable you to construct questions which combine the process with content and sample classroom activities were cited.

In Chapter VII, we will conclude our exploration of the cognitive processes and familiarize ourselves with the teacher's "periodic table" of thinking skills which will serve as a reference chart for day-to-day planning of instructional activities which promote process-oriented learning.

FOOTNOTES

[1] Based on material from pp. 13-25 in *Productive Thinking*, Enlarged edition, ed. by Michael Wertheimer, © 1945, 1959 by Valentin Wertheimer, reprinted by permission of Harper & Row, publishers.

[2] Benjamin S. Bloom, *Taxonomy of Educational Objectives, The Classification of Educational Goals: Handbook I: Cognitive Domain*, New York: David McKay, 1956, pp. 205-206.

[3] *Chemistry, An Experimental Science*, W. H. Freeman and Co., 1963. CHEM Study Project, University of California, Berkeley, California.

7

Completing the Cognitive Cycle

Up to this point, we have associated, compared, engaged in convergent and divergent thinking, synthesized, analyzed, and reasoned inductively and deductively. The wheel of cognition has been spinning and as we complete the cycle within the context of this chapter, we will be involved in the processes of classifying, categorizing, critical thinking, creative thinking, and conclude with concept formation. Having charted our cognitive course, we will begin with the process of classifying.

CLASSIFYING

When we establish an arbitrary system of groupings and subgroupings on the basis of the common characteristics of elements, we are classifying. Too often we mistake the process of categorization for classification. Too often, golden opportunities are lost when youngsters are given the task of "grouping" objects, words, ideas, etc., within an established system rather than carefully examining the data, arriving at their own criteria, and constructing their own classification system. Usually we give them fish, birds, ducks, whales, frogs and Linnaeus and they categorize using the Linnean system rather than having the opportunities to observe, compare, and experience the excitement of setting up their own grouping system.

Although few of us experience little difficulty in classifying, there are many who are not fully cognizant of the number of cognitive skills involved in the classification process. Let us work with a specific example. Assume that you were assigned the task of class-ifying the pupils in your class. How many different ways could you do this? How many different classification systems could you establish?

Any of the following would serve as the criteria for pupil-classification: height, weight, eye color, hair color, shape of nose, shoe size, chronological age, mental age, IQ, special talents, abilities, interests, achievement scores, socio-economic status, etc. Need we continue?

Obviously we have many different criteria which we can use to establish a large number of classification systems. Nor are we com-pelled to use but one criterion. However, how did we arrive at these criteria? Based on our knowledge of these children, on our *observa-tions,* on the *comparisons* we have made—on the similarities and differences we noted—we *induced* a series of generalizations which served as our criteria. Once having *selected* the criteria, we then proceeded to set up our classification system. The cognitive processes involved in classification included observation, making comparisons generalizing, selecting criteria (critical thinking), and then establish-ing the system. The process can by no means be viewed as simple. Therefore, when we provide our pupils with opportunities for class-ifying we are enabling them to utilize a variety of cognitive skills.

Behavioral Outcomes of Classification

In providing ample opportunities for classification, we serve to:

1. Provide pupils with a tool to organize and store information.
2. Reduce the need for memorization.
3. Provide for greater retention of information.
4. Enable pupils to perceive new and different ways of handling data.
5. Provide pupils with a tool to order and relate classes of objects, ideas, events, etc.

Sample Questions to Promote Classification

- Into what kinds of groups can you place these items, objects, ideas, etc.?
- What properties can you recognize by which these items may be separated into groups?
- Using your own ideas, make up your own grouping systems and then place these items in the groups (categorizing).

Content for Classification

The following is a list of some of the things which can be used for classification by elementary school children:

1.	Blocks	14.	Numbers
2.	Buttons	15.	Geometric forms
3.	Letters	16.	Arithmetic examples
4.	Pictures	17.	Plants
5.	Story books	18.	Animals
6.	Vocabulary words	19.	Rocks
7.	Sentences	20.	Shells
8.	Food	21.	Songs
9.	Clothing	22.	Poems
10.	Tools	23.	Stories
11.	Vehicles of transportation	24.	Newspaper articles
12.	Methods of communication	25.	Places
13.	Musical instruments		

For secondary school children we might utilize:

1. Writers, poets, statesmen, scientists, philosophers, etc.
2. Forms of governments.
3. Historical events, places, dates.
4. Scientific discoveries.
5. Animals and plant forms.
6. Artists, sculptors, artistic works.
7. Musicians, musical forms, and musical instruments.
8. Languages and grammatical structures.
9. Poems, plays, novels, essays, and short stories.
10. Values, feelings, interests, and appreciations.

CATEGORIZING

When we place objects, ideas, events, etc., in a given classification system, we are categorizing. For example, when the school librarian returns books to their proper place on the shelves, she is categorizing. When children in the classroom place their belongings in their assigned cubbyhole, they are categorizing. Placing our clips in the clip box and our pencils in the pencil box are examples of categorizing. When we compile lists of students to be placed in our established reading groups—the "bluebirds," the "green birds," and the "eagles"—we are categorizing. Categorizing involves having knowledge of given criteria, observing the phenomena with which we are dealing, and *slotting* those phenomena into established groups or categories. In practice we provide ample opportunities for this process.

Behavioral Outcomes of Categorizing

As a result of categorizing experiences, pupils are provided with:

1. A more ordered view of the environment.
2. An increased awareness of similarities and differences and of relationships between objects, ideas, events, etc.

Sample Question for Categorizing

Given the following known groups, place the items, objects, etc. in one or more of these groups.

Content for Categorizing

The examples given under classification are applicable to categorization.

CRITICAL THINKING

The term critical thinking brings to mind the old story about the orange picker who stood in the hot sun sorting his oranges and muttering, "Decisions! Decisions! Decisions!" There are few days which go by when we are not confronted with decision-making. Yet as teachers, we provide few opportunities for our pupils to make realistic, personally relevant decisions. We make the decisions and then proceed to establish the policy and procedures for classroom performance. Those decisions which pupils do share in making are usually ersatz and of little personal value. The class has decided to make a scrap book. The children have decided to publish a newspaper, write a play, construct a weather station, or raise money for X cause. In truth, too many times, those decisions were in the teacher's plan book the week before the pupils made them! Too many times, those decisions were based on the teacher's thoughts, attitudes, feelings, and beliefs. The game was to arrive at the decision the teacher wanted—the "right decision." Critical thinking is a *critical cognitive function*, critical in that, if properly used, it allows the child to find himself—to *become*—for he is able to begin to understand his beliefs, feelings, and attitudes and those of others. If properly used it can greatly contribute to the human education of human beings. The task is to understand the process and provide an environment and a "curriculum" for critical thinking.

We have defined critical thinking as a complex process involving the acquisition of data, the analysis of this data, the evaluation of this data by weighing the components either qualitatively or quantitatively, and making a selection or decision on the basis of this evaluation. Although theoretically the process is objective, in practice value standards are operating. Our feelings, attitudes, beliefs, and values enter into the process. This is as it should be, for the resultant decisions should be humanistic as well as rational—for are not feelings and values significant facts?

To provide a sample practice exercise in critical thinking, the following situation is presented: The board of education is exploring the concept of a four-quarter plan for year-round schooling. Many members of the board are of the opinion that it is wasteful of the taxpayer's money to close the school plant for two months, and more importantly that pupils would benefit from this opportunity.

In a newspaper release the following advantages were cited: The year-round plan would enable slow learners to work at their own pace and permit them to be graduated at the same time as their faster peers. Ambitious high school students could complete their studies in three years instead of four. Pupils interested in taking enrichment courses and advanced courses could do so. Pupils would be able to choose any quarter they prefer for vacations or might choose to attend all year. Teachers would earn higher pay.

The assistant superintendent has chosen a committee of teachers to review the four-quarter plan and to present recommendations to the board. You are a member of this committee. What is your recommendation?

Prior to making a decision, you would explore the statements made by the board members, investigate current programs where the plan is presently in operation, list the advantages and disadvantages of the plan for both pupils and teachers, and then confront the problem in terms of your feelings and attitudes toward the plan.

How do you feel about year-round teaching, did you plan to go to Europe, did you plan to advance your own education, did you plan to do "just nothing" and enjoy it? Are you parents who spend the summer relaxing with your children or pursuing your hobbies? On the other hand, would this plan give you an opportunity to work with potential drop-outs? Would you have a more positive effect on the "slow learner"? Would you spend more time on improving the curriculum? Would you experience more satisfaction as educators?

The recommendation you would make would reflect not only a careful analysis and evaluation of the data relevant to the plan, but also an assessment of your feelings, attitudes, and values relative to all factors related to the plan.

From the above description, it is evident that critical thinking is a complex process—complex not only in that it involves a variety of cognitive processes but in that it compels us to critically assess our feelings, attitudes, beliefs, and values and to clearly identify what we truly prize. In our classrooms, therefore, should it not serve our pupils in the same way?

Behavioral Outcomes of Critical Thinking

Meaningful experiences requiring critical thinking serve to:

1. Assist the pupil to make decisions on the basis of evaluating the components involved.
2. Assist the pupil in determining the validity of conclusions, beliefs, and opinions expressed by others.
3. Assist the pupil to look at his own beliefs, feelings, attitudes, and thoughts as related to a given situation, and allow him to substantiate his own ideas and beliefs and to decide for himself those values which he cherishes.

Sample Questions Which Promote Critical Thinking

The basic structure is displayed by the first example.

- Given two or more alternatives, which one would you choose and why?
- Given X problem and solutions 1, 2 and 3, which would you select and why?
- Given X issue and views 1, 2 and 3, select the view you would accept. Substantiate your selection.
- Given the following courses of action in X situation, which one would you choose to follow? Justify your choice.

- Given the following articles reporting Z event, select the one which best describes the actual occurrence. State the reasons for your selection.

Sample Content for Critical Thinking

Language Arts

- Which of these stories, poems, essays, reports did you enjoy most? Why?
- Which of these stories was most realistic? Why?

Social Studies

- Do you believe that men must have laws in order to survive? Why?
- Do you believe that Britain and its allies would have lost World War II if the United States had not helped them? Why?

Science

- Which of the following scientific inventions (X, Y, Z) was most beneficial to mankind? Why?

Mathematics

- How could we measure the size of this room? Which is the best method? Why?
- Bill has three ways to solve this problem. Which method do you prefer? Why?

CONCEPT FORMATION

Variations on the theme of concept formation appear to be numerous. An examination of hundreds of textbooks used in the schools yields the following generalization: few textbook writers are in agreement as to what constitutes a concept. These writers have labeled factual statements, rules, principles, and generalizations as concepts. It appears that the rule in operation is simply: when in doubt, call it a concept (for no one will know the difference!)

For practical purposes, our concept of a concept should be provided. We define a concept as a broad understanding or an enlarged mental image. For example, everything you and I know about love constitutes our concept of love. The knowledge we acquire, the experiences we encounter all serve to enlarge this concept.

Concepts may be concrete or abstract. A concrete concept is an understanding or mental image of an object that can be perceived by the senses; for example, the concept of a house, a train, a plane, a ball, etc. An abstract concept is an understanding or mental image "that has been acquired as a symbol ... for an intangible, for example the concept of square, circle, soft, ten, fast, long, over, etc."[1]

The process of concept formation is a complex one in that it involves a variety of cognitive functions such as comparing, categorizing, analyzing, synthesizing, and inductive reasoning. The result of this process is an enlarged understanding. The concepts we hold differ not only in terms of concreteness and abstraction, but also in terms levels of complexity. In essence, we operate on various conceptual levels, and these levels are a function of our total experiential background. In the teaching process, we use this knowledge of conceptual levels to gear our instruction to our learners.

For example, let us deal with the concept of heat. In giving a classroom demonstration on developing this concept with second grade youngsters, I am clearly satisfied when the following description is offered: "Heat is how it feels when I touch Mommy's oven when she is cooking." On the ninth grade level, I received the following response: "Heat is increased molecular motion," at which point I state: You are giving me words; I don't understand. Can you explain it further?

"Well," begins the student, "It can be best explained by the current theory of solids, liquids and gases, and their molecular structure. Until further evidence is available, we believe that in solids the molecules move slowly within a confined area; in liquids their molecular motion is greater and therefore they move more rapidly; and in gases, their molecular motion is still greater and they are able to spread in all directions unless confined in a closed container. Suppose, Mrs. Gerhard, I place this ice cube in your hand. You are now holding water in its solid state."

"Yes," I reply, "but it's dripping!"

"The heat of your hand," he continues, "is being transferred to the molecules and increasing their motion; the solid ice cube is being changed into water."

"Fine," I reply. "What do I do now?"

"Well, if you will transfer some of the liquid water into this beaker and heat the beaker with the Bunsen burner, the water will change to gas. Again you are adding heat. You are increasing the molecular motion of the water molecules and they now enter into the gaseous state for heat is increased molecular motion. Do you understand now?"

"Yes," I reply, "I understand your concept of heat. It was a wet experience, but well worth it."

Another illustration of conceptual levels is recounted by one of our teachers who had remained rather late at our workshops and rushed home to be confronted by her three hungry daughters ages five, seven and twelve. To keep them busy, while preparing dinner, she jotted a large 3 and a small 4 on a napkin and asked: "Which one is larger and why?" Her five-year-old replied: "Three, of course, it's bigger." Her seven-year-old replied, "Oh no! Four is larger because four things are more than three things!" Her twelve-year-old seemed perplexed and then in a very sophisticated tone asked, "Mother, which criterion are you using?"

While each of these youngsters demonstrated a concept of "large," the conceptual level differed, based on knowledge and experience. Which criteria are we using to select conceptual levels? Those which match the child and his abilities at time now. To do so, we must establish realistic expectations of what children at particular stages of development are able to conceptualize. The well-known cartoonist Charles Schultz[2] illustrates this beautifully in many of his Charlie Brown cartoons. Many of us may recall one in which Charlie and Lucy are gazing at the stars and the following dialogue ensues:

> Charlie: Just look at all the stars. Did you ever see so many? They're all over. . . . The sky is covered with stars . . . stars, stars, stars . . . as far as you can see. I wonder how many there are?
> Lucy: Ten?

To state that concept formation is basic to the educative process would be a masterpiece of understatement. For are we not constantly striving to enlarge our children's conceptual worlds? Are not all of our efforts directed toward establishing broad understandings which in turn promote broad appreciations, interests, attitudes, and value systems which characterize childrens' behaviors?

A great deal of work has been done in researching concept formation. We have but to review the extensive work of Piaget, Bruner, Oliver, Greenfield and others to discover that much is known and much more is yet to be researched. This should not serve to deter us, but rather, equipped with this knowledge, it should intensify our efforts.

To provide a sample practice exercise in concept formation, the following demonstration is offered. In our workshops, teachers have not only found this exercise useful in enhancing their own understanding, but have used it to model a variety of classroom activities which have been extremely successful.

THE MIB[3]

A Demonstration in Concept Formation

The following demonstration makes use of several of the cognitive processes such as: *comparing and contrasting; categorizing; analysis;* and culminates in a generalization based on the several trials *(induction)*.

Obtain a blank sheet of paper, and during each of the trials, use it to cover all of the remaining trials on the page. After choosing your answer, slide the sheet down to uncover the next trial which also contains the answer to the trial item you have just answered.

In each of the trials you will try to determine whether the figure is a "mib" or not. After a few trials you will begin to have hypotheses about what a mib is. You will gradually begin to have a concept of what a mib is and is not.

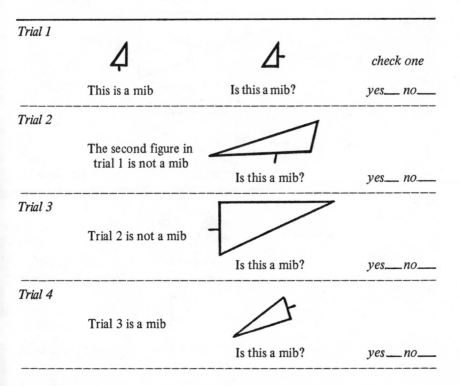

Trial 1

This is a mib   Is this a mib?   *check one*
                                               yes___ no___

Trial 2

The second figure in
trial 1 is not a mib

Is this a mib?   *yes___ no___*

Trial 3

Trial 2 is not a mib

Is this a mib?   *yes___ no___*

Trial 4

Trial 3 is a mib

Is this a mib?   *yes___ no___*

Trial 5

Trial 4 is a mib

Is this a mib?   *yes___no___*

Trial 6

Trial 5 is not a mib

Is this a mib?   *yes___no___*

Trial 7

Trial 6 is a mib

Is this a mib?   *yes___no___*

Trial 8

Trial 7 is not a mib

Is this a mib?   *yes___no___*

Trial 9

Trial 8 is not a mib

Is this a mib?   *yes___no___*

Trial 10

Trial 9 is not a mib

Is this a mib?   *yes___no___*

Trial 11

Trial 10 is a mib

Is this a mib?   *yes___no___*

Trial 12

Trial 11 is a mib

Is this a mib?   *yes___no___*

Trial 13

        Trial 12 is a mib

Is this a mib?   yes___no___

Trial 14

        Trial 13 is not a mib

Is this a mib?   yes___no___

Trial 15

        Trial 14 is not a mib

Is this a mib?   yes___no___

Trial 16

        Trial 15 is not a mib

Is this a mib?   yes___no___

Trial 17

        Trial 16 is not a mib

Is this a mib?   yes___no___

Trial 18

        Trial 17 is not a mib

Is this a mib?   yes___no___

Trial 19

        Trial 18 is a mib

Is this a mib?   yes___no___

Trial 20

        Trial 19 is not a mib

Is this a mib?   yes___no___

Trial 21

Trial 20 is a mib

Is this a mib?　　　　*ves___ no___*

Trial 22

Trial 21 is not a mib

Is this a mib?　　　　*yes___ no___*

Trial 23

Trial 22 is a mib

Is this a mib?　　　　*yes___ no___*

Trial 24

Trial 23 is not a mib

Is this a mib?　　　　*yes___no___*

Trial 25

Trial 24 is not a mib

Is this a mib?　　　　*yes___no_*

Trial 26

Trial 25 is not a mib

(Trial 26 is a mib.)　　　　Is this a mib?　　　　*yes___no___*

At this time, write out what you would consider to be a good description of a mib.

If you were successful, your concept of the mib was. A mib is a right triangle of any size, pointing in any direction, with a short perpendicular line attached to the shortest side of the triangle.

The Outcomes of Concept Formation

The outcomes of concept formation are quite apparent. The goal is to enlarge our pupils' conceptual framework in all content areas. The process is a neverending one—as our environment changes, new concepts arise, old concepts are discarded or modified, and the conceptual spiral continues.

Questions to Promote Concept Formation

The process of concept formation is a complex one involving numerous processes which we utilize as we "mibbed" along. Comparison, analysis and inductive reasoning were used in developing the mib. Therefore no one type of question serves the purpose. In concept formation, the nature of the concept we are developing determines the kinds of questions we combine to develop the understanding. The number and kinds of questions are a function of the concept.

A questioning pattern often used in developing a concrete concept involves the following series of questions:

1. What do you observe?
2. Describe the characteristics or properties of the object.
3. Compare it with other objects. What are the similarities; what are the differences?
4. How can you differentiate this object from others?
5. How would you classify it?
6. How would you categorize it?
7. Assume that I have never seen it before; combine all that you now know about it and tell me or show me in some way so that I will know what it is.

To best convey the value of this questioning pattern, let's use a concrete example. Suppose I want to teach you the concept of "bloop." How do you *obtain* this concept? *Naming* it does absolutely nothing. You would ask to observe it or you would ask me to describe it. What does it do? How is it used? You would compare it with familiar concepts you now hold; you would break it down into parts or components; you would attempt to classify or categorize it into a known conceptual framework; you would synthesize your data and then induce a general statement to convey the concept.

In working with young children we hear concepts described in terms of their functions—"a hole is to dig," "buttons are to close up and keep you warm," "mashed potatoes are so that we have enough for everybody"—are often heard.

To reiterate, the series of questions you use will depend on the concept being developed and on the conceptual level sought. In most cases, the cognitive skills will involve observation, description, comparison, classification, categorization, analysis, synthesis, and inductive reasoning.

Content for Concept Formation

The content area is vast. The following list is merely suggestive.

1. House	9. Grass	17. Heat	25. Government
2. Dog	10. Plant	18. Light	26. Democracy
3. Animals	11. Number	19. Electricity	27. Liberty
4. Train	12. Large	20. Energy	28. Equality
5. Car	13. Small	21. Cell	29. Happiness
6. Tree	14. Under	22. Atom	30. Hate
7. Flower	15. Over	23. Molecule	
8. Bush	16. On	24. Law	

CREATIVE THINKING

When we develop, organize, and reorganize ideas, objects, or words, and arrive at a product which is novel, original, unexpected, and imaginative in its new form, we are thinking creatively. Creative thinking is "new" thinking. In our approach, we accept creativity in its broadest sense. If the product produced by the pupil is *new* to *him*, not necessarily to us, the pupil is being creative.

All pupils can become creative thinkers. Every child possesses these abilities to some degree, and these abilities are capable of being increased by instruction. The more knowledge and experiences our children are provided with, the more creative they will be able to become.

The concept of creative thinking is no longer a new one. Excellent books on the subject are flooding our professional libraries. Numerous research studies have been published. Names such as Getzels, Jackson, Guilford, Lowenfeld, Maltzman, Parnes, Taylor, and Torrance are well known to all of us as key investigators in this area. Major creativity research centers have sprung up across the country. Industry has adopted procedures such as Osborn's brainstorming techniques and Gordon's "Operational Creativity." In sum —we have all become keenly aware of the need to develop a creativeness in people.

But do our schools reflect this awareness? We find creative youngsters in our kindergartens but conformers in our junior and senior high schools. Are we providing ample opportunities for our pupils to roam mentally, to free-wheel, to go beyond the commonplace, to invent, to be original, to be fluent and flexible with ideas, to "mess around" and explore, to "sit on the shelf" and imagine and dream?

Should schools for reality reject creativity? How many of the realities of today were but the dreams, visions, and fantasies of yesterday?

As educators we are proponents of creativity. We say it, we mean it, but what are we actually doing about it?

I recall visiting an art classroom in which youngsters were draw- ing pictures of an animal they had invented. One youngster was receiving assistance from the teacher. As the art period came to a close, the teacher asked each pupil to sign his name to the product he had created. This one youngster did. As I glanced down I read, "William Johnson and Miss Brown." We say it, we mean it—but!

How many of us have heard the following comments as teachers and as parents?

- "Follow the proper procedure. Do it the way it says in the book. Don't try to improve upon it."
- "When I was your age, we did it this way!"
- "Memorize the poem. Don't try to make up your own poems!"
- "Do as I say and stop asking those silly questions!"
- "Why, that's utterly ridiculous! How did you ever think of that?"
- "You have 20 minutes to finish that composition. Don't dream, write."

There are many times when we do not hear ourselves. We are so intent on covering content or developing a particular skill that we lose sight of the far more important objectives. We know what we are developing but we are unaware of what we are destroying.

In dealing with all of the previous cognitive processes, we ex- perienced the process by using one or more exercises. Therefore the following exercise is provided: Design a plan for rearranging the physical aspects of your classroom to provide an environment for creative thinking.

There is no one creative design which is "correct." Some will be more creative than others in the degree of originality demonstrated. Some will provide a greater variety of physical stimuli and resources to promote the creative process. However, a creatively designed classroom may contain the following components:

- The room is divided into a series of stations or centers. Different parts of the room serve as specific stations for art, science, music, reading, con- struction, and research, to mention but a few.
- The furniture is movable. The pupils can readily rearrange the chairs and tables without custodial assistance. Portable chalk boards, partitions, bookcases on casters are in use.
- Different kinds of furniture are used. The sizes and shapes of chairs, tables, bookcases, partitions vary. Stools, soft chairs, rugs, mats, cushions —regular or inflatable—are available.
- A large variety of resources is readily accessible to the pupils at all times. For example, the research area is equipped with reference books, maps,

globes, writing materials, audio-visual equipment such as cassette tape recorders, record players, a T. V. set, an 8mm projector, a slide projector, a portable screen, etc. The art center contains not only art supplies but a variety of commonplace materials such as cans of assorted sizes and shapes, boxes, rug and fabric swatches, wallpaper samples, old picture frames, old magazines, pieces of bark, stones, shells, etc.

- Learning areas vary in size to accommodate individual small groups and large groups of pupils. Carrels or small enclosures may serve as "work-alone" or retreat areas; other sections may become pupil-conference areas where two to five pupils may work together; and still other areas may accommodate larger numbers of pupils. A large area of free space should be available.

- Lighting devises may vary from desk lamps to adjustable fixtures which can be adapted to many needs.

- Storage areas are well organized and again readily accessible. In addition, pupils have their own places to store their materials, personal resources, and products.

- The room is attractive and reflects pupil creativity rather than "organized" confusion. How the room is decorated and what is displayed should be the result of the cooperative efforts of the teacher and pupils. The well-ordered, neat, meticulous classroom prearranged by the teacher displaying "educated" bulletin boards with "perfect" papers arrayed in symmetrical rows does not reflect a creative setting, but a "do-it-my-way" environment.

These components provide a fluid, flexible physical setup for releasing creativity. Creative climates will tend to produce creative children. Conventional arrangements convey the message—loud and clear: "Arrange your thoughts and actions along conventional routes."

Behavioral Outcomes of Creativity

Providing creative opportunities for pupils serves to:

1. Make children aware of their creative abilities.
2. Stimulate the production of new ideas, new products.
3. Stimulate an openness and sensitivity to the total environment, to the thoughts, ideas and reaction of others.
4. Promote problem-solving. (To use David Russell's term, creative thinking is "problem-solving plus.")
5. Stimulate a desire for learning.

Structuring Questions to Promote Creative Thinking

The following are sample items to serve as models:

- Make up a story_____.
- Create or design a_____.
- If you were a_____ , what would you do?
- Change the story.
- Invent_____
- Imagine that_____, what would happen?
- What would happen if_____?
- How would you feel if_____?
- What would you do if_____?
- Give an imaginative account of_____.
- Devise a system or procedure for_____.

Content for Creativity

The content to be utilized is vast. The following may serve as sample items:

1. Invent a language, a number system, a machine, a new society, etc.
2. Create a poem, a story, or a play that describes what happiness means to you.
3. Change the beginning, ending, or middle of this story.
4. Invent slogans to sell an idea or product you have created.
5. Devise as many different uses as you can for paper.
6. Imagine and describe what would happen if you could do anything you pleased.
7. Invent a cartoon character.
8. Describe what you would do if you were the teacher of a class.
9. Imagine that you have discovered a new planet. Describe what you would do with this new world.
10. Describe what would happen in a world without gravity.

THE "PERIODIC TABLE" OF THE THINKING PROCESSES

Having experienced and obtained a working knowledge of a variety of thinking skills, we are now ready to use them in planning our "units" of instruction. The following "periodic table" of the thinking processes is provided to serve as a reference for day-to-day use. The table contains each thinking process used in this approach, a definition, sample questions to promote the process, and sample items in each of the following content areas: language arts, social studies, mathematics, science, music, and art. Equipped with the table, you will be able to begin to structure questions to promote process

THE "PERIODIC" TABLE OF

The Thinking Processes and Definitions	Sample Questions	Applications to the	
		Language Arts	Social Studies
Association Relating objects or thoughts as they come to mind.	List all the things that come to mind when you think of _____.	communication books poetry play novel short story grammar dictionary reading speech	history geography topography map laws constitution government survival democracy liberty

THE THINKING PROCESSES

Following Content Areas:			
Mathematics	*Science*	*Music*	*Art*
number	earth	sound	a work of art
set	air	noise	balance
addition	fire	silence	symmetry
subtraction	water	note	color
multiplication	animal	pitch	form
division	plant	rhythm	beauty
geometry	energy	song	proportion
measurement	atom	lyric	media
circle	cell	strings	abstract art
area	experiment	opera	tools

THE "PERIODIC" TABLE OF

The Thinking Processes and Definitions	*Sample Questions*	*Applications to the*	
		Language Arts	*Social Studies*
Comparing Determining similarities and differences on the basis of some criteria.	List the similarities and differences between _____. Compare the following _____.	Two or more: words sentences stories poems newspaper articles authors poets prose and poetry characters settings moods	Two or more: historical events maps forms government presidents cultural regions religions climates documents explorations political organizations

THE THINKING PROCESSES

Following Content Areas:			
Mathematics	*Science*	*Music*	*Art*

Two or more:
number systems
solutions to a
   given problem
geometric forms
fractions and
   decimals
measurement
   systems
tools of
   measurement
theorems
arithmetic
   operations
equations
bases
	Two or more:
	animals
	plants
	animals and
	   plants
	kinds of
	   energy
	forms of
	   energy
	atoms and
	   molecules
	chemical and
	   physical
	   changes
	adaptations
	   of organisms
	   to their
	   environments
	hypotheses
	experimental
	   designs
		Two or more:
		composers
		instruments
		sounds
		rhythms
		compositions
		sections of
		   an orchestra
		types of
		   music
		music and
		   noise
		periods of
		   music
		melodies
			Two or more:
			works of art
			artists
			   early and late
			works of
			   artist X
			types of art
			art forms
			styles of art
			(realism,
			   impressionism,
			   cubism, etc.)
			media
			art in various
			   cultures
			styles of
			   alphabets
			colors and
			   moods

THE "PERIODIC" TABLE OF

The Thinking Processes and Definitions	Sample Questions	Applications to the	
		Language Arts	Social Studies
Convergent Thinking Arriving at one pattern or one solution out of diverse elements.	Find the correct solution or response to _____.	Spell the following words correctly. Punctuate the following paragraph. Name the authors of the following books. List five plays written by Shakespeare.	Provide the correct dates for the following events. Name the presidents of the United States. State the terms of X treaty. List the four causes of the Civil War.

THE THINKING PROCESSES

Following Content Areas:			
Mathematics	*Science*	*Music*	*Art*
Define a numeral. Identify the following geometric forms. Add the following numbers. Write the proof of the Pythagorean Theorem.	Define the following terms: *atom, molecules* etc. Identify the following rocks. List the organs of respiration. Draw and label a diagram of an animal cell.	Name the composers of the following compositions. List three famous compositions of Mozart. Define the following terms: *andante, allegro, piano, pianissimo,* etc. Name the notes on the following piece of music.	Name five old masters. Define the following terms: *symmetrical, asymmetrical perspective, proportion.* List the primary colors and complementary colors. Name five art forms

THE "PERIODIC" TABLE OF

The Thinking Processes and Definitions	Sample Questions	Applications to the	
		Language Arts	Social Studies
Divergent Thinking Offering at least two or more patterns, responses, or solutions to the same problem.	How many different ways can you _____?	How many different: a) ways can you use to communicate? b) endings can you write for story X? c) ways can you combine these words? d) titles can you provide for this poem, story, newspaper article, etc.?	What would have happened if: a) America had not been discovered until the 19th century? b) the Indians had refused to sell Manhattan Island? c) King John had not signed the Magna Carta? d) England had won the American Revolution? State two or more consequences.

THE THINKING PROCESSES

Following Content Areas:			
Math matics	*Sci n*	*Music*	*Art*
How many different ways cay you: a) use numbers? b) add numbers? c) measure the play area in the school yard? d) express X information in mathematical terms?	How many different ways can you: a) test hypothesis X? b) combine the following elements? c) control air pollution? d) classify these skills, animals, plants? e) use the material "Zerg" which has the following properties?	Given 4 beats, create as many rhythmic patterns as you can. How many different ways can you produce sound with these materials: strips of paper, rubber bands, wooden blocks, bottles, glasses of water, forks, and yourself?	In how many different ways can you: a) change the mood of a picture? b) express emotions through art? How many different: a) pictures can you create with the following shapes and lines? b) objects can you construct with your body?

THE "PERIODIC" TABLE OF

The Thinking Processes and Definitions	Sample Questions	Applications to the	
		Language Arts	Social Studies
Synthesis Combining and arranging parts or pieces into a whole to establish a pattern or product not clearly present before.	Combine the following _____ into a meaningful whole. Organize the following _____ into a report, summary, or table.	Combine the following unrelated words into: a) a sentence b) a paragraph c) a short story d) a poem Combine the following characters from X, Y, and Z books and construct a story.	Combine the following geographic data into a map. Combine the following data about "this newly discovered society" and state the interrelationships which you perceive.

THE THINKING PROCESSES

Following Content Areas:			
Mathematics	*Science*	*Music*	*Art*
Given the following arithmetic operations, construct a problem using all of them. Given the following tools of measurement, construct a plan for measuring the dimensions of your classroom. Given the following data, construct a graph which will best communicate this information.	Combine the following simple machines into a complex one. Given the following hypothesis and data, plan an experiment which would serve to test this hypothesis.	Given a number of notes, combine them into series of chords. Given a number of beats, combine them into a rhythmic pattern. Given the following notes, designate your own rhythm to form a melody. You may add words.	Given the following items ——————— construct: a) a mobile b) a collage c) a sculpture d) a diorama e) a mural f) an advertisement. g) a building Given the following poem and music, construct a picture to express your thoughts and feelings.

The Thinking Processes and Definitions	Sample Questions	Applications to the	
		Language Arts	Social Studies
Analysis Breaking down a concept, problem, pattern or whole into its component parts, systematically or sequentially, so that the relations between parts are expressed explicitly.	List the parts or components of _____. Describe the steps or procedures needed to _____. Analyze the given data and identify the significant components.	Analyze a variety of humorous, tragic, happy, or realistic stories and determine the factors which operate to make them so. Analyze the following story, novel, play and list the sequence of the main events.	Analyze the following artifacts and state your observations. Analyze the following description of a "good" community; identify and list the factors which contribute to making it good. Analyze the film on the Pueblo Indians; identify the key ideas in this film.

THE THINKING PROCESSES

Following Content Areas:			
Mathematics	*Science*	*Music*	*Art*
Given the following example of geometry in every day life—a tree, a snowflake, a daisy, a clock, a stop sign— analyze and identify the geometric forms in each. Analyze a picture graph, a bar graph, a line graph, and a circle graph and identify the title scale and approximate values of symbols, bars, or sectors.	Given the following formulas for a variety of compounds, state the elements found in each. Given the task of teaching your classmate how to use a microscope, list the steps you would demonstrate in the proper sequence.	Given the following melodies, identify: a) the time signature b) clef c) notes d) rhythm e) accidentals (sharps, flats, etc.) f) rests Given happy, sad, scary, or solemn music, identify the factors which create these moods.	Given slides of the following buildings, analyze them to determine the types of patterns or styles they display. Given the following familiar objects, break them down into basic geometric shapes.

THE "PERIODIC" TABLE OF

Th Thinking Pr)ᴄ ss s and Definitions	Sample Questions	A; ṗlicati) ns t .thᴄ	
		Language Arts	Social Studies
Inductive Reasoning Going from the specific to the general, often resulting in the formulation of a generalization, rule or principle.	Given the following specific data, what generalization, rule or principle can you formulate?	Provided with two lists of nouns in the possessive case, one list of nouns ending in s and one list of nouns not ending in s the pupils are asked to induce two rules namely that the possessive of nouns not ending in s is formed by adding an apostrophe and the possessive of nouns ending in s is formed by adding only an apostrophe.	Based on a variety of readings, films and/or filmstrips on the structure of a family, the pupils are asked to make a generalization as to the kinds of families which do exist, namely that families vary in the kinds and number of people they include.

THE THINKING PROCESSES

Following Content Areas:			
Mathematics	*Science*	*Music*	*Art*
After multiplying a variety of numbers by 10,100 and 1000, the pupils are asked to formulate a rule. Given a variety of triangles, the pupils are asked to measure the angles in each, determine the sum of the angles, and state a generalization.	Based on a variety of metals and non-metals, the pupils are asked to make a generalization as to the properties common to all metals. Given materials for bacterial growth, the pupils observe a variety of cultures and are asked to generalize as to the kind of media needed for this growth. (Pupils conclude that bacteria will grow on agar and any other media.)	After having experimented with a variety of ways of producing sounds, pupils are asked to generalize as to the basic ways of creating sound. Pupils conclude that all sound is produced in one or more of the following ways: vibrating strings, striking objects, blowing wind into tubes, etc.	After having painted with a variety of "tools" such as fingers, sticks, blocks of wood, branches, rope, brushes, rags, toothpicks, feathers, etc., pupils are asked to make a generalization in regard to "tools to paint with." They conclude that brushes are not the only tools but that there is a large variety of "tools" for painting.

THE "PERIODIC" TABLE OF

The Thinking Processes and Definitions	Sample Questions	Applications to the	
		Language Arts	Social Studies
Deductive Reasoning Moving from a generalization to arrive at a specific statement or conclusion.	*If* this generalization or principle or rule is given and X information is known, *then* what is concluded? Apply Z rule or Y formula to the following case. What are your *specific* conclusions?	Given the following rules of punctuation, pupils apply them to the following paragraph. Given the following proverb (generalization) and X story, pupils are asked to make a specific statement in terms of the proverb's relationship to the story.	Given the generalization that man requires laws in order to live, the pupils are asked to use this generalization by citing specific instances in which this generalization applies.

THE THINKING PROCESSES

Following Content Areas:			
Mathematics	*Science*	*Music*	*Art*
Given the following rule: if N represents any number then NXO = 0 and OXN = 0 Pupils are asked to apply it to the following specific statements: Ox2 = Δ Ox5 = Δ Ox35 = Δ	The pupils respond to the following: In all chemical changes, the substances lose their original properties and a new substance is formed. Which of the following are chemical changes? a) tearing paper b) melting ice c) burning wood d) eating candy e) stretching a rubber band f) breaking an egg.	Given the generalization that man expresses his feelings by music, the pupil is asked to identify specific instances in which this is the case.	Given the general statement that contrasts of light and dark color make some animals more interesting in appearance, pupils are asked to collect specific examples to demonstrate this statement.

THE "PERIODIC" TABLE OF

The Thinking Processes and Definitions	Sample Questions	Applications to the	
		Language Arts	Social Studies
Classifying Establishing an arbitrary system of groupings and sub-groupings on the basis of common characteristics of elements.	On the basis of some common characteristic or characteristics, place these items, objects, ideas, etc., into groups.	Group the following: letters sounds words sentences pictures stories poems essays authors verbs newspaper articles titles	Historical events Dates Presidents Forms of government Cities States Countries Cultures City governments Natural resources Methods of transportation Methods of communication Documents

THE THINKING PROCESSES

Following Content Areas:			
Mathematics	*Science*	*Music*	*Art*
Numbers	Animals	Tones	Colors
Geometric forms	Plants	Beats	Media
Fractions	Rocks	Chords	Shapes
Problems	Planets	Scales	Subject matter
Arithmetic	Cells	Sounds	Landscapes
examples	Organs	Pitch	Portraits
Measurement	Functions	Melodies	Abstract art
systems	Senses	Qualities	Artists
Theorems	Forces	Composers	Buildings
Axioms	Sounds	Musical	Styles of
Sets	Elements	compositions	architecture
Sub-sets	Compounds	Instruments	Contours
Equations	Mixtures	Operas	Design
		Styles of	
		music	

THE "PERIODIC" TABLE OF

The Thinking Processes and Definitions	Sample Questions	Applications to the	
		Language Arts	Social Studies
Categorizing Placing objects, ideas, events, etc., into a *given* classification system.	Given the following *known* groups, place the items, objects, etc., into one or more of these groups.	consonants vowels nouns common nouns adjectives adverbs fiction non-fiction editorials columnists features news items.	Forms of government democracy dictatorship monarchy Methods of transportation land sea air Methods of communication oral written aural Branches of government Executive Judicial Legislative

THE THINKING PROCESSES

Following Content Areas:			
Mathematics	*Science*	*Music*	*Art*
Numerals	Matter	Types of	Landscapes
Numbers	organic	music	Portraits
rational	non-organic	vocal	Still lifes
irrational	Forms of	instrumental	Realism
integers	energy	sacred	Impressionism
fractions	Sources of	religious	Cubism
decimals	energy	secular	Verbal art
real	Rocks	national, etc.	Non-verbal art
imaginary	igneous	Musical instru-	Mixed art
negative	metamorphic	ments	Commercial art
positive	sedentary	strings	Graphic art
Equations	Animals	percussion	Useful arts
linear	protozoa	woodwind	Media
quadratic	fish	brass	Styles of
Geometric forms	amphibians	keyboard, etc.	architecture.
	reptile	Functions of	
	birds	music	
	mammals	Elements	
		of music	
		Types of dance	
		forms in	
		music	
		Composers and	
		compositions.	

THE "PERIODIC" TABLE OF

The Thinking Processes and Definitions	Sample Questions	Applications to the	
		Language Arts	Social Studies
Critical Thinking A complex process which involves analysis, weighing of components either quantitatively or qualitatively, and *making a selection* or *decision on the basis of evaluation.*	Given two or more alternatives, which one would you select and why? Evaluate the following _____? What were your reactions to this _____?	Pupils are provided with a book, a play, a short story, a poem, etc., and are asked to evaluate the work. Did they like or dislike the work? Why? Given two or more newspaper accounts of a given event, pupils are asked to evaluate each account and select the one which they view as most accurate. Pupils prepare criticisms of a given piece of writing and are then asked to compare their products and defend their views.	In our school we have rules to govern our behavior. Which of these rules do you think are very important? Which would you discard? Why? Having discussed George Orwell's *1984*, the following question is raised: Do you think our government should put a telescreen in everyone's home? Give reasons for your answer. Bill states that there would be less conflict if all people had but one religion. Jane feels that each person should have the right to choose his own. Which viewpoint do you hold? Why?

THE THINKING PROCESSES

Following Content Areas:			
Mathematics	*Science*	*Music*	*Art*
Given three different methods of measuring the school yard, pupils are asked to select the most precise method and substantiate their choice. Given the interest rates at a variety of banks, pupils are asked to select the bank which offers the highest return and substantiate their selection with data.	Given a variety of theories of the birth of the solar system, pupils are asked to select the one which is most acceptable to them and substantiate their choice. Given a list of scientific inventions, pupils are asked to list these inventions in terms of their value to man. Given a hypothesis and two or more experiments, pupils are asked to select the experiment which would best test this hypothesis and state the reasons for their choice.	Pupils review the scores of two or more musical compositions, select the one which is most difficult to perform, and state the reasons for their choice. Pupils examine the construction of a group of musical instruments, decide which offers the greater versatility and why.	Given a variety of art products, pupils are asked to evaluate these products, select those which they like or dislike, and justify their responses. Pupils evaluate their own art work and identify their strengths and weaknesses.

The Thinking Processes and Definitions	Sample Questions	Applications to the	
		Language Arts	Social Studies

Concept Formation
 	
A complex process involving a variety of thinking processes such as comparing, analyzing, synthesizing, interpreting, classifying, inductive reasoning, resulting in a broad understanding.
	Concept formation involves a series of questions which result in the development of a broad understanding.
	1. What do you observe?
	2. Describe the characteristics of X.
	3. Compare it with other objects, ideas, events, etc.
	4. How would you classify or categorize it?
	5. How would you communicate what X is or means to someone who knows nothing about it?
	To test for concept formation the common question is: Explain and demonstrate what is meant by —————.
		Explain and demonstrate what is meant by:
		language
		prose
		poetry
		grammar
		a novel
		a play
		an essay
		an editorial
		noun
		pronoun
		adjective
		adverb
		preposition.
			Explain and demonstrate what is meant by:
			social studies
			history
			geography
			topography
			government
			law
			culture
			religious
			   freedom
			American
			   nationality
			evolution
			revolution
			constitution
			Bill of Rights

THE THINKING PROCESSES

Following Content Areas:			
Mathematics	*Science*	*Music*	*Art*
Explain and demonstrate what is meant by:	Explain and demonstrate what is meant by:	Explain and demonstrate what is meant by:	Explain and demonstrate what is meant by:
a number	science	sound	art
a circle	matter	noise	balance
a square	space	silence	form
a rectangle	energy	note	proportion
a set	force	pitch	media
a sub-set	life	rhythm	abstract art
a square root	hypothesis	lyric	beauty
an exponent	theory	vibration	color
a negative number	adaptation	key	perspective
an equality	change	notation	symmetry
an equation	control	harmony	foreground
a theorem	atom		background
a model	molecule		
	mass		
	density		
	gravity		

THE "PERIODIC" TABLE OF

The Thinking Processes and Definitions	Sample Questions	Applications to the	
		Language Arts	Social Studies
Creative Thinking Developing or reorganizing ideas, objects words, etc., and arriving at a product which is novel, original, unexpected, and imaginative in its new form.	• Create or design a _____. • Make up a story _____. • If you were a ____ what would you do. • Change the ____. • Invent a ____ • Imagine what would happen if _____.	Invent a new language. Change the beginning or ending of X poem, story, play, etc. Imagine that you have become a famous person; write a newspaper account of your accomplishments.	Create your own account of a new explorer who discovered an unknown culture. Invent what you would consider a utopian society.

THE THINKING PROCESSES

Following Content Areas:			
Mathematics	*Science*	*Music*	*Art*
Invent a number system and demonstrate how you would use it. Imagine that you are Gauss; write a short account of a day in your life. Pretend you are a geometric form. Describe your feelings.	Describe what would happen in a world without: (a) gravity (b) light (c) air (d) plants (e) water Describe what life would be like on a flat world. Imagine you are an atom. Describe what you would do.	Using music, how would you describe: (a) air (b) water (c) fire (d) light (e) electricity (f) largeness (g) smallness (h) roundness (i) freedom (j) discovery Select a poem or short story and invent a song which expresses your feelings about it.	Create a picture which expresses: (a) happiness (b) sadness (c) excitement (d) frustration (e) fright Given the following lines and shapes, create: (a) a landscape (b) a portrait (c) a still life Select a color and pretend that you are that color. Describe your thoughts and feelings.

Having reviewed the preceding table, we are now prepared to construct units to promote process and content goals. The first and crucial step in this process is the task of specifying these goals as behavioral objectives—objectives which clearly state the processes a child will use as he interacts with content and what behaviors the child will demonstrate as a result of these learning experiences. Chapters 8 and 9 will provide you with this essential tool, a tool which if properly used will systematize and strengthen your total instructional program.

FOOTNOTES

[1] Carter V. Good, ed., *Dictionary of Education,* prepared under the auspices of Phi Delta Kappa, (2nd ed.), McGraw-Hill Book Company, Inc., New York, Toronto, London, 1959, p. 118.

[2] From *Peanuts* by Charles M. Schulz, ©1953 United Feature Syndicate, Inc.

[3] From *Psychology and Teaching,* by William C. Morse and G. Max Wingo © 1955 by Scott, Foresman and Company, pp. 364-366.

8

Specifying Educational Objectives

A Blueprint as a Beginning

In Chapter 3 a blueprint was presented which proposed educational objectives for the future. The blueprint consisted of general goals, namely the active acquisition of knowledge; the development of broad and specific tool skills; the utilization of the cognitive processes; the development of a positive self-concept, of self-direction, of social effectiveness, and of positive attitudinal sets toward and interests in learning. Each of these goals was described in detail with one purpose in mind—that after reading this description you would understand the goals as I understand them and this would enable us to communicate with greater precision. The rationale for each of these generic goals was spelled out in down-to-earth terms. It may appear that the task of goal-setting has been completed, but—"this, my friends, is only the beginning."

Our own experiences have served to make us well aware of the fact that general goals are essential, but that they are by no means sufficient. They are merely broad descriptions of the purposes of education. They present an overview and are excellent statements for public relations pamphlets, but they are of little use to us as professional teachers who operate at a highly specific level.

Specificity Is Reality

For us, specificity is reality. Whether we are administrators, teachers, guidance counselors, or school psychologists, our actions, reactions, and interactions are specific. As educators we do not interact with pupils in general, but with specific pupils who demonstrate specific entry behaviors, who possess specific characteristics, specific needs, and specific interests. As teachers we instruct in specific content areas and our total behavioral and instructional pattern is one of intentional, purposeful activity geared to specific youngsters. If this is the case—and indeed it is, general goals stated in all-encompassing terminology serve to establish only overall purposes and directions, but do not delineate the specific objectives to be achieved and the specific routes to be taken. To verbalize that we want our youngsters to acquire knowledge, tool skills, or problem-solving skills is indeed admirable, but definitely inadequate when we settle down to the realities of classroom practice. It is time we placed the instructional focus where it should be—on the pupil, and on his behaviors as he interacts with the specific content whether that content be a parcel of knowledge, a tool skill, or an attitude to be developed. We must be able to establish explicitly the specific behavioral outcomes the pupil will demonstrate as a result of the instructional process. This is by no means an insurmountable task nor is it a new concept. How many times do we have to reinvent the wheel? The concept of defining clearly stated behavioral objectives can be traced back to the 1920's when individuals who were concerned with evaluation and test construction viewed the statement of behavioral objectives as a basic tool to enable them to devise and/or select valid evaluation procedures. A pioneer in this area was Ralph W. Tyler, who in an article on constructing achievement tests stated:

> Each objective must be defined in terms which clarify the kind of behavior which the course should help to develop among the students; that is to say, a statement is needed which explains the meaning of the objective by describing the reactions we can expect of persons who have reached the objective. This helps make clear how one can tell when the objective is being attained since those who are reaching the objective will be characterized by the behavior specified in this analysis.[1]

In addition to Dr. Tyler's writings, we can readily turn to Nolan C. Kearney's *Elementary School Objectives,* to Will French and associates' *Behavioral Goals of General Education in High School,* and to others such as Bloom, Mager, and Krathwohl who have succeeded in refocusing our attention on this indispensable tool. For specifying behavioral objectives is precisely this—a tool which enables us to transform education into a more systematic, meaningful, and relevant process rather than allowing it to remain the haphazard, global process of glittering generalities and high-sounding beliefs which expresses little and impresses few. It has taken us approximately 50 years to rediscover this tool, and fortunately educators throughout the country are beginning to apply it to classroom practice.

More than ever before, general goals are being transformed into functional pupil objectives. Teachers and curriculum designers are stating objectives as a series of *operations* which the pupil will perform as he acts upon specific content to acquire knowledge or to develop specific skills. Numerous school systems have involved their staffs in preparing these objectives which describe in precise terms the specific observable behaviors which the pupil will demonstrate as a result of a teaching-learning activity.

Transforming General Goals into Specific Objectives

How this is done involves a process of self-questioning and thoughtful analysis. Many of us have started with the following questions: What will the pupil be able to do as a result of a specific teaching-learning experience? What is the specific purpose of any educational activity in terms of the pupil's behavior? How will the pupil's behavior change? What will he be able to do when he has completed this or that activity or series of activities? What behavior will he demonstrate? Is this behavior observable? Will I, the teacher, be able to measure it? Am I primarily concerned with a pupil's behavioral outcome or a product he produces? Are there instances when I can judge pupil performance only by the resultant product? If so, what are they?

When we begin to confront these questions and to construct a series of statements describing the anticipated pupil behavioral change, we are specifying objectives. We are clearly delineating the pupil's objective or in some instances the product which is indicative of his attaining this objective.

Illustrations of Specific Behavioral Objectives

At this point a few concrete illustrations may be appropriate. Let us examine a few samples of goals which are not specified in terms of pupil behaviors and then transform them into behavioral terms.

Suppose we select a content area such as science. A common goal in science education has been that pupils "acquire knowledge of the scientific method." To transform this goal into a specific behavioral objective we must ask ourselves: What precisely does having a knowledge of the scientific method mean in terms of pupil behaviors? How does the pupil demonstrate this knowledge? How do I know he knows? Does having a knowledge of the scientific method mean the pupil will be able to list the sequential steps involved in this method? Does it mean that given a new problem the pupil is able to apply the scientific method and arrive at a tentative solution or at a variety of possible solutions to the problem? Does it mean that in viewing a film dealing with an experimental approach, the pupil is able to identify those steps which were trial and error and those which were representative of the scientific method? There is little doubt that each of these behaviors are indicators—some poor, some better—of the pupil's "acquisition of knowledge of the scientific method." Therefore, the objective stated in behavioral terms would read: The pupil acquires knowledge of the scientific method as demonstrated by any of the following observable behaviors:

1. Listing the steps of the scientific method.
2. Solving a new problem by applying the scientific method.
3. Differentiating between the trial and error process and the scientific method and identifying each method in written or oral form.

The above statement clearly identifies the observable pupil behaviors. As teachers, we are then able to determine whether he does or does not have some knowledge of the method. Of course, behavior Number One, which requires listing, merely tells us he is able to recall the steps of the method; behavior Number Two tells us he is able to apply the method to a problem-solving situation, and behavior Number Three tells us simply that he does "know" what the method is as opposed to trial and error. Which of these behavioral outcomes we would specify for a particular child would be based on our knowledge of the child. However, the point being emphasized at this time is that a goal such as the pupil's acquisition of knowlege of the scientific method can be operationalized and stated as a series of pupil behaviors which now are meaningful and useful to both pupil and teacher, in that the objectives to be achieved are clearly stated and are observable, enabling both teacher and pupil to determine where they are going and when they have gotten there.

For a second illustration, let us utilize the area of foreign languages. A general goal in this area may read as follows· The pupil will acquire a command of the Spanish language. But—what precisely does the term "acquire a command" of the Spanish language mean in terms of pupil behaviors? Does it mean that the pupils will be able to engage in simple, smooth-flowing conversations in Spanish? Does it imply that pupils will be able to translate simple articles taken from Spanish newspapers into English? Does it mean that pupils will be able to write descriptions of an event in Spanish utilizing correct grammatical forms?

"Acquiring a command" of the Spanish language obviously encompasses all of these behaviors and many more. However, the statement *the pupil will acquire a command of the Spanish language* conveys little practical meaning to teachers and pupils unless we specify the observable pupil behaviors or pupil products which demonstrate the achievement of this goal. This broad goal can readily be broken down into hundreds of specific pupil behaviors requiring an instructional period of one to four years before we are able to say the pupil has "acquired a command" of the Spanish language. Samples of some specific behavioral objectives might read as follows:

> Given simple articles from a Spanish newspaper, the pupil will be able to translate these articles into English with at least 85% accuracy.
> Given topics such as *my home, my family, my friends,* the pupils will be able to engage in a smooth flowing conversation in Spanish.
> Given topics such as *my school, my hobbies, my ambitions,* the pupil will be able to write a short composition of 200 words in Spanish with a minimum of 85% accuracy.

The preceding illustrations should have served to differentiate between broad goals and specific behavioral objectives. The broad goals merely designate a general area; the specific objectives pinpoint precisely where the pupils are going and what they will achieve.

The "Whys" of Specifying Objectives

The key question, however, remains to be answered, namely, "Why specify objectives?" Or should the key question read, "Why specify objectives in education?"

It is interesting to note how specific we are in dealing with matters outside the realm of the learning process or merely tangential to it. For example, few of us would construct a house or a school without highly detailed blueprints, nor would we build a bookcase or design a dress or suit without specific plans, but how many of us have walked into our classrooms with our objectives "in mind"? How frequently in workshops in the past five years I have heard experienced teachers discard the need for specifying objectives. "I have taught for 15 years! I know my objectives. There is no need for me to write them down in terms of pupil behaviors!"

But what happens when I am so bold as to ask these teachers to state their objectives? The objectives which emerge are descriptions of content; rarely are they statements which describe what the pupil will be able to do as a result of interacting with this content. Objectives such as the following are heard: "I am teaching the Civil War." "I am teaching protozoa." "I am teaching *Lost Horizons.*" Usually at this time I am silent, for I am tempted to state quite openly that 15 or 20 years ago I too taught the Civil War, probably to protozoa, and had lost my horizons. I maintain my equilibrium and cautiously ask that old, old question, "To whom do you teach the Civil War?" The forthcoming reply of course is, "To the children." Then the final question emerges: What do you want the children to be able to do as a result of being exposed to *Lost Horizons,* or protozoa, or the Civil War, or rational numbers, or what have you? What specific outcome do you want the child to demonstrate as he interacts with this content? Do you want the child to list the causes of the Civil War? Do you want the child to compare the causes of the Civil War with other civil wars? Do you want the child to prepare an account of the Civil War as viewed by a Northerner, by a Southerner? What specific pupil outcomes are you concerned with? Are you concerned with the pupil's ability to read a given textbook and to regurgitate its contents relative to the Civil War? Are you concerned with the child's ability to process data on the Civil War, make comparisons, analyze different resources, critically think about the issues of that time? Are you concerned with the child's feelings about the issues of that war, about the conflicting values of those times? Or are you merely concerned with the happenings which constitute the Civil War? Or, let us take it one step further or backward, are you concerned with the scores the pupils will receive on the tests you administer to record their "progress"? How well do they fill in the missing blanks or how proficient are they in the multiple-guess questions relative to the Civil War? What are our real objectives? What objectives will withstand the test of time; what objectives will be retained, will be meaningful, will change the child into a more effective human being in today's society?

When exposed to this barrage of questioning, when given ample time to discuss their responses, few teachers can honestly state that they are primarily concerned with the content. Of course, how children interact with content, how children's behaviors change when they are exposed to and involved with content are the real objectives. But many teachers explain they have lost sight of these objectives. Their training at the college level, their own experiences as pupils, their initiation into X school requiring them to complete the boxes of a lesson plan book, specifying the precise pages to be covered in X text, the precise topics to be listed, the precise day for testing, have served to misplace the focus. Few if any of those lesson plan books contain statements of what the pupil will be able to do! In fact few if any make any reference to the pupil! Therefore, there should be little surprise or disappointment when teachers initially fail to react positively to the great discovery of specifying objectives in terms of pupil behaviors.

They have been well trained to ignore the pupil, and this training has been reinforced by many outdated requirements such as the sacred lesson plan booklets for the "substitute." I doubt if many administrators have given much thought to the detrimental effects these planbooks have had on conditioning teachers. How many times the planbooks, the firm schedule, the specific grouping procedures have served to provide the false semblance of a smooth-flowing, well-run school plant. For this is precisely what we have reduced education to—a school plant—a content-centered and procedure-centered factory. We have not created a living learning world teeming with human beings striving for realistic behavioral change and behavioral growth.

Therefore, we should not be astounded at the teacher's response to the concept of specifying behavioral objectives. However, when teachers attempt to grind out behavioral objectives, when they roll up their sleeves and persist, the clarity which emerges affects every aspect of the instructional process and serves to change the total pattern.

During the process of specifying objectives and planning for instruction, questions and comments such as the following are frequently heard:

"Why am I emphasizing facts 1, 2 and 3? Shouldn't I be developing concept A instead?"

"Are these facts relevant or are they mere details to be memorized and then forgotten? What real purpose is there in the child's involvement with this content?"

"Are not content A and B equally good in achieving this objective? Which content selection will serve the child in attaining more than one objective?"

"Aren't all of these objectives requiring the child to recall information? Shouldn't I be preparing objectives which involve higher cognitive levels such as comparison, analysis, classification, induction, and critical thinking?"

"Why am I using this diagnostic test? It doesn't test for the objectives I have listed."

"By golly, it's relatively easy to construct a post test by using the list of objectives. You really are testing for what you have taught!"

"The behavioral objectives I have just constructed will require more than one word fill-ins or multiple choice test items. These old tests must go!"

"I've just reorganized my instructional sequence in teaching skills X and Y. Listing the pupil's behavioral objectives did it. It is more logical and efficient this way. I have no need to review and reteach."

"I've had a great deal of trouble in planning this unit but I finally hit upon it. I really wasn't clear about what I wanted the kids to be able to do."

"Sure, I can use any one of these four content areas or others; the objective is to develop group responsibility on the part of the youngsters."

"It doesn't matter what country is selected as a vehicle, the geographical concepts and their relationships are to be developed by the youngsters. The pupil objective is concept formation."

"You don't understand! The objective is that the pupil will think creatively and produce his own product, not that he will correct every misspelled word. When the objective is to have the pupil learn to spell certain words correctly, that's fine. But you have to be clear in your own mind what the objective is. You also have to be certain that you do not combine two objectives where one will inhibit or destroy the other."

"These objectives require that the child *actually performs*—not that he writes or verbalizes. You don't test a kid on swimming by asking him to write an essay on 'How I Swim!'"

"I just want the kid to square dance. I'm not going to test him on each turn and twist he makes. The objective is as specific as it should be. The pupil will be able to square dance. How specific you get depends on how specific you want the pupil's behavior to be!"

"I've compiled a list of objectives, each with a variety of alternatives. I'm going to have the youngsters select from these alternatives. If I'm going to promote some self-direction, I should provide the kids with opportunities to make choices."

"It is not an insignificant objective. Look at it this way—one of our major goals is to develop self-directive youngsters. Right? Well, the objective states that: *Given oral or written directions, the pupil will be able to follow these directions.* A youngster cannot be self-directive or self-instructive unless he can follow directions. Following directions is a very important skill."

"I thought this business of specifying objectives was just verbal garbage. I felt we were just substituting the objectives game for the plan book game. But boy, was I surprised! This specificity gets to you!"

Merely from these teacher comments and questions the "whys" of specifying objectives clearly emerge. Many of these "whys" will be expanded upon as we proceed. However, at this point it should be evident that in getting specific with objectives:

1. We compel ourselves to carefully analyze our objectives and select those which we judge to be most relevant to today's reality.

2. We state these objectives in terms of specific pupil behaviors or pupil products which are observable and measurable. (Those which are not readily observable can be made observable by a "backdoor" approach which will be dealt with in Chapter 9.)

3. We are able to select those diagnostic tests which match our objectives to determine whether the pupil has already achieved these objectives in part or fully and what deficiencies exist.

4. We are able to plan a series of instructional sequences which are logical and efficient, by which our pupils will attain these objectives.

5. We are able to select and/or construct post tests which match these objectives, thereby enabling us to evaluate whether the pupil has attained them and the degree of success he has experienced.

6. We are able to better assess our own instructional patterns and decisions and make the needed revisions.

In sum, getting specific with objectives affects the total instructional process. This specificity becomes a thread which runs through the entire fabric from establishing behavioral objectives to selecting diagnostic instruments—to planning instructional sequences—to evaluating pupil performance. As teachers, we begin the process of systematically "making the match." We match the diagnostic instruments to the objectives; we match the instructional activities to the objectives; we match the evaluative instruments to the objectives. And of course, it goes without saying we start the match with the child. Our knowledge of the child—his abilities and his needs—determines which objectives, which instructional activities, which media, which evaluative instruments will be utilized. These processes —the process of becoming specific with objectives and the process of making the match—serve to systematize and refine the teaching-thinking-learning process. They clarify and sharpen the process and bring us closer to reality—for the match between education and reality has yet to be made.

FOOTNOTES

[1] Ralph W. Tyler, *Constructing Achievement Tests,* The Ohio State University, Columbus, Ohio, 1934, p. 18.

9

Preparing Objectives for Classroom Use

How to Specify Objectives
in Behavioral and Measurable Terms

Up to this point, we have talked about and around objectives, but we have not pinpointed the mechanics and procedures which are involved. We are now at the how-to-specify-objectives stage. It seems appropriate to state precisely what your behavioral outcomes will be as a result of interacting with the contents of this section of the chapter.

Key Objectives and Sub-Objectives

Provided with the background information in Chapter 8 and the practical activities in this section, you will be able to write pupil objectives in behavioral, observable, and measurable terms. In other words, you will be able to state precisely what the pupil will be able to do as he interacts with some specific content. The statements will describe *observable* behaviors and specify how these behaviors will be measured. This is the key objective. However, before you are able to achieve this objective, there is a series of objectives which are pre-requisites, serving to make the attainment of the key objective easier. These sub-objectives are listed below. You will be able to:

1. Compare a set of objectives and differentiate between one which is clearly stated and one which is ambiguous and subject to a variety of interpretations.
2. Identify the "loaded" terms which promote ambiguity in poorly stated objectives.

3. Define and illustrate the terms *overt* and *covert behavior.*

4. Operationalize covert behaviors by listing overt behaviors or products which clearly demonstrate that the covert behavior has taken place.

5. Define and identify cognitive, affective, and psychomotor behaviors.

6. Identify the cognitive, affective, and psychomotor components in a given set of behaviors.

7. Construct specific objectives.

8. State affective objectives in observable terms.

9. Construct objectives designating realistic mastery levels.

10. Identify and apply the relationship between specified behavioral objectives and the construction of valid test items to measure the attainment of these objectives.

11. Combine and apply all of the above skills by specifying objectives in observable and measurable terms for classroom use. This constitutes the key objective.

Differentiating Between Ambiguous and Clearly Stated Objectives

Let us begin with the first objective—that of differentiating between a clearly stated objective and one which is ambiguous and subject to a variety of interpretations. Which of the following is a more clearly stated objective? Why?

a) A general knowledge of American History encompassing the period from 1910 to 1969.

b) The pupil will be able to state at least two major reasons for U. S. involvement in Viet Nam and explain each briefly. (Maximum number of words—100).

A general knowledge of American History encompassing the period from 1910 to 1969 is certainly not a clearly stated objective. Whose objective is this? The pupil's? The teacher's? What knowledge is to be dealt with? For what purposes? What is the learner to do with this knowledge? How is the attainment of this general knowledge to be measured? Were ten teachers of social studies to be given this objective, would they arrive at the same interpretation? Obviously not. The statement, if we can call it that, is not an objective. It conveys very little and is reminiscent of the worthless "survey" courses prevalent at the college level.

The second (*b*) is a more clearly stated objective. It clearly conveys what the pupil will be able to do. Any of the ten social studies teachers referred to above would clearly "know" what the pupil should be able to accomplish. The instructional strategies would vary, but the objective and therefore the outcome would be identical in all of the ten classrooms. Objective *b* clearly communicates.

Identifying "Loaded" Terms

Let us proceed with Objective 2, that of identifying the "loaded" terms which promote ambiguity in poorly stated objectives.

Consider the following familiar statements taken from many "experimental" and commercial curricula:

a) The pupil will develop an understanding of grammar.
b) The pupil will develop an appreciation of music.
c) The pupil will understand our cultural heritage.
d) The pupil will enjoy art.
e) The pupil will grasp the significance of the U.N.'s efforts at promoting peace.
f) The pupil will have faith in democracy.
g) The pupil will know Newton's Laws of Motion.
h) The pupil investigates the relationship of mass and weight.
i) The purpose of the study is to see the shape of the magnetic field around two bar magnets.

Do these objectives focus on the pupil? Are the behaviors clearly stated? Are you able to pinpoint them as they occur? Do these objectives readily suggest specific instructional activities in which the pupils may engage? Would these objectives serve as useful guidelines for teachers working independently of you? Would they all arrive at the same interpretation?

These objectives, except for *i*, certainly focus on the pupil. The behaviors are stated: developing an understanding, developing an appreciation, understanding, enjoying, grasping the significance of, having faith in, knowing, investigating, seeing. But—how in heaven or in the classroom—do we "know" that John or Bill has developed an understanding or an appreciation, or that Mary enjoys, grasps the significance of, has faith in, or is investigating and does see? Those behaviors are not observable; the words describing them are "loaded" terms—loaded with ambiguity—for the teacher cannot say with any degree of precision that these behaviors are taking place.

In considering the instructional activities to be utilized to achieve any one of these objectives, we find that few parameters are given. Developing an appreciation of music or understanding our cultural heritage leaves the field wide open. Were we to consider the phrasing of these objectives and give thought as to how other teachers, working independently, would interpret these objectives, most of us would conclude that the interpretations would be varied. It would be most unlikely that we would all arrive at the same interpretation.

Avoiding "Loaded" Terms

Objectives *a* through *i* were obviously poorly stated objectives. The major reason was the use of "loaded" terms which promotes ambiguity, for they are not descriptive of observable behaviors. Therefore, in constructing objectives we avoid terms such as the following:

understands	sees
understands the meaning of	develops an insight
really understands the meaning of	becomes familiar with
appreciates	covers
knows	thinks
enjoys	learns
grasps the significance of	realizes
really grasps the significance of	comprehends
has faith in	develops the concept of
values	develops an interest in
investigates	

Defining and Illustrating Overt and Covert Behaviors

The "loaded" terms listed above are examples of covert behaviors, behaviors which are not directly observable but are hidden. We do think. However, the act of thinking is not observable. We do experience anxiety. However, the act of being anxious is not always observable. Processes such as learning, knowing, enjoying, comprehending are examples of covert behaviors—behaviors which occur, but are not *directly* observable. Therefore in constructing behavioral objectives which are observable we attempt, whenever possible, to avoid these "loaded" terms. We use terms which describe overt actions, namely, observable behaviors.

Consider the following objectives and compare them with the previous ones. How do they differ?

a) The pupil is able to write a short paragraph of 75 words describing the theme of poem X.
b) The pupil recites the conjugation of the verb, *faire*.
c) The pupil solves quadratic equations.
d) The pupil constructs a simple machine.
e) The pupil compares the Civil War with World War I by listing five ways in which they were similar.
f) The pupil contrasts the effects achieved by using water colors with the effects achieved by using oils by stating these different effects

The comparison yields observable results. An analysis of objectives *a* through *f* indicates that the terms used clearly describe overt or observable behaviors; the pupil writes, recites, solves, constructs, compares by listing, and constrasts by stating. Therefore, in constructing objectives we utilize terms such as:

writes	compares by listing
recites	contrasts by stating
discusses	analyzes by stating or recording
states	selects
cites examples of	differentiates by listing
lists	explains in written or oral form
illustrates	identifies
describes	names
constructs	points to
solves	defines

All of these terms describe behaviors that are observable or products that are observable. When the pupil produces a written or an oral statement, constructs a graph, a geometric object of specific dimensions, or a simple machine, we have a product which is both observable and measurable. The pupil either does or does not demonstrate X behavior; he either does or does not produce a product which is indicative of a specific behavior. There is no guesswork or conjecture on our part as teachers.

Operationalizing Covert Behaviors

However, when a behavior is covert as exemplified by comparing, contrasting, or analyzing, we are able to make it observable by coupling it with an overt behavior or product. We construct our objectives so that the pupil compares by listing the similarities and differences, or he analyzes by stating or recording his results, or he creates by turning out a product which is new to him. Without the observable product, we could not be certain that he has compared or analyzed or created. The major problem with covert behaviors is that we are compelled to rely on products or a series of related behaviors to serve as indicators that the hidden behaviors have probably occurred.

Defining and Identifying Cognitive, Affective, and Psychomotor Behaviors

As previously stated in Chapter 5, both overt and covert behaviors may be classified into three domains—the cognitive or mental domain, the affective or emotional domain, and the psychomotor or neuromuscular domain. Our objective is to define the three behavioral domains and identify those behaviors which may be designated as highly cognitive, highly affective, and highly psychomotor.

Let us review the definitions of each of the behavioral domains. The cognitive domain includes all behaviors which involve primarily mental or intellectual processes—the processes of thinking, of knowing, and of problem-solving. The affective domain includes all behaviors dealing with emotions, attitudes, values, interests, and appreciations. The psychomotor domain encompasses manual, motor, neuromuscular, or physical skills.

Based on the above definitions, review the following behaviors and categorize each one by placing a "C" in front of those which are illustrative of the cognitive domain, an "A" in front of those which are of the affective domain, and a "P" in front of those which are of the psychomotor domain. When doubtful about a particular response, use the criteria of highly cognitive, highly affective, and highly psychomotor.

1. _____ The pupil turns a page.
2. _____ The pupil uses a dictionary

3. _____ The pupil associates the words *le soleil* with *ole sol*.
4. _____ The pupil interprets Marlow's *Faustus*.
5. _____ The pupil enjoys reading,
6. _____ The pupil laughs at your jokes.
7. _____ The pupil states the "right answer."
8. _____ The pupil writes on the desk top with his penknife.
9. _____ The pupil strongly defends his values.
10. _____ The pupil selects an alternative which he will pursue.
11. _____ The pupil compares a circle, a triangle, and a square by stating the similarities and differences.
12. _____ The pupil compares two teachers and rates each one in terms of his own criteria.
13. _____ The pupil types his name.

Applying the criteria of "highly" cognitive, "highly" affective, and "highly" psychomotor, the "right answers" should have read as follows:

1. P	7. C
2. C	8. P
3. C	9. A
4. C	10. C
5. A	11. C
6. A	12. C
	13. P

But—if we were highly critical in analyzing each of the 13 behaviors, our responses would read as follows:

1. __P__ The pupil TURNS a page. No problem, this requires a motor skill, the act of grasping and moving the page. Definitely psychomotor.
2. __C__ The pupil USES a DICTIONARY. Possibly, no problem. The use of the dictionary is a skill requiring knowledge of a procedure.
3. __C__ The pupil ASSOCIATES the word *le soleil* with *ole sol.* This is recall. *Le soleil* brings to mind *ole sol.* Definitely cognitive.
4. __C and A__ The pupil INTERPRETS Marlowe's *Faustus.* Interpreting is a cognitive process involving a reordering and rearrangement, providing a new view of the material. Of course, in the process of interpreting, the pupil may become emotionally involved. Interpretation may include emotional components. Highly cognitive but possibly affective as well.
5. __A and C__ The pupil ENJOYS reading. Enjoyment clearly indicates the affective domain. Of course, the pupil had to acquire reading skills prior to experiencing enjoyment. The behavior is highly affective and contains cognitive components.

6. __A and C__ The pupil LAUGHS at your jokes. Affective! However, to laugh at a joke implies that one "understands"—that a humorous meaning has been communicated. The behavior is highly affective yet does contain cognitive components.

7. ___C___ The pupil STATES THE "RIGHT ANSWER." Convergent thinking. The pupil recalls the correct response. A low level cognitive behavior!

8. __A not P__ The pupil WRITES on the DESK TOP with his PENKNIFE. Writing is a motor skill and a tool skill involving knowledge. But—what prompts a youngster to write with a knife on a desk top? Boredom? An intense dislike for school? This behavior is obviously more affective than anything else.

9. __A and C__ The pupil STRONGLY DEFENDS his VALUES. Highly affective, for to value something is to experience strong feelings as to the worth of something and to accept and behave in terms of this value. However, in many cases do we not intellectualize in the process of developing a value? Are not the thinking processes involved to a limited extent?

10. __C and A__ The pupil SELECTS an ALTERNATIVE which he will pursue. Selecting an alternative implies making a choice or decision which is usually based on internal or external criteria or both. Of course, one makes decisions by carefully weighing the available information; essentially, by thinking critically. However, are there not times when there are emotional components which strongly influence that choice or decision? The behavior is highly cognitive and may contain affective factors.

11. ___C___ The pupil COMPARES a circle, a triangle, and a square by stating the similarities and differences. Highly cognitive.

12. __C and A__ The pupil COMPARES two TEACHERS and RATES each one in terms of HIS OWN CRITERIA. The pupil is utilizing comparison and critical thinking, but will his feelings toward the teacher influence his rating? Affective components? Highly probable.

13. __P and C__ The pupil TYPES his NAME. Typing is a manipulative skill. Spelling one's name is a tool skill involving knowledge of the alphabet Highly psychomotor but contains cognitive components.

Operating within the framework of "highly" cognitive or affective or psychomotor presented few or no problems in classifying behaviors. But when we move away from a gross view and analyze specific behaviors, we find that few behaviors are solely or purely of one domain. In the majority of the behavioral patterns we demonstrate, we are usually climbing two or more ladders simultaneously. Or we may move from a rung on the cognitive ladder to a rung on the affective ladder and then back to the cognitive one.

When we state that certain behaviors appear to be primarily associated with one particular domain, we are simply classifying them in terms of our definitions and nothing more. It is merely a convenient system for arranging them and working with them. It makes the task of specifying behavioral objectives easier.

For example, let us assume that our major goal is to further the development of higher cognitive skills in our pupils. It is clearly evident that unless we have specific knowledge of the cognitive domain, unless we have some precise definitions of the cognitive skills we seek to develop, we will be unable to translate this goal into behavioral objectives or to plan an instructional program to produce these objectives. On the other hand, if one of our major goals is to focus on the development of specific affective behaviors—particular attitudes; interests, appreciations, and values—operational definitions of these terms, wherever possible, are needed.

Two handbooks which provide extensive and detailed information in these areas are readily available. Bloom's *Taxonomy of Educational Objectives, Handbook I* deals with the cognitive domain. Krathwohl's *Taxonomy of Educational Objectives, Handbook II* deals with the affective domain. In the 1966–67 winter issue of *Illinois Teacher of Home Economics*, E. J. Simpson has presented a tentative schema for the classification of educational objectives in the psychomotor domain. All three resources merit careful study.

Although, as stated previously, few behaviors are purely cognitive, affective or psychomotor, the classification of these behaviors into three domains serves to facilitate the process of specifying objectives.

Specifying Cognitive Objectives

To date, the cognitive domain has received the most extensive coverage of the three. The availability of this information has made the specification of cognitive objectives a relatively easy one in comparison with affective objectives. The task of specifying low level cognitive skills is simple. In fact, the more simple the objective, the more simple the procedure. The more insignificant the objective, the more simple the procedure.

For example, if our objectives are of the rote-recall variety and we want Johnny to name the ten water holes in territory X or ten important facts about musical genius Y, the process of specification is just that. The pupil will be able to name the ten water holes in territory

X or the pupil will be able to state, in written or oral form, ten important facts about musical genius Y.

However, if our objectives focus on the higher cognitive processes such as inductive or deductive reasoning, analysis, divergent production, or critical thinking, the process of specifying objectived becomes more complex.

Let us assume that our objective is to promote the pupil's use of inductive reasoning as he interacts with specific content. Our objective would read as follows: Given a series of specific situations, objects, or ideas, the pupil will be able to formulate a generalization or rule which is applicable to all. If we wish to operate at a level of greater specificity in terms of the use of inductive reasoning, and relate our objective to one particular classroom activity, our illustration would read as follows: Provided with essential data and an outline map containing X's, designating areas adjacent to water, the pupil will induce the proportional generalization that many great civilizations arose in areas adjacent to water.

Let us assume that our objective is to promote critical thinking. We have previously defined critical thinking as a complex process involving comparison, analysis, the weighing of components either qualitatively or quantitatively, and making a selection or decision on the basis of evaluation. We have stressed that while the process is necessarily objective, it can have subjective or emotional components which enter into the evaluation. A specific behavioral objective focusing on critical thinking might be the following: Given question X and arguments A and B, the pupil will be able to select the argument he considers to be the stronger one and state the reasons for his choice. Another specific objective, again focusing on critical thinking, would be: Given candidates A and B for position X and their qualifications, the pupil will be able to select the candidate he considers best qualified for the position and state the reasons for his choice.

An objective, such as "the pupil will make a value decision" involving critical thinking coupled with emotional components, may be stated as follows: Suppose you were given $1,000, describe what you would do and cite the reasons for your decision.

It is evident that in specifying higher level cognitive objectives, we experience little difficulty—if we have clear-cut definitions of the cognitive processes involved—and we are able to describe the products the pupil will produce by which we will measure the occurrence of these processes.

Stating Affective Objectives in Observable Terms

When we attempt to tackle the specification of affective behavioral objectives in observable and measurable terms, problems arise. Here we are dealing with the so-called intangible learning outcomes. These outcomes are not as observable and as measurable as having correctly punctuated a paragraph, written a composition, sewn a seam, used a microscope, executed a hand stand, or named five of Shakespeare's plays. Here we are dealing with feelings and emotions, with interests, attitudes, values, appreciations, and social and self-adjustments—the covert behaviors which defy precise measurement and are so crucial to the development of an individual.

Few if any of us would question the worth of affective goals such as the development of a positive self-concept, positive attitudes towards education, social effectiveness, and self-direction. Few of us would toss aside the development of human values, appreciations, interests, and attitudes as functions of the school. As educators and more importantly as human beings, we know that feelings are facts—significant facts—which produce significant results. And moreover, we know that these affective behaviors are not as intangible as we would so conveniently like to believe. The label should be *less tangible.* Surely, we have difficulty in communicating these behaviors meaningfully to others, but they do exist and we are, in part, responsible for their development.

Not a day goes by when these factual feelings fail to make their impact on us. We "know" that Billy is interested in reading; that Johnny enjoys folk music; that Tony is afraid of mathematics; that Ann raises her hand only when she knows the "right answer"; that Mary is anxious, fears failure, and will not attempt to tackle anything new; and that Ken is insecure and feels that "nobody cares and everybody is doing it." Yes—we know and we pay verbal homage to our affective goals but our problems persist for we are unable to define these goals with any degree of precision, to describe how we are going to promote their development, and finally, how we are going to measure and evaluate them.

Of course, anxiety levels can be measured by galvanic skin impulses, respiration rates, and perspiration rates. Or if time were available—and it rarely is—we could administer interest inventories, adjustment inventories, and attitude scales. We could utilize anecdotal records, case studies, interviews, sociograms, observation techniques, and checklists. Or we could continue to resort to the man-at-the-church technique. This technique is best illustrated by the following brief account:

A policeman, in making his rounds one night, noticed a man pacing around in front of a church scrutinizing the ground. He approached the man, who continued to pace, and then leaned against the large lamp post in front of the church. Finally the policeman asked: "Anything wrong?"

"Yup!"

"Lost something?"

"Yup!"

"What was it?"

"A watch."

"There's no watch here! Where did you lose it?"

"Back there, behind the church."

"Then why are you looking here?"

"Well—there's *light* here!"

Limiting our objectives to the "light" areas and avoiding the dark areas has been a common practice. Obviously, the dark areas are not as dark as we have been led to believe—for we have been able to identify the Billys who demonstrate interest in reading, the Johnnys who enjoy folk music, the fearful Tonys, Anns, Marys, and the insecure Kens and many others. What has been lacking is a method of stating less tangible objectives and clearly identifying the behaviors which are indicators of these affective outcomes. A method of this type is available. Robert Mager has developed one which he describes in *Developing Attitude Toward Learning*, and James Popham of U.C.L.A. has developed another which is available as a film strip. Both are similar to the one used in the Behavioral Outcomes program.

The method can best be described by beginning with a commonplace example which many of us as parents have experienced: our children's interest in or enjoyment of a particular kind of music. This enjoyment of music—let's use folk-rock as an example—is an affective behavior. But how do we know that they enjoy folk-rock? We have only to observe their behaviors which serve as indicators. I "know" that my children enjoy folk-rock music, as demonstrated by the following behaviors:

- They have the record player going constantly. Folk-rock, what else?
- They spend most of their allowance and earnings on folk-rock records.

- They attend concerts, music festivals, and jam sessions.
- They stand for hours waiting to be admitted to a concert.
- They will stand at a concert rather than leave if seats are not available.
- They rarely miss a T. V. program featuring folk-rock singers.
- They subscribe to a folk-rock music magazine.
- They play these songs on the piano and clarinet.
- They compose their own music and lyrics.
- They talk folk-rock to death.
- They have formed a folk-rock band.

What we have succeeded in doing is taking an affective outcome, such as enjoying music which can serve us equally well as an objective, and identifying the particular behaviors which are indicators in that they clearly demonstrate that the "enjoyment" outcome has indeed occurred. As parents, of course, we had inside information. But the procedure in the classroom is the same and consists of the following steps:

1. We state the specific affective trait we want the child to acquire or further develop.
2. We identify a child (or children) who possesses this trait.
3. We observe and talk with this child or children and list the behaviors which serve as indicators of this trait.
4. To check our behavioral indicators, we identify and observe a child (or group of children) who lacks this trait.
5. Equipped with these indicators, we select those which are appropriate, in that we can gear specific instructional activities to promote them.
6. We plan our instructional activities in terms of our newly formulated affective objectives.

Illustrations of Affective Objectives

A few samples of affective objectives stated in observable and measurable terms should be helpful at this time.

The pupil will recognize the worth of each individual as demonstrated by:

a) giving assistance to his peers without being asked
b) acting courteously to his peers
c) working cooperatively with his peers
d) agreeing or disagreeing with members of the peer group without making any negative remarks or demonstrating hostility
e) listening to his peers without interrupting them
f) using tact in replying to his peers

   g) sharing ideas freely with his peers
   h) expressing appreciation of another pupil's efforts by his statements

This objective will be measured by teacher observations of pupils' in-class behaviors utilizing the items listed above as a checklist.

The child will develop qualities of leadership and social responsibility as demonstrated by:

   a) readily initiating new ideas and changes in the classroom
   b) offering constructive suggestions to the class
   c) helping peers by clarifying ideas, problems, etc.
   d) treating classmates as equals
   e) initiating cooperation of peers by being a model of cooperative behavior
   f) organizing activities
   g) tactfully directing others
   h) responding positively to peer members
   i) contributing to solving another pupil's problems by offering ideas and suggestions

A checklist including the items listed above will serve as the measurement instrument.

The pupil will demonstrate the development of more positive attitudes toward and an interest in classroom activities as measured by:

   a) asking a great many questions in class
   b) reading many more books than those required
   c) bringing to class on a voluntary basis materials and resources which relate to classroom activities
   d) initiating new ideas relative to these classroom activities in terms of projects, etc.

This may be measured by:

   a) a checklist
   b) a log kept by the teacher
   c) an "attitude" inventory administered in a *pre* and *post* format

To sum up, affective objectives can be formulated as observable and measurable learning outcomes. We have but to specify the affective trait we wish to develop, identify pupils who possess this trait as well as those who lack it, compare and elicit those behaviors which are indicators of this trait. Combining the traits to be developed and the behavioral indicators by which we are able to assess their attainment, provides us with affective objectives. Those of us who are highly critical and precision-minded will view these affective objectives as crude. Crude they may be at this point in time, but they are both practical and useful to the classroom teacher, for they are both practical and useful to the classroom teacher, for their provide her with a preliminary framework for an affective beginning.

Designating Realistic Mastery Levels

Thus far, throughout this chapter, we have stressed the practical value of formulating objectives in behavioral, observable, and measurable terms. We are able to identify and specify what the pupil will be able to do as a result of a given learning experience. But we have failed to incorporate one important component—one which designates how well the pupil will be performing. And moreover, how well is *well*?

Consider the following sets of objectives. Compare the *a's* with the *b's*. As a teacher, which one is preferable? Why? Put yourself in the pupil's seat. Which one is preferable? Why?

1. *a*) The pupil will demonstrate his ability to apply his knowledge of physics by constructing simple machines.
   b) The pupil will demonstrate his ability to apply his knowledge of physics by constructing at least two simple machines.
2. *a*) The pupil will be able to use a microscope correctly.
   b) The pupil will demonstrate his skill in using a microscope by viewing at least two slides and making an accurate diagram of each.
3. *a*) The pupil will demonstrate his appreciation of the poems of Carl Sandburg by writing an essay.
   b) The pupil will demonstrate his appreciation of the poems of Carl Sandburg by selecting at least three poems which he enjoyed and writing an essay, using a minimum of 200 words.
4. *a*) The pupil will be able to solve quadratic equations.
   b) The pupil will be able to solve at least 8 out of 10 quadratic equations.

Not 8 out of 10, but 10 out of 10 teachers and pupils prefer the "*b*" objectives. The reason is simply that most of us, if not all, want to know not only where we are going but when we have gotten there. And we want to know what *there* means. Have we mastered this objective? Have we met the minimal level of acceptable performance? Is our performance rated as an A, B, C, or F—if that means anything? Have we attained 100% or 80% or 50% accuracy?

Focusing on Objective 4 *b* we note that it clearly communicates the minimal level of acceptable performance, namely 8 out of 10 correct solutions. Solving 10 out of 10 indicates 100% accuracy, which is not required in this case, while solving fewer than eight equations indicates that more work on quadratic equations is required.

Establishing mastery levels or minimal standards of acceptable performance is essential if we are concerned with sound instruction and realistic learning. It eliminates the need to solve the "Mastery Maze" or resort to games pupils play such as the Idiosyncrasies Game (discover the teacher's idiosyncrasies and capitalize on them), or the Expectations Game (guess what great expectations the teacher has for you), or the Research Game (do a little research; ask the kids who had her last year what her requirements are). The establishment and use of performance standards benefits all. The pupil knows precisely what his objectives are, when he has achieved them, and the degree to which he has mastered them. He knows whether he is to move on to the next objective or whether additional effort is required. No games need to be played. The objective and the mastery level have been specified with clarity.

However, a question persists. Does the mastery level as specified in objective 4*b* or 3*b* or 2*b* apply to all pupils? Will all pupils be required to solve 8 out of 10 quadratic equations? If we do accept the concept of individual differences, the answer is a firm no. Mastery levels need to be determined for each child, for there is no one learning size.

Our experiences have demonstrated that mastery decisions are best left in the hands of the individual teacher. Her knowledge of her pupils, of the structure and sequence of the content and/or skill area, enables her to "make the match" and to set realistic mastery levels and revise them as needed. To establish performance levels in a vacuum without matching them to the child's abilities is an exercise in futility resulting in frustration for both pupils and teachers. Teachers have found that initially, mastery levels were hypotheses— to be confirmed or revised—and as their knowledge of the child increased, the mastery match became more precise.

Unquestionably, there are specific sequential skill areas which require a high degree of mastery for all pupils in order for learning to take place; however we must confront reality—the reality that children differ in their developmental levels and will learn at different levels of complexity. To equate mastery with perfection or total and complete achievement of a given learning task is utopian.

By establishing individual mastery levels, extensive benefits are derived. Equipped with objectives in terms of realistic performance standards, pupils are able to acquire knowledges and skills at their own rate, experience feelings of satisfaction from these initial successess, build upon these successes, become more self-confident, and continue their efforts. The cycle renews itself as long as the "match" matches.

For the teacher, the mastery match results in more time available to work with individual pupils, fewer discipline problems, less need to provide for remedial instruction, and increased professional satisfaction.

Applying Specific Objectives
to Test Construction

Pupils are caught, not only in the mastery maze, but also in the testing daze. Corridor conversations and educational research yield the following:

- "She teaches one thing; she tests for another! Why bother studying?"
- "Passing her tests is a matter of chance! Any resemblance between what goes on in class and what is covered on her tests is purely coincidental!"
- The goals stated by the teacher were not the same as the goals for which the teacher tested.[1]

It would seem logical that in the process of testing we would test for what we have taught, that our tests would reflect our specific behavioral objectives. This, however, is not the case in actual practice. In practice, teachers do attempt to gear their instruction to their general objectives, but when they reach the stage of test construction the relationship between these goals and the preparation of test items is completely lost or forgotten.

Initially, the purpose of this tool was to insure the construction or selection of valid test items. Do the tests measure the pupil objectives? Are we utilizing the objectives to guide us in test construction? And if not, shouldn't we be doing so?

Having prepared a set of properly stated objectives, it is not difficult to select or construct test items which match and measure these objectives. Let us examine the following:

- The pupil will be able to spell 90% of words from spelling list B correctly.

  The test is right there. We dictate the words from list B and the pupil spells or misspells.

- The pupil will be able to solve 8 out of 10 quadratic equations.

  We test on quadratic equations. He solves or fails to solve the given equations. We do not ask him to describe the nature of quadratic equations or their practical value or how they originated. We simply test him on his ability to solve them.

- The pupil will demonstrate his ability to induce generalizations when provided with data.

  In this case, we are not concerned with the process of recall as involved in spelling words correctly or going through the acquired steps of solving quadratic equations. Here, we are concerned with the process of inductive reasoning or generalizing. Our test item would not center on the situation covered in class from which the pupil elicited a generalization, for this would reduce the process to one of recall. Our test item must match our objective. Is the pupil able to *generalize,* not *recall a specific generalization*? Therefore, we construct a test item which provides him with new data and requires him to induce a generalization from this data.

- The pupil will be able to utilize divergent thinking.

  In this case, again our objective is the use of a cognitive process. As previously defined, divergent thinking involves offering various patterns, responses, or solutions to a problem. Our test item, therefore, would provide a new problem, not one encountered in the classroom, and the pupil would be required to cite two or more solutions to this problem.

- The pupil will be able to sew a straight seam using a sewing machine.

  The test item would involve the actual performance by the pupil and observation on the part of the teacher.

In all of the examples cited, the specific objective designated the behavior and the content to be measured. Therefore, provided with these objectives, it is a relatively simple task to construct test items which measure these objectives. If the purposes of our tests are to determine the degree to which our pupils have achieved their objectives and to provide us with information to plan for further instruction, then our tests must reflect these objectives.

Normally—we TEST to diagnose; we OPERATE to expose our learners to educational experiences; we TEST to determine the results of this exposure, and then we EXIT. The TOTE pattern, although originally proposed by Miller, Galanter, and Pribram as descriptive of the productive thinking process, is applicable to the teaching process. Effective teachers Test, Operate, Test, and Exit, but unless our tests match our objectives we are engaged in an exercise in futility.

IN SUMMARY

The purpose of this chapter was to provide the necessary information and practice to enable you to specify behavioral objectives. Operating on the assumption that this objective has been achieved, we will proceed with the task of constructing learning units which promote both process and content objectives. This is the subject of Chapter 10.

FOOTNOTES

[1] Isobel L. Pfeiffer, "Teaching in Ability-Grouped English Classes: A Study of Verbal Interaction and Cognitive Goals," Kent, Ohio: Original report from author, Kent, Ohio, 1966, also in "Of Special Significance." *The Journal of Teacher Education,* 17:384-86; Fall, 1966

10

Constructing Learning Units
to Promote Content and Process Goals

The subject of this chapter is the *learning unit.* The purpose is to provide you with:

- the concept of a learning unit
- the essential steps in constructing effective learning units
- a table of specifications to enable you to obtain a "process profile" of your teaching style
- a brief discussion of the effects of the "process profile" on classroom methodology
- a detailed description of the behavioral outcomes methodology as a multi-process approach enabling you to apply a large variety of methods, materials, and media to promote both process and content objectives

The Learning Unit Versus the Lesson Plan

The term *learning unit* is usually associated with the lesson plan. Although the learning unit has many of the same components as the lesson plan, it is distinctly different in that it conveys a different philosophy of education, a different focus on what promotes "real" learning, a different methodology in the structuring of activities and questioning procedures, a different view of the role of the teacher, and a different emphasis on the kinds of pupil behaviors which should be the outcomes of education.

For those of us who have taught for many years, the task of constructing "lesson plans" is no longer exciting or intriguing. The reason is quite evident. We have only to glance at the plan books distributed at the beginning of each school year and at the number of small boxes into which we are required to slot our plans for pupil growth. Lesson planning has been reduced to a routine, rigid procedure of "put it in the box." On a weekly basis, the 30 or more boxes containing plans for the week's instruction are approved and initialed by the principal and the task is done.

The process of constructing learning units can not be viewed as this type of lesson planning. It can be viewed, however, as creative in-depth pupil-centered planning. It is challenging and exciting, as demonstrated by the teachers whose desire for finding a better way has led them into this process and whose results provide the impetus to continue.

Only when we have constructed and utilized learning units in our own classrooms can we make a realistic assessment and evaluate the outcomes for both pupil and teacher.

THE ESSENTIAL STEPS
IN CONSTRUCTING EFFECTIVE LEARNING UNITS

We are once more at the "how is it done" stage. Before we proceed, we should focus on the term *learning unit.* To most of my readers, I am saying nothing new when I stress that learning is what the pupil does and instructing is what we as teachers assume we do. Therefore, a *learning unit* places the focus where it should be—on the pupil, on his interactions with content, on his *processing* of knowledge and skills, on his use of the thinking skills in order to learn—for learning is to *think*! However, as has been previously emphasized, one thinks and thereby learns in a content environment: one processes a variety of knowledges, skills, and experiences. Given this framework, we will begin by examining the five basic steps in constructing a learning unit.

Step 1—Prepare a Preface Page

We prepare a preface page by summarizing the *broad general* objectives (knowledges, skills, relationships, appreciations, attitudes) of the entire unit. These broad objectives represent the integration of the learnings of the whole unit.

To illustrate, we will use an actual example of a preface on a unit on water.

PREFACE

The purpose of this unit is to provide the pupil with ample educational opportunities to investigate the topic of water as an indigenous aspect of his own community and how it affects him.

Exploring the disciplines of biology, chemistry, physics and their interrelationships, the pupil will conduct a study of local water focusing on its properties, problems, distribution, and uses in the community.

The broad outcomes of the unit, in terms of pupil behaviors, will include:

1. a knowledge of the problems of procuring and distributing potable water.
2. a knowledge of the methods of the removal and effective treatment of waste materials to the end that river and shore waters are conserved for re-use and recreation.
3. a knowledge of a body of significant facts, relationships, and generalizations about water as developed from the various science disciplines.
4. a demonstrated increased curiosity about and interest in both science and community.
5. a demonstrated maturing ability to learn through the use of the cognitive processes.
6. an increased skill in the use of laboratory techniques and systematic methods of investigation.

The preface, in addition to providing us with a general framework, serves a "sharing" purpose. Usually when a group of teachers becomes involved in constructing learning units, they find it most useful to exchange and share units. The units are reproduced and placed in the library. They are made available to all teachers who have received training in the Behavioral Outcomes Approach. Teachers have only to read the preface page to determine whether the unit will be useful to them. Many teachers adapt these units to the needs of their pupils, and as a result a variety of different versions of the "same" unit is produced.

Step 2—Construct a Content Outline

Having stated in broad terms what our general objectives are, we now concentrate on specifying the content which our pupils will process to achieve these goals.

The content outline represents a sequential listing of the material to be dealt with in the unit. We arrange the content in a *logical* sequence. We state the major concepts and then proceed to list the sub-concepts under each major concept. The concepts are arranged so that concept one is a precondition for concept two. This logical arrangement minimizes the need for the pupil to review or relearn an earlier concept as he progresses through the unit. Whenever possible, we employ a sequence that begins with concrete experiences and moves toward the abstract level.

When we have completed our first draft of the content outline, we examine it to ascertain whether we have a valid rationale for each of the major items. In essence, we ask ourselves why we have included each major item and of what significance is it to the pupil in terms of the general objectives.

If we cannot answer the question, "why have we selected this particular segment of content?" the item is discarded. For unless we can readily and clearly substantiate our curricular decisions and communicate to our pupils the value and importance of the content or skill we are seeking to develop, we should not be teaching that content or skill. Our pupils have the right to know why they are learning specific skills and content. We would not be confronted with "compulsory miseducation" if we spent more time in answering our children's "Why do we have to learn_____?"

Step 3—Specify the Pupil's Objectives in Behavioral and Measurable Terms

Equipped with an outline of content which, at this point, we view as logically sequenced and relevant to our general goals, we construct a series of specific objectives in behavioral and measurable terms. With the content outline as a guide, we clearly state what the pupil will be able to do as a result of his interactions with each of the content items and how we will measure these results.

For example, were we dealing with a unit on numbers, the first content item listed might be a definition of the term *number*. Therefore, the first objective would be stated as follows: Provided with a variety of activities involving the concept of *number*, the pupil will be able to construct his own definition of *number*.

We continue this process of specifying pupil objectives until we have covered all items in our content outline. We must keep in mind that this "content" outline should contain no only knowledges, skills, and processes, but also appreciations, interest, attitudes, and values. The result is the basic framework of our learning unit. We now have a list of the behaviors which the pupil will demonstrate as a result of his activities in this unit. In sum, we know what specific pupil outcomes we will be looking for, and we are able to move ahead to the planning stage.

Step 4—Specify Methods, Activities, Questioning Patterns, Materials and Media

In Step 4, we clearly spell out the instructional methods, the learning activities, the questioning patterns, the materials and media which will be used by both pupils and teachers to achieve each of the specific objectives. At this point *process* takes over. We cannot select methods of instruction, learning activities, questioning patterns, materials, or media until we have made decisions as to the specific thinking or process skills which we wish to promote in our children. The processes which we choose to emphasize will determine our methods and strategies; our selection of pupil activities, materials, and media; and the kinds of key questions which we will utilize to initiate and propel the learning process.

Here an example is clearly in order. Let us assume that our objective is "to develop an awareness" in the pupil of the variety of geometric forms in the environment. How do we develop this "awareness?" Which of the thinking processes do we "want" the child to use? The child can develop this awareness by using inductive reasoning, deductive reasoning, creativity, analysis, comparison, and synthesis, or we can save him the trouble of thinking and use the "show and tell" approach.

For example, we can use a series of objects and pictures and point out the variety of geometric forms, both obvious and hidden, in these objects and pictures. Or we can utilize a film on "Geometric Forms In and Around Us" and have the pupils summarize what they have seen and heard. Show and tell again, but this time on film! Or we can have the youngsters construct a variety of geometric forms and create many different objects, people, plants, etc., with these forms, then have them relate their work to actual phenomena around them, and finally induce a generalization that all the phenomena we view contain combinations of geometric forms. Or we can provide the children with the generalization that all phenomena contain combinations of geometric forms and ask them to collect specific items which "prove" or "disprove" this statement. The "process" alternatives are many. The "awareness" can be developed inductively, deductively, creatively, via synthesis, etc. But the process or combination of processes which we select for pupils to employ to achieve the objective will determine our method, the pupil activities, the materials, the media, and the kinds of question we will ask.

When we ask the child to *create a variety of geometric forms* and *to synthesis them in a variety of different ways* and then *relate what he has done to phenomena about him* and compare and *induce a generalization,* we have structured activities and questions which promote creative thinking, synthesis, divergent production, comparison, and inductive reasoning into one lesson. We have achieved *both* process goals and the specific content objective. How can we compare this approach with "show and tell," or "Turn to Chapter 3, page 40, and read 'Geometry Around Us' and answer questions 1-5"?

But to return to the point, *the processes we select determine the methodology, activities, and materials* to be used. Therefore, many teachers have sought to specify their objectives by designating the process the pupil will use as an integral part of the objective. For example, the pupil will be able to make the generalization that _____. This clearly states that the pupil will use the inductive approach. Or the pupil will provide three or more predictions from X data. Again the methodology and materials are obvious. The pupil will be given data and resources and will use an analytical as well as a divergent-thinking approach.

You will note that in each of the above cases, reference was made to the pupil using a specific approach. This is truly the case. We, as teachers, select the approach or method, but it is the pupil who uses it. We "use" it in the sense that we continue to structure questions and activities to guide the pupil in the process or processes.

Therefore, in Step 4 when we specify methods, learning activities, questioning patterns, materials, and media, we are creating more than a content-methods match; we are creating a *content-process-methods match.* We are selecting the content the pupil will interact with, the thinking process he will use in this interaction and, *based on the thinking process or processes,* we select the methods and activities which will enable the pupil to achieve the objective.

If he will acquire knowledge by inducing a generalization from specific bodies of data—then the method is inductive. If he will acquire specific data by breaking down a whole into its parts, the method is analytical. If he will examine and analyze data in order to make a decision or select an alternate, the method is one of critical thinking. In the Behavioral Outcomes Approach, we have a variety of methods which we select and structure to enable our pupils to achieve their objectives.

Additional attention will be given to methods later on in this chapter. At the present, let us assume that we have completed the first four steps of unit construction. First, we have prepared a preface providing a general overview of the unit. Second, we have constructed a content outline which is arranged in a "logical" sequence and which—based on our professional judgment—is relevant to our pupils' needs. Third, we have translated the content of the unit into specific pupil behavioral objectives. Fourth, we have selected the specific thinking processes which we wish to promote and designed our methods, activities, questioning patterns, and materials to fit these processes. We are now ready to proceed to Step five, that of identifying in written form the thinking processes which the pupils will use in achieving each objective.

Step 5—Identifying the Thinking Processes

This step is a relatively easy one if we have made the proper match in Step 4. To obtain a concrete picture of the total process and to fully understand Step 5, let us look at the format of a learning unit as well as at a sample unit. Let us assume that we have before us a preface page, a content outline of the total unit, a list of the specific pupil objectives for the total unit, and that now we are ready to synthesize the unit. The form we use is shown on page 196. The column headings clearly designate what is to be placed in each column. For example: in Column 1, we insert our first content item; in Column 2, the pupil objective dealing with that content item; in Column 3 the methods, activities, questions, etc. which the pupils will use to achieve this first objective, and finally in Column 4 we identify the thinking processes the pupils will use to achieve this objective.

Now to clarify the process of unit construction further, let us examine the sample unit on pages 197, 198 and 199. We will note that the content, the objectives, the methods and activities, and the thinking processes have been arranged in the proper columns. If we focus on Column four, we note that six different thinking processes are used by the pupils to achieve objective one. Now, we are concerned with Step 5 which is identifying the thinking processes to be used by the pupil. Obviously they have been identified and placed in Column 4, but the question is how was this accomplished. Notice that each process in Column 4 is in line with a specific question or activity in Column 3. We simply analyze the structure of the question and the activity designated in Column 3 to identify the thinking process or processes.

For example, in the sample lesson the first question was "What do you think of when you speak of change?" Obviously, we are asking the pupils to associate. In the second question, when we ask for many different ways in which an object or organism could be changed, we are providing for divergent thinking. In the third question we are asking "How do we know that something has changed?" This calls for analysis. Therefore Step 5 is accomplished by closely examining the structure of the questions we ask or what kinds of questions a particular acitivity involves and pinpointing the thinking process. When in doubt as to the specific process involved, we have only to refer to the "periodic table" of thinking processes and match the structure of our questions with the samples provided. As we become proficient in using the processes, we will have little need to match the table.

The sample unit which we have examined differs greatly from the usual plan found in "plan" books. Within this sample unit, in order to achieve three specific objectives, the pupils are provided with opportunities to use a variety of thinking processes—eleven processes in all—ranging from association to critical and creative thinking. To those of us who have constructed and utilized units of this type, the process outcomes are well worth the effort.

To sum up, we have examined the following five basic steps used in constructing a learning unit:

Step 1—Preparing a preface page.
Step 2—Constructing a "logical" content outline.
Step 3—Specifying the pupil's behavioral objectives.
Step 4—Matching the methods, activities, questioning patterns, and materials to selected process objectives as well as the content objectives.
Step 5—Identifying the thinking processes.

Given these basic steps, teachers frequently ask a very practical question, namely, "how long is a learning unit?" The response is congruently practical: "As long as you see fit to make it." The length of the unit will depend on many factors—the importance of the concepts to be developed, the number of sub-concepts essential to

Teacher
School:
Grade:

BEHAVIORAL OUTCOMES LEARNING UNIT PLAN

Subject of Unit:

(Column 1) Content Outline	(Column 2) Pupil Behavioral Objectives	(Column 3) Methods, Activities, Materials, etc. Structure and spell out the method. Relate it to the pupil objective	(Column 4) Cognitive Process

Teacher: M. Gerhard
School: Fox Run School
Grade: Fourth Grade

Subject of Unit: Physical and
Chemical Change

BEHAVIORAL OUTCOMES LEARNING UNIT PLAN

(Column 1) *Content Outline*	Column 2) *Pupil Behavioral Objectives*	(Column 3) *Methods, Activities, Materials, etc.* *Structure and spell out the method.* *Relate it to the pupil objective.*	(Column 4) *Cognitive Process*

I Changes
  A. Physical
  B. Chemical
	I The pupil will be able to differentiate between a physical and chemical change by:
	
	A. constructing his own definition of each
	
	B. citing at least 5 examples of each kind of change
		I *Introduction of Concept of Change*
		  A. *Key Questions*
		
		  1. What do you think of when you speak of change?
		  2. Select any object or organism and list the different ways it could change.
		  3. How do we know that something has changed?
		  4. What do you think a physical change is? a chemical change?
		
		II *Silent Demonstration to be Performed by Teacher*
		  A. Directions:
		  You will now observe a series of ten demonstrations of changes; the first five will be physical changes, the last five will be chemical changes.
		
		  1. Observe carefully.
		  2. Note your observation.
		  3. How is each object being changed?
		  4. What actually did change?
		  5. From your observation, attempt to arrive at your own definitions of a physical and chemical change.
			
			Association
			Divergent Thinking
			Analysis
			Association
			
			Observation
			Analysis
			Analysis
			Comparison
			Induction

Teacher: M. Gerhard
School: Fox Run School
Grade: Fourth Grade

BEHAVIORAL OUTCOMES LEARNING UNIT PLAN

Subject of Unit: Physical and Chemical Change

(Column 1) *Content Outline*	(Column 2) *Pupil Behavioral Objectives*	(Column 3) *Methods, Activities, Materials, etc.* *Structure and spell out the method.* *Relate it to the pupil objective.*	(Column 4) *Cognitive Process*

		6. Cite 5 new examples of each kind of change.
		B. Silent Demonstration
		  1. Breaking potato chips
		  2. Breaking an egg
		  3. Bending glass
		  4. Stretching a rubber band
		  5. Tearing paper
		  6. Burning a wooden splint
		  7. Burning magnesium ribbon
		  8. Adding H_2SO_4 to sugar
		  9. Burning paper
		  10. Adding Phenothalen to ammonia water.
			Deduction

	II The pupil will compare his own definition with others and select the "best" one using his own criteria.	III *Comparison and Critital Thinking* When pupils have completed their observations and written their definitions and examples of each kind of change, have groups of pupils compare and discuss their results and select the best definitions.	Comparing Critical Thinking
	III The pupil will demonstrate his acquisition of the concept of change by:	IV *Constructing Novel Changes* A. Given the sample item: *What would happen if our clear air changed into dense fog?* ask pupils to create a series of "What-would-happen changes."	Creative Thinking

BEHAVIORAL OUTCOMES LEARNING UNIT PLAN

Teacher: M. Gerhard
School: Fox Run School
Grade: Fourth Grade

(Column 1) Content Outline	(Column 2) Pupil Behavioral Objectives	(Column 3) Methods, Activities, Materials, etc. Structure and spell out the method. Relate it to the pupil objective.	(Column 4) Cognitive Process
	A. creating a written series of "what would happen changes?"	B Pupils are asked to plan two physical and two chemical changes to be demonstrated to the class. (Teacher will check each change prior to demonstration.)	Synthesis and Concept Formation
	B. demonstrate two physical and two chemical changes		

the development of the total concept, the characteristics of the pupils, and the amount of time available. In many cases teachers have divided a learning unit into parts. Part one may encompass a period of one week and may be used with pupils who have a relatively short attention span and who are capable of mastering the basics of a concept rather than working toward an in-depth understanding of that concept. This is essentially the beauty of the approach. It is "tailorable." The teacher's professional judgment, her knowledge of the subject matter, and more importantly of her pupils will determine the length of the unit. In a superficial manner the length of the unit is comparable to the length of a girl's skirt. We may recall the days when the question, "What is the acceptable length of a girl's skirt?" prompted the response, "It should touch the middle of her knee." The criterion was *her* knee. The criteria for the length of the learning units are far more complex, but we must not lose sight of the *key* criterion—that of matching the unit to the needs and characteristics of the pupil.

However, there are two critical steps which have not been dealt with and the lack of which reduces the total learning process to "black-box" education. The steps are obvious: the construction of a pre-test and a post-test. Pre-testing and post-testing our pupils enables us to plan realistically and to tailor our units to our pupils. This pupil-unit match is the most crucial one. How we construct and utilize pre- and post-tests and incorporate them into the learning unit will be the subject of Chapter 11. It is sufficient at this time to point out that the diagnostic pre-test and the post-test are integral components of the learning unit.

Obtaining a "Process Profile" of Your Teaching Style

If we return once again to the sample learning unit on pages 197 and 198-9 and closely analyze column 4, which lists the processes pupils use, we are able to discover a great deal about our teaching style. In fact, we are able to obtain a "process profile" of our instructional patterns. For the processes listed in Column 4 simply reflect the kinds of methods and strategies we employ, the kinds of questions we ask, and in essence mirror our philosophy of education, our view of the teaching-learning process, our perceptions of our pupils and of our role as teachers.

As many of us have discovered, one doesn't have to ask a colleague for a written statement of her philosophy of education if one observes her in the classroom over a period of time and speaks with her at informal meetings. The living philosophy is apparent in every action and reaction of the teacher as she works with her pupils and as she expresses her educational viewpoints at informal occasions. An analysis of our learning units similarly reflects our instructional pattern in the classroom. In Column 3 of the learning unit we find our methodology, and in Column 4 we find a list of processes which serve as an index of our style. Therefore by using the data in Column 4 and recording and tallying the kind of processes we attempt to promote in our learning units, we obtain a "process profile" of our teaching style. For this purpose we utilize a table of specifications which is shown on pages 202 and 203.

Using the Table of Specifications

You will note that across the top, we list the cognitive processes with which we are working and in Column one, we list all of the specific objectives of the unit. We then proceed, in terms of each objective and focusing on section 4 of our learning unit, to record and tally the number of times we have "used" (structured for) each cognitive process. After recording and tallying our results for a number of objectives, we discover a pattern.

For example, if we use the sample learning unit on pages 197, 198, and 199 and record and tally our results as shown on pages 202 and 203, we find that the teacher's "process" profile is extremely broad. In acquiring the concepts of physical and chemical change, pupils utilized 11 cognitive functions. The teacher had provided a multi-process approach.

Most of us, in our initial attempts in unit construction, find that our patterns are not diverse but extremely narrow. Our process profiles demonstrate that many of us are the "who-what-where-when" or the convergent teacher. We structure for the recall of specific facts rather than for a variety of higher cognitive functions.

Early experiences in constructing learning units clearly indicated that I was a highly inductive teacher. The activities which I selected and the questions which I asked consistently required inductive reasoning on the part of the pupils. My students were not being given ample opportunities to use a variety of thinking processes. There was a need for me to explore other methods, approaches, and questioning patterns.

To Obtain a "Process Profile"

Processes

	Analysis	Inductive Reasoning	Deductive Reasoning	Classifying	Categorizing	Critical Thinking	Concept Formation	Creative Thinking
	XXX	X	X					
						X		
							X	X

Total No. of Processes in Unit – 11

TABLE OF SPECIFICATIONS

Subject of Unit: Physical and Chemical Change

Cognitive

Pupil Objectives	Association	Comparing	Convergent Thinking	Divergent Thinking	Synthesis
I The pupil will differentiate between a physical and chemical change by: (A) constructing own definition (B) citing at least 5 examples of each change.	XX	X		X	
II The pupil will compare his own definition with others and select the "best" one, using his own criteria.		X			
III The pupil will demonstrate his acquisition of the concept of change by: (A) creating a series of changes in written form; (B) creating and demonstrating changes.					X

Broad Pattern—contains four or more processes
Narrow Pattern—contains one to three processes

Some teachers find that the nature of the content they are teaching requires a specific process pattern. For example, in the area of solid geometry, deduction is used extensively. However, in all of the content areas at the elementary school level all processes are applicable. Teachers seek to provide as large a variety of processes as possible. When they find that excessive use of one process is evident, methods and questioning patterns are revised.

The most efficient method of insuring that a large number of processes is utilized is to plan two sections of a learning unit and to screech to a halt. The table of specifications is then used, and the teacher examines the process profile which is emerging. If too much emphasis is being given to one process, methods and questioning patterns are restructured. Therefore, there is no need to revise a total unit; the teacher is able to diagnose her process profile as she plans the unit and to make the necessary adjustments to broaden the pattern.

The effects of the "process profile" on methodology are profound. The mirroring effect of the table of specifications results in the redesign of teaching strategies and in the development of a variety of problem-solving approaches. Teachers seek to diversify their process patterns. They become divergent methodologists! "How many different approaches can we use to develop concept X or skill Y or attitude Z?" Workshops become creative centers where teachers hitchhike on each others' ideas and pool their experiences and resources. "We are attempting to promote process in our youngsters and in the process we are processed." Or to put it more aptly, as David Hawkins states, "The potter (in this case the teacher) molds the clay and in the process not only is the clay transformed, but so is the potter."

The Development of Process Methodology

After examining samples of their process profiles and attempting to expand the spectrum of processes in their learning units, teachers are surprised at the wide variety of alternative approaches that are available to them. The repertoire of approaches which emerges may be labeled *process methodology*. It becomes quite apparent that the Behavioral Outcomes Approach does not involve one method or one prescribed technique. Teachers are confronted not only by the reality of individual differences in their pupils but also by those within themselves. They develop process approaches which meet their individual' needs and their personal styles of instruction. They fully realize that no one approach will serve to promote the attainment of a specific outcome with all kinds of children, nor will one prescribed approach serve as the most effective and efficient mode of instruction for all teachers. They develop process approaches based on process and content objectives and match them to the individual needs of their pupils and themselves. They utilize inductive, deductive, creative, and critical thinking approaches as well as multi-process methods such as the inductive-deductive approach, where pupils not only induce generalizations but move beyond their generalizations to arrive at additional specific data. In sum, the teacher's goal of promoting the development of a large variety of thinking skills in pupils by diversifying their profiles serves to produce a variety of multi-process approaches.

Adapting Conventional Methods to Process

Nor does the teacher ignore the so-called conventional methods such as the lecture, discussion, recitation, project, self-selection, and "discovery" approaches. However, she does not use them in the traditional sense. Of course, when we speak of "the traditional sense," we recognize how ambiguous our terms are. We have only to review the research on teaching methods undertaken by Dr. Robert Travers and others to realize that terms such as "lecture" and "discussion" are rather vague. For as Drs. Travers & Wallen state, "One man's lecture may be another man's discussion."[1]

However, be that as it may, the process teacher is by no means an extremist; she does not expect her pupils to rediscover all existing knowledge. There is a need for information-giving, but that information must be processed by the pupil. Therefore, lectures are given, but they are followed by thought-provoking questions which stimulate pupil interactions with that content.

In a similar vein, discussions are encouraged, but these discussions are pupil-centered. Too many of us have witnessed "discussions" where the ball bounces at the precise angles determined by the teacher, from teacher to pupil A, and then back to the teacher and then to pupil B. This ping-pong of discussion is controlled and dominated by the teacher. Foul balls are called and the game rarely gets out of hand. Should a pupil attempt to serve, the game screeches to a halt. It would appear that one of the most important functions of a discussion would be to provide ample opportunities for pupils to express their own views and values and to maximize their inter actions with each other.

Discussion time for the process teacher signifies a time for listening, for encouraging responses, for the use of non-verbal cues, for involving as many pupils as possible, and for really "tuning in" on the youngsters.

To state that discussions should center on issues relevant to the pupil would appear to be superfluous, yet how many of us, as teachers and parents, have listened to our children's reactions to an issue discussed in class? To put it bluntly, the children couldn't care less or failed to view it as a real issue. Of course they participate, for if one participates one is meeting the requirements of the course. In sum, discussions of this sort teach our children to play the game—or, to put it crudely but in down-to-earth terms, "to beat the system."

In a recent workshop, I listened to a well-known professor and researcher give the following advice to a large group of teachers and administrators: "If we are to keep our youngsters in school, we must teach them first to beat the system and then to obtain an education!"

There will be no need to teach them to beat the system if the system is sound and reality-based, if the outcomes we teach for do indeed match the outcomes of the real world, if the issues we discuss are indeed real issues, if the truths we expound are the truths we live by. Need we go on? Yes—to a process and reality-centered approach to education.

To return to our discussion on discussions. The pupil-centered discussion dealing with relevant issues is a method employed by the process teacher. The recitation method, however, is not used as extensively as in the conventional classroom, for recitation clearly implies that the teacher asks a qeustion with the intent that the pupil respond with the precise answer the teacher has in mind. The purpose of recitation may be served equally well or better by giving the pupils an objective test. There are right answers to specific questions. Pupils acquire specific knowledges and skills and should be able to demonstrate these knowledges and skills, but it is far more efficient to utilize a short objective test to achieve this purpose than to waste precious time for oral recitation.

The project method when properly applied is a valuable approach. It is an excellent method to promote self-direction. When pupils are given opportunities to plan their own projects, to work together cooperatively or on an individual basis, to evaluate their own results by establishing or selecting their own criteria, the process of education is truly in "process." However, the project method should not be reduced to a series of teacher-directed activities for the purpose of displaying X number of products on P.T.A. nights. The pupil-initiated, -directed, and -evaluated project is the only meaningful one.

We are all too familiar with the assigned projects as exemplified by numerous school science fairs, where parents "help" and Johnny returns with a "homemade" computer, an electric eye, or a model of a motor which contains everything but a neon sign! When we think about a project of this type, we are forced to but one conclusion: How little was gained in that "A" rating of the project and how much was lost in the child's receiving parental "assistance"!

The self-selection and self-discovery methods are naturals for the process teacher. But again the caution signals are evident. The key word is *self*. We must not only exercise care, but we must also establish optimal conditions to insure that pupils have the real freedom to make selections by themselves and to discover for themselves. Cook-book "self-discovery" and teacher planned self-selections are frauds which we as professionals should not accept. If we plan to structure discovery, then let us call it just that and not mislabel the process.

The Use of Inquiry Training

In addition to the methods described up to this point, a modified version of the inquiry method developed by Dr. Richard Suchman is utilized by process teachers in the area of science.

For those of my readers who are not familiar with inquiry training, a brief description is in order. In 1960, Suchman developed a sequence of inquiry training.[2,3] The goal was to develop within youngsters a systematic approach for discovering information. Children were being provided with opportunities to confront a problem, ask questions of the instructor relative to the problem, collect data, formulate hypotheses, verbally test these hypotheses, and generate a theory explaining their observations or arrive at a possible solution to the problem.

For example, one type of situation used by Suchman is one in which the children are exposed to a short silent film. One of the best known of these films is "The Bimetallic Strip." The children view a bimetallic strip held over a Bunsen burner. The strip bends downward. The strip is then submerged in a beaker of liquid and straightens out. The strip is then placed over the Bunsen burner and this time bends upward. The strip is returned to the beaker of liquid and again straightens out. The question which is then raised is, "What is happening here and why?"

The pupils are usually amazed to see the strip bending upward. This observation does not fit their expectations! They have no conceptual scheme at this time to explain what they have seen. Suchman calls this "a discrepant event," discrepant in that it fails to match what the pupil knows.

The pupils are then told that they may ask any questions which they wish about the phenomenon they have observed; however, they are to word their questions so that the teacher's responses will be "yes" or "no." For if they are permitted to ask any question, they might ask, "What is happening here and why?" and the purpose of the lesson would be destroyed.

Each pupil may ask as many questions as he wishes. He may "sit on the shelf" and think. When the pupil formulates a theory to explain what he has observed, he may test his theory by using the teacher as his laboratory and source of information.

Observing an inquiry lesson is a mind-opener, for we listen to "children in process"; they ask their own questions; they formulate hypotheses and verbally test them; they theorize. Here we observe learning at its best, for the children are using their minds not as sponges sopping up data which is being transmitted but as sharp tools dissecting, analyzing, and synthesizing data.

Those of us who have adopted the inquiry technique and have become adept at using it, have found it to be a rewarding experience for our pupils and for ourselves. But—one must keep in mind that the purpose here is not to teach substantive content, but to teach the process of inquiry.

Modifying Media

The focus on inquiry and process methodology has served to modify the use of media and has resulted in more creative applications of these media in the classroom. For example, the use of "silent" films, "silent" filmstrips, "silent" transparencies, and 'silent" teacher demonstrations has served to increase pupil inter-action with content. A film is shown without the sound. Pupils analyze the film and provide their own sound. The film is then replayed with the sound providing pupils with the opportunity to confirm their analyses. During the replay, pupils listen as they have never listened before. They are intent on knowing how accurate their analyses were.

The "silent" filmstrips are simply filmstrips shown without the written messages. The filmstrips are inserted into the projector so that these messages are masked and come into view after the pupils have given their own responses. Our "silent" transparencies may be unlabeled diagrams, maps, or any sort of pictorial material which is open-ended requiring the pupils to interpret, classify, analyze, predict, and do their own labeling.

In sum, the behavioral outcomes methodology is a multi-process approach. The teaching strategies are diverse, incorporating a broad range of thinking skills. Conventional methods such as the lecture, the discussion, and the project are adapted to promote process. Self-discovery, self-selection, and inquiry techniques are integral parts of the program. The learning units clearly reflect *process methodology.* The differences between these units and the conventional lesson plans are obvious. The learning unit focuses on both process and content objectives. It mirrors an open, loosely structured learning environment in which pupils are a part *of* the educative process, not apart *from* the process. The pupil is viewed as an interacter rather than as a receiver of information and skills; the teacher's role is seen not as an information-transmitter but as a diagnostician, a guide, and a partner in the learning process. The learning unit, therefore, is precisely what it has been labeled—a process-centered and pupil-centered vehicle to promote learning. However, the effectiveness of these units is a function of the teacher's ability to serve as a diagnostician, for unless she is able to pretest her pupils and tailor these units to meet their individual needs, her efforts have been in vain. Therefore in Chapter 11 we will deal with test construction, in terms of practical procedures teachers can employ to pre-test and post-test their pupils. Having a vehicle, be it a well-constructed learning unit or a car is fine, but unless we know where our passengers are going and when they have gotten there, why take the trip?

FOOTNOTES

[1] Norman E. Wallen and Robert M. W. Travers, "Analysis and Investigation of Teaching Methods" in *Handbook of Research on Teaching*, N. L. Gage ed., a project of the American Educational Research Association, (Chicago; Rand McNally and Company, 1963), p. 481.

[2] Digested from Richard J. Suchman's "Inquiry Training in the Elementary School," *Science Teacher*, November, 1960, 27, pp. 42-47.

[3] Richard J. Suchman, "Inquiry Training: Building Skills for Autonomous Discovery," *Merrill-Palmer Quarterly*, 1961, 7. pp. 147-169.

11

Testing for Thinking and Subject Mastery

In Chapter 10 the pre-test and post-test are identified as essential components of the learning unit. The learning unit, in and of itself, regardless of how well it is constructed, is of little worth unless it meets the specific needs of the pupils. The match between the pupil and the learning unit has to be made. Unless the objectives of the learning unit are congruent with the needs of the pupil, the teaching-learning process is reduced to a shot-gun approach at most—or a vacuous process at least. The pre-test is the tool which enables us to make the match.

EFFECTIVE TEACHING THROUGH PRE-TESTING

The pre-test is the yardstick or gauge which enables us to determine where the pupil is in terms of the specific objectives of the learning unit. The pre-test is precisely what its name implies—it is a test administered prior to instruction in the classroom.

I can recall the amazement of a new staff member on the second day of the school term when she discovered that I was "testing" my pupils. "How can you test them when you haven't taught them?" I refrained from saying, "Madam, these children were not born yesterday! They have acquired knowledges, skills, and attitudes before Gerhard." Instead I explained that the test I was giving was not the kind of test she had in mind—that it was a survey which provided me with essential information enabling me to teach more effectively and efficiently.

It was obvious and is obvious that few teachers are familiar with the pre-test as a classroom tool. Essentially it serves as a "surveyor's" tool, for it enables us to map the territory—realistically. It provides us with information in terms of what the pupils know; it identifies their strengths, their weaknesses, their misconceptions. It identifies pupils with similar needs, allowing us to group the pupils for specific purposes; it designates a series of launching points from which individual pupils or groups of pupils can enter the learning experience It eliminates the review syndrome which so many children are needlessly subjected to and which serves to produce problems which can readily be avoided. It provides us with a series of tentative hypotheses about our pupils. We obtain a sketchy profile of each child which becomes more distinct as we interact and learn together. We have a basis for prescribing specific sections of the learning unit for each child or groups of children. We are not making blind decisions as to what the "class" requires or what is "good" for all children. Nor are we administering any test. The pre-test clearly and distinctly reflects the objectives of the learning unit. It is a teacher-constructed instrument. It is not designed by ETS or SRA. We structure it to obtain specific information which we need to tailor the learning unit to the pupil's needs. It is a diagnostic tool. By no means is it an all-encompassing tool. Nor for that matter is any test an all-encompassing tool. The pre-test is geared to the "content" objectives of the learning unit and it serves a distinct function. It assists the teacher in making the crucial match between the pupil and the learning unit. After utilizing pre-tests, modifying learning units, and prescribing specific sections of these units for specific groups of learners, teachers have difficulty in understanding how anyone could possibly instruct pupils without first employing this type of diagnosis. *To test before you teach* becomes a must.

The following teacher comments are clearly indicative of the results of pre-testing which insure more effective teaching and learning.

"After pre-testing my pupils, I could no longer utilize whole class instruction as I had previously. I began to use grouping for specific purposes. Based on the pre-test results, pupils were grouped temporarily to achieve specific objectives. When these objectives were attained, pupils were regrouped. I no longer viewed the class as a whole, having one "learning size.""

"My expectations of what specific pupils could do were more realistic. Therefore, pupils were able to experience success in learning. I had fewer discipline problems."

"I began to focus on the individual pupil, on what he was able to do, on his strengths and his weaknesses."

"I began to focus on myself and my own teaching procedures. I realized that I needed a larger variety of both methods and materials to meet the diverse needs of my pupils."

"The pre-test led to the selection of more valid teaching procedures and materials."

In sum, teachers who began to use the pre-test were unable to regress to teaching without some form of diagnosis. The pre-test was the essential preliminary step to the learning unit.

How to Construct a Pre-Test

If we keep firmly in mind the purposes of our pre-test, the procedures used in constructing this instrument are both logical and "relatively simple" in that our goal is to produce a teacher-made test rather than a product produced by a professional test constructor.

Our purpose is to diagnose the pupil in terms of the specific objectives of the learning unit. These objectives may be limited to knowledges and skills or may include attitudes, interests, appreciations, and values. We may also include other objectives which are the pre-conditions or readiness tools which the pupil should have prior to working with the specific learning unit.

The results of our pre-test should serve to identify the specific strengths and weaknesses of the individual pupil and should serve to designate the specific entry points for individuals or groups of individuals into the learning unit. We are well aware of the fact that these results are tentative, that the pupil profile we obtain is a hypothesis to be confirmed and modified as we proceed in the teaching-learning process.

In constructing a pre-test, we use the following procedure:

Step 1. *Utilize the List of Specific Behavioral Objectives of the Learning Unit*

We begin with the list of specific behavioral objectives of the learning units as our framework. We list these objectives *in order of their importance*. For example, our list of objectives as applied to any content area may read as follows:

(a) The pupil is able to *express* concepts, generalizations, and principles in his own words.

(b) The pupil is able to *apply* concepts, generalizations, and principles to novel situations.
(c) The pupil is able to *identify relationships.*
(d) The pupil can *attack a problem* and *plan a method* or methods to arrive at a solution to the problem.
(e) The pupil *recalls essential facts.*
(f) The pupil reads popular material and *sifts out facts from theories.*
(g) The pupil *demonstrates use of special skills* and *tools.*

Of course the above list deals with knowledge and skill objectives. The teacher may include affective objectives which attempt to elicit the pupil's attitudes, appreciations, interests and values relative to the content of the learning unit. Although we are well aware of the many difficulties involved in measuring affective behaviors via pencil and paper tests, many of us have found it useful to include items of this type initially and to compare the results later on, on the basis of classroom observations. Therefore, we start with our list of specific behavioral objectives and prepare test items, objective and subjective, which measure the extent of the pupil's "knowledge" of each of these objectives. Some teachers have found it useful to construct a two-way table with one axis representing the subject matter content and the other representing the types of behaviors or mental and affective processes that the test is intended to elicit. Each cell in this table is then used to record the number of test items constructed. Other teachers have simply used a checklist of objectives and recorded the number of test questions constructed next to each objective.

Step 2. *Utilize the Measurability Factors as Stated in the Objectives*

We tailor the questions by utilizing the measurability factors as stated in the objectives. For example, in those cases where we have specified minimum levels of acceptable performance, we make certain that our test items will reflect attainment of these levels. If a pupil is to solve four out of five linear equations, then the test must contain five linear equations. Since our pre-test is to determine which of the objectives the pupils have mastered as well as those to be mastered, a sufficient number of items must be included to reflect mastery of each objective.

Step 3. *Provide an Adequate Sampling of the Unit's Objectives*

In constructing test items to measure each of our objectives, we must be certain that we have provided an adequate sampling of the unit's objectives. Relying on one item per objective has proven inadequate for our purposes. In the main, we have found that our pre-test should contain a sufficient number of test items to test for each of the objectives based on the importance of that objective as well as on the mastery criteria. Of course, the test should not be too lengthy, but we must keep in mind that for diagnostic purposes, unless our sample is adequate our results will not be reliable.

Step 4. *Sequence Test Items*

We arrange the test items in terms of the sequence of objectives in the learning unit. This converts the test into a miniature of the learning unit. It enables us to conduct an item analysis more efficiently and to obtain specific information in terms of part scores. We are not concerned with the total score that any pupil obtains. We are concerned with his performance in terms of each objective.

Step 5. *Check the Total Process*

When we have completed the task of constructing the pre-test, we check to ascertain whether we have (*a*) sampled all of the objectives, (*b*) utilized the measurability factors, (*c*) provided an adequate sampling of all objectives, and (*d*) sequenced the items in terms of the learning unit.

Problems in Selection of Test Items

In pre-test construction, teachers are concerned with the kinds of test items which will best suit the purpose of diagnosis. The weaknesses and strengths of completion, multiple-choice, true and false, and matching items as well as the essay type questions are apparent.

The decisions in terms of types of items which can best be constructed by teachers and which will in all probability best reflect the pupil's present status are the following:

1. In most cases, the specific behavioral objective clearly designates the structure of the test item. For example, when pupils are asked to *define, describe, list, identify, compare, cite examples of,* the test item simply requires that behavior in written form.

2. In those cases where the objective requires recall of information or convergent thinking, the completion type item is utilized. The item is designed so that it is short and definite and has only one correct response. However, in constructing completion items, the teacher clearly realizes that she is focusing upon recall of information rather than on more complex cognitive behaviors, such as the application of principles to new situations. Her emphasis in this case is primarily on factual details.

3. A modifiable form of multiple-choice items is acceptable. The modification is simply that in the process of making a choice, the pupil is required to state the reason for his choice. The purpose here is to attempt to eliminate the multiple-guess weakness inherent in this type of item. All too often, test-wise pupils learn to identify the weak distractors and deduce the correct response.

4. The true and false format is utilized, but again in a modified form. The pupil is required to supply evidence as to why the false items are false or to transform false statements into true statements. Teachers avoid the use of specific determiners such as "only," "never," "all," "every," "none," "no," and "always." Again, an attempt is made to overcome some of the weaknesses in this type of item. Teachers are impressed with the fact that essentially, true and false items serve to measure pupils' ability to recall specific information; that these items are difficult to construct; and more importantly, that few true-false items are easily constructed which serve to measure generalizations, broad principles, or relationships which are far more important that the minute specifics they do measure.

5. For our purposes, the essay is most suitable for it provides an excellent means to measure concept formation, generalizations, understandings, principles and relationships, as well as factual information. This is not to state that objective types of test items cannot be utilized for this purpose. However, the process of constructing objective items to measure concepts and generalizations is by no means simple. Therefore, for our purposes, the essay question is used extensively. It is highly structured, and restrictions are incorporated in the question which serve to limit the length of response and thereby reduce the amount of teacher-time needed to measure the response. Since our purpose is diagnostic, we are not interested in a total score, but in an item-analysis of specific behaviors. Therefore in evaluating the essay, we apply a modified form of the analytical method of scoring. The teacher, in constructing the essay items, records the specific responses sought for each item. She analyzes the response and identifies the component parts. As she reviews each pupil's response to the item, she notes the various subparts of the correct response as well as those which are missing, and scores accordingly.

In addition, she is aware of the pitfalls or sources of rater unreliability such as the "halo effect" and the influence of extraneous factors. Most of us are aware that on objective tests, a teacher's bias, either in favor of a pupil or against him, has little or no effect on the scoring process. But this may not be the case when rating an essay item. Therefore, to reduce the "halo effect" teachers score the essay items anonymously, paying no attention to the pupil's name. In addition, teachers rate all responses to each test item at one time and then proceed to the next test item. This tends to minimize the "halo effect" and provides a comparision among the various responses made to a specific item. The influence of extraneous factors such as handwriting, organization of material, and the quality of grammar, spelling, and punctuation must be dealt with. Here, the teacher must decide whether these factors are to be evaluated separately or if they are part and parcel of the specific objectives to be measured.

In sum, the pre-test, which serves as a diagnostic tool to determine where each pupil stands in terms of the specific objectives of a learning unit, may be constructed by using a variety of objective test items as well as a series of brief, precise, and highly structured essay questions. The type of test item selected will depend on the nature of the specific behavioral objective to be measured. In constructing a pre-test, the teacher utilizes the specific behavioral objectives as a framework, arranges these objectives in order of importance, tailors the test items in terms of the measurability factors stated in the objective, provides an adequate sampling of each of the objectives, sequences the test items so that they reflect the arrangement of the learning unit, and then proceeds to administer the test and conduct an item analysis of the results. The item analysis then enables her to prescribe the specific learning activities of the unit which will be meaningful and relevant for each pupil or group of pupils in her class.

Sample Pre-Test Items

The pre-test items we construct or select will vary in terms of our objectives. In the areas of skill development and knowledge, the task is relatively simple and the content is clear-cut. In the areas of process and affect the task is more complex.

Let us begin with a simple skill objective such as: The pupil will be able to spell the 15 "new" words in X reading assignment.

Having acquainted the pupils with the purposes of pre-testing (as will be described in detail later on in this chapter), the teacher may simply dictate the words to the pupils as they write them. Following the correction process, each pupil is provided with his own list of words which require mastery. Some teachers have put these word lists on tape, thereby enabling pupils to pre-test themselves. The teacher may then correct the pupil's work or provide him with an answer sheet for self-correction.

Let us cite another example, this time dealing with a skill segment in mathematics. One of our objectives in this unit may read as follows: The pupil will be able to write large numbers encompassing the millions range. (Mastery level—85% accuracy) The pre-test items in this case may consist of the following:

I. Write the following numbers as word statements:

1. 56
2. 830
3. 9,542
4. 1,001
5. 33,402
6. 434,799
7. 6,900,000
8. 66,342,846
9. 256,684,023
10. 15,230,070,000

II. Write each of the following in number form:

1. Six thousand, two hundred twenty-five.
2. Eight hundred seven thousand, two hundred fifty.
3. Five thousand, four.
4. Fifty-four thousand, four hundred two.
5. Four million, two hundred thousand, ninety-nine.
6. Seventy-four.
7. Fifty million, four hundred thirty-two thousand, six hundred twelve.
8. Three hundred thirty nine million, four hundred fifty thousand, sixty-four.
9. Three hundred twenty.
10. Eight million, three hundred thousand.

Now let us assume that we are dealing not with a skill objective but with the development of a concept on a primary level. Our objective in this case may be: The pupil will be able to demonstrate his concept of "under" by identifying objects in an "under" position or placing specific objects in an "under" position.

In this case the pre-test item may consist of a series of pictures in which the child is instructed to circle objects which are *under* a chair, table, desk, etc. In constructing this item we make certain that other objects in these pictures are present which are *over, next to on the side of, on top of* the chair, table, desk, etc. Or we may simply use a performance test rather than a pencil and paper instrument by which we require each child to manipulate concrete materials to demonstrate the concept of *under*.

Now let's assume our learning unit encompasses another process objective. This time one of our objectives is: The pupil will create a short poem. What type or types of pre-test items may we construct? For the child to create a poem, he should have some knowledge as to what constitutes a poem. Obviously our pupils vary in their experience and knowledge. Therefore in constructing the pre-test items, we may wish to obtain many kinds of data such as: What is the child's concept of a poem? What kinds of poetry is he familiar with, if any? Does he like poetry, and if so what kinds? What kinds of people in his opinion write poetry? Does he believe kids can write poetry? Does he think he is able to create a poem? Therefore pre-test items such as the following may be used:

I. List at least five words that come to mind when you think of the word, *poem*.

II. Suppose you had to describe the idea of a poem to someone who has never heard or seen one; what would you say?

III. Check any of the following statements below in each of the categories which best applies to you.

☐ A(1) I have read many poems.
☐ A(2) I have read few poems.
☐ B(1) I have read poems only in school.
☐ B(2) I have read poems in school and at home.
☐ C(1) I enjoy reading poems.
☐ C(2) I don't like reading poems.
☐ D(1) I feel that poems are only for grownups.
☐ D(2) I feel that children can enjoy poems as well as grownups.
☐ E(1) I have tried to write poems.
☐ E(2) I have only tried to write poems when my teachers asked me to do so.
☐ F(1) I don't think pupils my age can write poems.
☐ F(2) I think pupils my age can write poems.

IV. If you have any favorite poems, list their names below.
If you have no favorite poems, leave this question blank.

In sum, the preceeding pre-test items are merely samples to guide us in diagnosing our children and in tailoring the learning units and transforming them into realistic and relevant experiences. Teachers who have utilized them find them to be indispensable tools.

Preparing Pupils for Pre-Testing

In preparing pupils for the pre-test, we utilize the direct approach. The purpose of the pre-test is clearly communicated. We inform the pupils that this test differs from the tests which they are accustomed to, and that it is a preliminary survey which provides information enabling the teacher to determine what to teach them and where to begin. Test anxiety is reduced when pupils are informed that they will not be marked or assigned grades. In fact, there probably will be few questions which the children will be able to answer with any large degree of certainty. They should feel free to leave many questions unanswered when they are unable to respond. If their ideas are vague or if they are guessing, they should record this on their paper. This test is not a weapon (nor should any test be viewed as such), but a useful tool for the teacher to use to enable her to teach more effectively and efficiently. This is a teacher's test to guide her in selecting appropriate activities for her pupils.

Pupils' Reactions to Pre-Tests

Elementary school children accept the pre-tests readily. As the year progresses, the pupils look forward to the pre-test of the next unit, and to having the teachers share their results with them. Children are interested in knowing where they are and in assisting in charting their own progress.

At the junior high school level the initial reactions are mixed. "Is she kidding?" "I know what tests are for. Those files in the main office are full of them." It appears that these test-taking, test-wise students are reacting as we reacted as students to the testing maze.

Possibly the following verse, although written humorously, best reflects their view of tests at the onset of the program.

"We've a splendid testing system. If you'd like it I shall list 'em,"
Said the city superintendent with a holy little smile.
"We measure kids and test kids to see what things
Infest kids, and then repeat the process every
Little while.
We give grammar tests and hammer tests and also Katzenjammer tests,
And German tests and vermin tests, the best we can compile,
Appreciation, condensation, information, lubrication
To say nothing of vocation—Oh, a tall, tall pile.
Our tests are often mental, but they may be merely dental
Or sometimes environmental (about the domicile).
Versatility and ability, then utility, then debility—

With indefatigability we choose the latest style.
Constitution, restitution, home pollution, destitution,
Go-to-college, moral knowledge—just wait a little while;
Aptitudes and attitudes but seldom the beatitudes
For measurement of platitudes serves only to beguile.
Physiology, sociology, entomology, and geology,
For present-day psychology says these things we should compile;
Metaphorical and clerical, historical, hysterical,
Our tests are quite numerical, and very much worthwhile.
Spelling tests and yelling tests—no, I'm not selling tests,
But schools that seldom use them are very, very vile.
We give our tests, record our tests (I wish we could afford more tests),
And I keep them—keep them—in a great, large file."

—Anonymous

But as the pre-testing process continues the pupils' reactions are not only extremely favorable, but also serve to motivate the teachers. With the older pupils as with the elementary school children, they want to know the extent of their progress; they want to obtain knowledge of their results; they welcome real substantial feedback.

Many of the teachers use the pre-test for a dual purpose. First, to determine the content-wiseness of their pupils, and second, to stimulate interest in the unit and motivate the pupils. The results are indeed surprising. In some classrooms, following a pre-test, teachers find they are bombarded with questions about the unit; pupils are enthusiastic about getting started; outside resources are requested and the classroom is swamped with materials pupils bring from home which they think will be relevant to the new learning unit.

For many pupils, it is a new experience to view a test as a useful measuring device rather than as an anxiety-producing weapon which is part and parcel of the school environment The pre-test becomes a very personal experience for the pupils, but the post-test (which we will deal with now) is a still greater challenge and an adventure to test real learning.

THE CONTENT-PROCESS POST-TEST

The content-process post-test is a test which attempts to measure both content achievement and process usage at the close of a specific learning unit. It is not synonymous with a typical content or skill test. It does not measure merely the rote recall or recognition of a body of knowledge or skills. It is not concerned with the pupil's ability to parrot the "educated" notebook or "The Text." It is concerned with measuring far more important objectives such as: can the pupil demonstrate his knowledge and understanding of specific concepts, generalizations, and principles by expressing them in his own words, by applying them to new situations, by identifying relationships, by solving new problems, and by viewing them in a variety of different contexts? Has the pupil been involved in the process of "knowing" or has he remained back there filling a memory bank? The content-process test measures his ability to process the specific content he has learned by providing him with totally new or novel situations which he has not encountered in the classroom in an effort to determine if he "really knows" and "understands." The content-process test therefore is a challenge and requires a different type of study and preparation on the part of the pupil than the conventional test which emphasizes recall and convergent production.

When teachers in their day-to-day instruction focus upon process, when pupils are encouraged to be divergent thinkers, analysts, synthesizers, and critical thinkers as well as creative thinkers, one does not test them with an instrument which emphasizes rote recall. Our tests reflect *what* and *how* we teach. If we teach one way and then proceed to test in another way, we are educational charlatans. If we firmly believe that real education involves both process and content and that content becomes part and parcel of an individual when it is processed, then our tests must indeed reflect both content and process. However, we must exercise care in not reducing content and process to a rote process. If a particular concept or understanding is developed in class in which our pupils utilize induction or deduction, we do not pattern our test item in the post-test so that pupils must repeat the same cognitive process or processes to arrive at a solution. For there is danger that the student might repeat the process, as taught, in a rote fashion. To follow a procedure such as this is to reduce the process approach to a rote approach and to destroy the process goals of education.

Constructing a Content-Process Post-Test

The following sequence of steps is utilized in constructing a content-process test:

Step 1. *Utilize the Content Outline*

Arrange your content so that you list the key concepts, generalizations principles, data, and tool skills in a sequential and logical order. This sequence may be listed as part of a test table in which the content serves as the Y axis or vertical dimension of the table.

Step 2. *Utilize the Specific Behavioral Objectives*

List the specific behavioral objectives, cognitive and affective, and arrange them along the X axis or horizontal dimensions of the test table.

Step 3. *Construct Test Items*

Combine both content and process objectives by constructing test items. Whenever possible, present problems and create situations which center upon the cognitive processes in which pupils must use the content and where you can identify how they are thinking. Check the methods column of your learning unit to make certain that you are not requiring pupils to utilize the same cognitive process with the same content as was developed in class. Do not present the same situations utilized in the classroom. Create new or novel situations which compel the pupils to apply their concepts and generalizations to unfamiliar situations.

Step 4. *Utilize the Measurability Factors as Stated in the Objectives*

Where you have specified quantitative or qualitative conditions, make certain that your test items reflect these specifications.

Step 5. *Provide an Adequate Sampling of the Unit's Objectives*

As in the pre-test, make certain that each of the objectives is included in the test and that there is a sufficient number of items representing the key objectives as well as a minimum number representing the others. Combine a number of objectives into one test item. There is no need to test for each one separately. Record the number of test items in the table as they relate to content and process. A rapid perusal of your table will inform you of the adequacy of your sampling as well as your inclusion of all objectives.

Step 6. *Weigh the Test Items*

At this point you will assign specific weights to each of the test items. The weights you assign will be a function of the importance of the objective and the criteria you will utilize in evaluating each response. In a content-process test, unlike an objective test, it is rare that we encounter an all-or-none type of response requiring the usual weighting of 1 or 0. In dealing with cognitive behaviors, we are more likely to use a scale of values based on the levels of response available. Therefore, we might assign a maximum of five points for the best response, four for the next best, and so on down to 0 for the poorest. In all probability, this system is more defensible than any of the special weighting systems that are commonly used. The values assigned, therefore, will depend upon the criteria established by the teacher, the number of levels of response that are anticipated to specific questions, the relative importance of specific questions as opposed to others which are considered secondary, and the questions viewed as more difficult by the teacher as opposed to those deemed simpler. Since for our purposes, we are not attempting to construct a "professional" test, teachers are quite capable of establishing their own criteria based on their objectives and assigning weights to the test items.

Step 7. *Review the Entire Test*

Check the entire test to make certain that you have:

a) included the key content and basic skills.
b) incorporated all of the specific pupil behavioral objectives.
c) constructed test items that involve novel or new situations.
d) utilized the measurability factors as stated in the objectives.
e) provided an adequate sampling of the unit's objectives.
f) weighted the test items in terms of importance, difficulty, your criteria of performance.

In addition, make certain that you have specified directions clearly, and that wherever possible you have provided the pupil with sample items to reinforce these directions. One of the criteria of a good cognitive test, which we have found most useful, is its ability to be used as a learning unit. If it can be used for the purpose, then it does indeed reflect the teacher's pattern of instruction and it is a *test that teaches.*

Illustrations of Post-Test Items
Used in Content-Process Tests

The following are sample test items which may be used in content-process tests. Some of these items are very specific and illustrate the measurement of specific content and process objectives; others are general in format and, therefore, can be adapted to a wide variety of content areas although the processes are a function of the structure of the test item. You will note that in all cases, content is applied by the pupil to a new or novel situation. The situations utilized as test items were not encountered in the classroom. In some cases, the general items contain blanks or refer to descriptions, slides, pictures, or pictorial representations which are not presented in this book. In these cases, teachers are free to utilize their own resources to complete the test item.

Each test item is preceded by a general description of what pupils were exposed to as well as the specific objective to be measured by the item.

A. *Content Area—Art*

The pupils have have completed a learning unit on the principles of composition.

The objectives to be measured: The pupil will be able to apply the principles of composition in analyzing unfamiliar pictures.

Item 1. Projected on the screen, you see two pictures in which the artists have applied the basic principles of composition.

a) Analyze these pictures and describe and identify the principles utilized.

b) Compare these pictures and record both the similarities and the differences.

c) Select the one which you prefer and state the reasons for your preference.

B. *Content Area—Biology*

The pupils have completed two learning units; one dealing with the classification of animals and another dealing with animals and their relationships to their environments.

The objectives to be measured are:

(1) The pupil will be able to apply his knowledge of the classification of animals to a new situation.

(2) The pupil will demonstrate his knowledge of the varieties of ways in which animals adapt to their surroundings.

Item 2. Below you will observe pictorial representations of six animals. It is obvious that they are figments of someone's imagination. However, let us assume that they are real. Study the pictures carefully. Compare the animals, noting their similarities and differences. Then, classify these animals into two groups.

a) State your classification system.

b) Describe the basis or criteria for your classification system.

c) Arrange all six animals in a hierarchy starting with the most simple or primitive and ending with the most complex. State the reasons for your specific arrangement.

d) Select any three of these animals and describe the environmental conditions in which each should live. Give specific reasons for your choice of environment in each case.

C. *Content Area—General Science*

The pupils have completed learning units dealing with chemistry, matter, energy, work, magnetism, electricity, light, sound, and atomic energy.

(1) The pupil will have acquired the skills of

(a) measuring the volume of an irregularly shaped object

(b) determining the density of a substance

(c) determining the weight of a substance

(d) detecting radioactivity

(e) determining the acidity of a basic nature of a substance

(2) Given the specific characteristics of a substance, pupil will be able to apply and interrelate the generalizations learned in the above-mentioned units and invent three practical uses for this substance.

Item 3. "Bloop" is an irregularly shaped solid which has been recently discovered.

    I. How would you find the following characteristics of "Bloop"? Describe your procedure briefly.

    A. the volume of this sample of "Bloop"

    B. its density

    C. its weight

    D. radioactivity

    E. acidic or basic

    It was found that when a small piece of "Bloop" was submerged in water, it dissolved.

    F. What problem does this present in regard to one of your above procedures?

    G. How can this problem be solved?

    II. Following careful experimentation, let us assume that "Bloop" was found to possess the following characteristics. Utilizing these characteristics, list and describe three possible practical applications in which "Bloop" could be used.

Characteristics

    A. "Bloop's" electrical conductivity exceeded that of gold, silver, and copper.

    B. It was extremely light and did not oxidize.

    C. Its coefficient of friction with most common materials was extremely low.

    D. It would react with sodium, releasing a tremendous amount of light energy, but no heat.

    E. When a strip of "Bloop" was connected with any metal at room temperature, a large electric current would flow.

    F. In a moving magnetic field, it produced a tremendous amount of electricity.

    G. Sound waves passing through it were highly amplified.

    H. When bombarded by slow moving neutrons, it became fissionable, transforming a small part of its mass into a tremendous amount of energy. Its by-products were not radioactive.

D. Content Area–Mathematics

The pupils have completed a series of units dealing with measurement. The objective to be measured: The pupil will be able to creatively apply a variety of different methods of measurement to a specific situation.

Item 4. Invent four different ways of determining the height of the Washington Monument.

E. *Content Area–Language Arts*

The pupils have completed a learning unit on the daily newspaper and the weekly news magazine.

The objective to be measured: The pupil will be able to identify the functions served by a daily newspaper and those served by a weekly news magazine.

Item 5. Below you will find two articles describing a current news event. One article was taken from a daily newspaper, the other from a news magazine. Read each article carefully and identify which was the newspaper article and which was the magazine article. State the reasons for your response.

F. *Content Area–Social Studies*

The pupils have completed a learning unit which dealt with the methods and materials utilized by social scientists.

The objective to be measured: The pupil will be able to analyze data and to make inferences from this data.

Item 6. Man's behaviors and actions mirror his values and his beliefs. Below is an account of a man's actions. Analyze this account and describe what you think this man values and what he believes in. Substantiate your responses by citing specifics from the account.

The preceeding six test items serve to emphasize the nature of the content-process test. In each of the cases, the pupil must apply his knowledge to a situation not previously encountered. This type of test has proven far more valuable in testing understanding than the usual content-centered variety. Possibily many of us will agree with that old saying, "Knowledge is like fish; it doesn't keep very well unless it is used."

How Pupils and Teachers Benefit from These Novel Tests

The pupil benefits derived from these content-process tests are significant. Few of us will dispute the fact that how a teacher tests will determine to a large extent the kind of preparation and study pupils will engage in.

As our pupils state, they really have to prepare for these tests; they really have to understand—"You can't fake it," "You have to know your stuff." Rote memorization and verbalism are not sufficient. To be able to apply generalizations to new situations, to be able to suggest a variety of solutions to a problem, to be able to make valid decisions based on evidence cannot be done without a thorough knowledge and understanding of the content

Although in the majority of cases these tests are pencil and paper tests rather than performance tests, the pupil performance in terms of process and content is clearly evident.

Pupils view these tests as real, relevant, meaningful, challenging, and "brain-draining," and most importantly not only as test situations but as learning situations. These are tests that teach.

Teachers, in general, find the process of test construction difficult at first but as they move beyond these initial attempts, they are amazed at their creativity in producing problem-solving situations which serve to interrelate a wide variety of topics in their content area.

Many who have had little or no background in tests and measurements turn to the literature to learn more about test construction. Needs which have not been previously identified become apparent. Teachers begin to understand the limitations of tests and to perceive the results as partial and as descriptive of time now. Greater care is exercised in the selection and construction of test items. The perspective of teachers is broadened. Few hold the content-oriented test as sacred as they previously did. The content-process test has arrived.

I recall that at the close of our first year in the program I visited a school and found one of our teachers unloading her desk and filing cabinet directly into the wastebasket. "You're not leaving?" I asked in despair. "No," she replied, "but these tests are! I'm past the stage of having my pupils run the testing maze. I've seen what content-process tests have done for my children and I have no intention of using tests which focus purely on recall."

In addition, the content-process test yields a great deal more information about the individual pupils and teachers. Teachers enjoy "marking" these tests. "It's amazing to discover the number of solutions pupils arrive at—solutions which I never would have thought of!"

In sum, the content-process test demonstrates substantial benefits for both pupils and teachers. The cycle of specific clear-cut behavioral objectives; of "matching" methods, materials, and media with tests which clearly reflect the objectives; the process-oriented teaching style; and the teacher's realistic expectations based on pre-test data and classroom observation is complete. The teachers and pupils experience the total process and now "see" the whole—a whole which is meaningful, relevant, realistic, and systematic, and which produces positive results for all involved in the process. "Testolotry," to use Dr. Bannish Hoffman's term, does not exist in this approach. Here the quest for tests is met. Here we are using tests as tools for specific purposes, and the results are not stored in our great big files but are utilized to make the match—the match that can make the difference between success and failure in our classrooms—the match that makes the difference between "Schools for Children" or Procustean Schools.

12

Developing Responsive Pupils
and Responsive Environments

We are equipped with general goals of education. Yet we know —this is not sufficient. We specify pupil objectives in behavioral and measurable terms. Yet we know—this is not sufficient. We expend time and effort and construct learning units to promote process and content and incorporate pre-tests and post-tests and then utilize these in our classrooms. But—this is not sufficient. For one essential ingredient is lacking—that of creating a responsive environment, an environment in which pupils are free to interact realistically with the human and material resources which are provided.

Here again, it would take little effort to be caught up in a web of words. What, precisely, do we mean by a responsive environment? Who is interacting responsively with whom and how is this environment created in a classroom?

Defining the Responsive Environment in Terms of Pupils

First—we will define the responsive environment in terms of the pupils. A responsive environment is one in which pupils are given the freedom "to be" and "to become." Pupils "know" that they are viewed and valued as distinct individuals. They have no need to play specific roles in the classrooms. They are able to shed their role of the stereotyped pupil. They are not afraid to ask their own questions, to make mistakes, to initiate requests, suggestions and activities—for what they are and what they have to offer are welcomed in the classroom. They have no need to play the game, make the right moves, or learn to beat the system. They are not in a state of anxiety or fearful that their actions or reactions are constantly being evaluated and recorded. They are not subjected to rigid routines or precise procedures which are valued more than they are. They do not view the teacher as a taskmaster or a disciplinarian. The atmosphere they are provided with is one in which they are truly free to learn. They graviate toward it because it centers on them as real people. The message in this environment is clear—You, the pupil, count. You are somebody!

The Teacher and the Responsive Environment

Second—we will define the responsive environment in terms of the teacher, for the teacher *is* the responsive environment. She is the key factor in the classroom. Her total pattern of influence, everything she does from the moment she greets her pupils in the morning until she dismisses them in the late afternoon, determines the responsiveness of the classroom environment. Her role as a person, as a diagnostician, as an instructor, as an observer, and as a participant in human interactions and transactions, creates an environment which either is conducive to real learning or promotes only mechanistic training.

The teacher, therefore, by demonstrating a specific pattern of behaviors, is able to create an environment in which pupils voluntarily respond to the learning stimuli in her classroom. The pupils respond to her as an authentic individual, to each other, and to the activities and resources provided. To reiterate—she will create either a responsiveness to learning and continuing education in her classroom or a training regime which her pupils will learn to accept and live with until they are released at the close of the term.

So many of us, despite our good intentions and dedication to the profession, have failed to see the vital importance of our total pattern of behavior, of our "whole person" impact on our pupils. Few of us have had the opportunity to see ourselves in our classrooms. We tend at times to be so task-oriented, so content-oriented, so procedure-oriented, that we lose sight of the individual human beings we deal with. It is not that we lack the humanistic elements crucial to teaching; it is that these elements have been subverted, in some cases by a system which has been imposed upon us and which continues to monitor us in terms of outdated concepts of teacher effectiveness, and in other cases by our early training in "teachership."

I can readily recall a meeting at which a teacher was aghast at what appeared to be a laissez-faire attitude of an administrator. She would not allow "things to just happen" in her classroom. "When my pupils pass the threshold of room 307, they know what is expected of them. All talking stops at that threshold. They enter and immediately go to their assigned seats. Their homework assignment is on the board. They have exactly five minutes to copy their assignment. Attendance is taken and the lesson begins. At the end of the 45 minutes, I have accomplished the prepared objectives. The pupils have completed their work, taken notes which summarize the lesson, and know how they are to prepare for the next day. I come prepared to class and so do my pupils. There is no guesswork or floundering in my classroom. The procedures are established the first day they enter my room. They know what I expect of them and what they can expect of me."

How many teachers "run" a classroom in this manner and are convinced that they are indeed doing a superb job? How "laissez-faire" is an administrator who questions an approach in which clearly defined roles, procedures, and pupil expectations are established the first day of school prior to the teacher obtaining any knowledge of her pupils? How "laissez-faire" is an administrator who prefers an open-structured environment where the pupils involved are more important than the silence at the threshold, the assigned seats, the homework assignment for "all," the specific pattern of instruction, the "summarized" notebook, the hands on the clock which determine the learning time and closure time by which pupil mastery is "achieved," and the teacher satisfaction which is derived from putting the ribbon on the "learning" package?

I am no longer able to view this administrator as "laissez-faire," but ten years ago, I was extremely sincere in the viewpoint I expressed. As were many teachers, I was trained in the "art" of teaching. In the forties, when I entered teaching, the three-year probationary period was still in effect as it is today in numerous school systems. My supervisor's expectations were clearly apparent. The required teaching environment was spelled out in an observation check list. The range of expectations encompassed my personal appearance; the physical appearance of my room (seats arranged in neat rows, blackboards washed daily, shades lined up at matching heights, floors litter free, bulletin board with perfect papers arranged in straight lines, desk at the center of the room, windows open for proper ventilation); the homework assignment on the board; the presentation of the lesson following a precise format of assignment, motivation, teacher presentation, pupil recitation or activity, medial summary, change of activity, final summary, and dismissal. My ability to adapt to this pattern determined my permanent status as a teacher. Little wonder that so many teachers today demonstrate this training pattern in the classroom, for this type of experience is still prevalent. But we as professionals can change this pattern, and we must do so if our schools and universities are to be relevant.

To define the responsive environment in terms of the teacher, we must specify the kinds of behaviors she demonstrates in the classroom. How do we convey to pupils that we value them as individuals, that we want them to be themselves, that making mistakes is a vital part of the learning process, that their questions and ideas are indeed welcome and that essentially we are all human beings searching for better ways to live and to create a better world? The answer is, in large measure, available to all of us. It consists of employing a set of specific behaviors which we, the teachers and administrators, demonstrate—behaviors which become the day-to-day actions and reactions and transform us into *models* for pupils to emulate. These behaviors, which will be set forth in the following pages, are by no means new. They are abstracted and inferred from the extensive research studies of Flanders, Hughes, Lewin, Lippitt, White, Medley, Mitzel, Miller, Rabinowitz, Openshaw, Rosenfeld, Lander, Ryans, and many others. When these studies were analyzed and synthesized they yielded data that was useful in creating a social-emotional or psychological climate which is conducive to real learning. Following 15 months of full-time research in this area under a grant from the Fund for the Advancement of Education, I have attempted to apply the teacher behaviors from these and other studies to classroom situations. The behaviors listed are stated in basic terms. We have found that they work—but they work only when we work hard at making them an integral part of our behavioral pattern of influence.

How Teachers Create a Responsive Environment

To create a responsive climate, the teacher demonstrates and employs the following behaviors:

1. *Accepts pupils' ideas.*[1] Demonstrate verbally or nonverbally that you are receiving the message.
2. *Develops pupils' ideas.*[1] Expand upon what they are offering or assist them in clarifying and further developing their ideas.
3. *Accepts pupils' feelings.*[1] Feelings are facts. Again, demon-

strate that you have received the message. Don't toss them aside with a curt remark and proceed with the sacred lesson plan.

4. *Develops pupils' feelings.*[1] Make certain that you understand how they feel. Ask questions to assist them in communicating their specific feelings.

5. *Gauges when to pursue pupils' feelings and when to take no action.* Here, you, as the professional, must make the decision, based on your knowledge of the child.

6. *Gives freedom.* Initially, when pupils are given freedom, they are not always ready to take it. They do not become autonomous in a short period of time. Therefore, you guide them and assist them in the process. It is surprising how frequently they hold the reins on themselves.

7. *Praises rather than criticizes.*[1] It is so easy to be critical and the results are so obvious. You accomplish much more by enhancing the child's self-concept than by destroying it with criticism. When children are not succeeding, it is time you reevaluated your objectives in terms of the pupil and the methods, strategies, and activities which you have provided. It is time to be critical of your program rather than of the child. Provide alternatives; if praise is not merited, remain neutral in your actions rather than critical.

8. *Encourages.*[1] When you encourage, you are demonstrating your belief in the child and his ability. Nothing is achieved when you abruptly tell a child that he couldn't possibly succeed in a task. Again, you may have mismatched the child and the task and you may have to break down the task into sub-tasks. This is readily done and then encouragement should accompany the act.

9. *Insures a level of success for the pupils.* This takes us back to the match of pupils and objectives and pre-test data. To many of us this is old hat, but it is of major importance. Children will succeed in our classrooms if we provide opportunities for success. This initial success will spur them on. Stop focusing on the syllabus, the sacred text, the test in your files; focus on the child, make the match so that some measure of success will ensue. Children progress at different rates—we accept this. Children achieve at different levels—we accept this. Therefore, we must act on these assumptions until they are proven to be fallacious.

10. *Listens.*[1] How many times do you and I listen and not hear? Listening to our youngsters provides us with a wealth of information not found in the permanent records. By really "tuning in"

on our children, we obtain the vital data which will enable us to instruct them as individuals.

11. *Allows for pupil talk. Doesn't talk most of the time.*[1] From our own experience, we have found this is a most difficult task to accomplish. When you have grown accustomed to information-giving, the initial frustrations in monitoring yourself and reducing the amount of teacher-talk are great.

12. *States the pupils' goals with clarity.* There is sufficient research evidence to indicate that pupils will demonstrate increased achievement when clear-cut goals have been communicated.[2] Pupils must know where they are going and why they are going there.

13. *Accepts pupils' mistakes.* If you are to create a climate where pupils are to be themselves and are accepted as human beings, then mistakes must be received as a valuable part of learning. Accept the mistakes without reprimand, but focus on why the child made the mistake.

14. *Makes her own mistakes.* Demonstrate that you are human. Don't hide your mistakes. Be real rather than wear the facade of perfection.

15. *Doesn't seek instant closure.* Since one of our major goals is the development of process, provide children with time to process information. Don't anticipate instant responses to a problem. Pause —give children time to process the content, to formulate complete responses.

16. *Constantly assesses her expectations of the pupils.* If you will recall the Rosenthal study referred to earlier in the book, you are aware of the effects of the self-fulfilling prophecy. Exercise care in establishing pupil expectations; keep in mind that their expectations must always be in process and, therefore, require constant revision.

17. *Is authentic.* So many of us wear our professional role of teacher well. We erect our wall and hold our pupils at a safe distance. We are excellent actors and actresses; our performances are superb. At 3:30 or 4 o'clock we return to our real selves. We are doing our pupils a major disservice. The time to be real, to be oneself, to demonstrate one's wholeness and individuality is in the classroom. Our children should know us and view us as total individuals, with thoughts, feelings, values, and beliefs which may not coincide with theirs but which are there nonetheless. Our relationships should be honest, not based on the role-functions of the teacher as stated in X

manual. We have to break down the artificial barriers we have created.

At an ASCD convention a well-known educator described a teacher-training program being implemented at his institute. A potential teacher and a youngster were teamed for the day. The teacher was not to directly instruct the child but simply be his companion for the day. The teacher was a bit dismayed, but the child took the teacher by the hand and smiled with assurance. "Don't worry," the child said, "We'll make it." Do we make it or do we play a role?

In sum, the 17 guidelines provided in this chapter will serve to create a responsive teacher who in turn will transform pupils into responsive learners.

The task is by no means an easy one. The act of changing our behavior patterns in terms of our differing personality traits requires a great deal of effort. But—we have been realists. Equipped with the desire to create this responsiveness, we developed our own styles of accepting and developing pupils' ideas and feelings; we provided freedom gradually; we praised and encouraged; we focused on insuring some level of success for each pupil; we learned to listen and to encourage pupil talk and interaction; we stated clear goals; we accepted mistakes and made our own mistakes. We did not seek instant closure but "opensure"; we were cautious in regard to pupil expectations; and we were able to assist our pupils in many more ways than previously for we found that we knew our pupils. The task of being authentic was, of course, an individual one and each of us proceeded in our own fashion. We succeeded in putting these guidelines to the test: the results were extremely positive in terms of both pupil and teacher outcomes.

The Effects of Responsive Environments on Pupils and Teachers

What happens to pupils who are taken out of stereotyped and highly controlled environments and placed in a responsive climate?

My first experiences in attempting to become a responsive teacher are best suited to describe the results. My schedule indicated that I had five groups of youngsters: three "average" groups, one "slow" or "difficult" group and one which was "accelerated."

Initially, all pupils couldn't believe it! They knew the rules of the game and I was obviously a subversive teacher. And then changes occurred. Pupils who had been apathetic the previous year were actively participating. My "slow" or "difficult" students were in class promptly, ready to work. Activities which they initiated were carried through to completion. Early successes paid off. Children who thought they couldn't achieve, did achieve. Requests for working on their projects after school were numerous. Pupils were open in their reactions. "This year was different!" "We are learning more." "We are really interested." "We know that we are doing better than before."

My "slow" and "difficult" children were motivating me; they were no longer frustrating and depressing me.

The "average" and "accelerated" youngsters responded equally well. The children were more willing to tackle tasks and problems. They brought materials to class which were not requested. They asked their questions; they designed their projects. The previous year, a total of 20 youngsters from my six classes volunteered to enter our science fair. This year, there were 60 youngsters. Room 307 was never neat or totally in order, but the activity and noise were education in process. Our laboratory was directly over the principal's office—but I had only to scan his face when he entered the room to know that he was equally responsive and totally supportive of what he had seen. I knew that my pupils and I were both changing and growing. My satisfaction in teaching was heightened. Each day was challenging and exciting for me.

It would appear from the above description that only secondary school pupils respond in this fashion. But, you may ask, how do elementary school youngsters respond? In precisely the same way! These children come alive. Robot-like behaviors disappear. Personalities emerge. Personal contributions flow. In language arts, music, art, social studies, mathematics and science, children open up, become involved and interact.

During the first three years as I moved through the elementary schools to demonstrate the approach using "borrowed" classes, the teachers were amazed at what their children demonstrated. As one teacher put it, "It was as if someone touched a hidden spring and released the true vibrations." Children who were limited participators and passive observers were transformed into seekers, talkers, and doers.

In sum, all kinds of pupils respond in a responsive environment. They develop a more positive self-concept; they learn because they want to learn in this type of setting; they achieve; they interact freely with their peers and their teacher. They experience the success and joy of learning.

For the teacher, classroom life becomes challenging and exciting. She experiences satisfaction. She grows because she is constantly challenged and motivated by what she experiences as she interacts with her pupils. She obtains increased knowledge about her pupils, about herself, and about human interactions and transactions. There is no one role to play. There are no repetitions of the same experience period after period, for she is dealing with different groups of individuals and they are responding authentically. The game is over. Education is in process.

FOOTNOTES

[1] Ned A. Flanders, *Helping Teachers Change Their Behavior,* Ann Arbor, Michigan: School of Education, University of Michigan, October, 1965 (revised edition).

[2] Edmond J. Amidon and Ned A. Flanders, "The Role of the Teacher in the Classroom," Ann Arbor, Michigan: School of Education, University of Michigan, 1963 (Mimeo).

13

Strategies for Starting

All aspects of the Behavioral Outcomes Approach have been described in detail: the philosophy, the blueprint of educational objectives, the cognitive processes and their applications, the specification of behavioral objectives, the construction of learning units, pre-testing and post-testing, and the development of a responsive environment. These aspects have been delineated on a practical level and in operational terms. The extensive benefits derived from this approach for both teachers and pupils are clearly evident. Therefore, we are now at the most relevant point of the continuum—that of implementing this approach in our own schools with our pupils. We are now equipped with basic tools to create "Schools for Children," to put into operation the teaching-thinking-learning process, to create responsive environments and thereby develop responsive pupils, and to fulfill the realization that *learning is to think.*

In order to initiate this approach and to experience a large measure of success at the early stages of implementation, the following strategies for starting are presented. These strategies should serve as guidelines enabling teachers to develop the approach gradually and systematically so that competencies in all aspects of the program result prior to the total implementation.

Practical Guidelines for Implementing the Approach

Step 1. *Select a Content Area*

If you are a teacher in the elementary school, select the content area in which you are most competent. If you are a secondary school teacher, you are most likely a specialist in one or two areas. It is wise to start in content area in which you are extremely knowledgeable and secure.

Step 2.   *Develop Skill in Utilizing the Cognitive Processes*

Working within the content area you have selected, begin to develop skill in structuring questions to promote specific cognitive processes. Concentrate your efforts on using two or three processes per week. Listen to and observe your pupils' reactions when they are stimulated and encouraged to think. Use "pausing" behavior. Pause after you ask a question. Explain to your pupils that the pause is to provide them with time to think about their responses and to enable them to give complete answers rather than short responses which do not reveal their thoughts and knowledge. Start your pupils off by using processes they are relatively familiar with, such as comparison and classification. Then move ahead to divergent thinking, analysis, induction and deduction and the other processes. Practice structuring questions on your feet in response to pupils' questions and replies. Attempt to develop the technique of answering a question with another question, enabling the pupil to arrive at his own answer to his question. Minimize the "who-what-when-where" type of questions. Refrain from responses such as "No, you are wrong!" Instead, ask the child a question by which he will reevaluate what he has said and will correct himself. When you sense that a pupil is wavering and uncertain, respond with a "Possibly," and give him time to obtain and process additional data.

It would be naive to say that developing this skill in cognitive questioning is simple. In fact, it was interesting to note that during the first few months in which we piloted the program, all of the participating teachers identified this as their major weakness. We found that only by concentrating our efforts on one or two processes at a time in one content area were we able to develop competence. Therefore, in year-round workshops which followed, teachers utilized the one–process–one–content area approach and met with success.

Similarly the development of "pausing behavior" on the part of the teacher took time and in many cases required the cooperation of the pupils. During my early experiences with "pausing behavior" I equipped the third-grade pupils with signs which said *PAUSE!* When the youngsters felt I was racing on without giving them time to think, they would hold up the sign. I would smile, nod my head, and pause.

The usually restless youngsters became actively involved. We all worked at it together, and these youngsters were excellent teachers. I learned to pause.

Step 3. *Create a Responsive Environment*

Construct a checklist of factors which foster a responsive environment. Identify those factors which you feel need further development in your classroom. Concentrate your efforts on these factors. The use of a tape recorder or video-tape recorder has proven effective for many teachers in monitoring their own behavior privately. By listening to a tape or viewing a video-tape of our own behavior, many of us were amazed to discover the discrepancies between what we assumed we were doing and how we were actually operating in the classroom. By using the checklist in conjunction with our tapes, we were able to analyze our behavioral patterns and observe the changes as they took place.

Step 4. *Construct a Brief Learning Unit*

Having developed some proficiency with cognitive functions and fostered a responsive climate, construct a learning unit of a week's duration. Outline the content, specify the pupil objectives for the week, briefly list the learning activities, and structure and key questions. Use your table of specifications to determine your process profile. Using these few objectives as a framework, construct a short pre-test and post-test.

Step 5. *Prepare Your Pupils for the Pre-test*

Explain the purpose of the pre-test to your pupils. Answer all questions relative to this "survey."

Step 6. *Pre-Test*

Pre-test the pupils, analyze the results, group your pupils in terms of their needs, and tailor the unit to these needs.

Step 7. *Introduce the Learning Unit*

Utilize the learning unit, allowing each group of pupils to work on their specific objectives. Make certain that all the resources listed in the unit are readily available. Guide and assist each group as needed.

Step 8. *Post-Test*

As each group of pupils completes the unit, administer the post-test items based on their specific objectives.

Step 9. *Provide Pupils with Knowledge of Results*

Review the results of the post-test with your pupils. Identify those objectives in which some pupils may require further work.

Step 10. *Continue the Process of Unit Construction*

As you observe the results of this approach with your pupils, you will find that the process of unit construction will propel you into expanding your efforts. Regressing to old methods will be a difficult task, for the stimulation and challenges encountered with these teaching-thinking-learning experiences will promote a chain-reaction.

In sum, the results experienced by your pupils and the personal satisfaction you will derive from this approach, will leave you no recourse but to continue.

The Administrator's Role in the Implementation Process

The guidelines provided will enable teachers in all content areas and at all educational levels to utilize the Behavioral Outcomes Approach. However, we must not lose sight of the vital role of the administrator in the implementation process. The administrator's key function is to establish a responsive and threat-free environment to enable teachers to test this approach. The administrator must keep firmly in mind that the test is not of the teacher but of the approach and its application in a given setting. When he views the innovations in this light he will create a climate that is conducive to change.

In the Behavioral Outcomes program, many administrators have attended workshops not as auditors but as participants. They have written learning units, "borrowed" classes in their schools, and taught sections of their units. These experiences have served to sensitize them to all the operational aspects of the program. They have fully experienced the process, the initial frustrations, and the ensuing satisfactions. As a result they were well equipped to provide concrete assistance and realistic encouragement to their staff. In describing the program to parent groups and in obtaining community support, they were able to demonstrate the kind of enthusiasm which comes only from firsthand experience. In essence, behaviorally-oriented teachers supported by behaviorally-oriented administrators is the most desirable combination.

In some schools, teachers intrigued with the approach planted the seeds and perceptive administrators nurtured their efforts. In other schools, the administrator initiated the approach and was supported by a flexible and receptive staff. What is most significant is not who introduced the approach but that the approach was implemented and with measurable success.

CONCLUDING STATEMENTS

The task is ours. As educators we have the responsibility of restoring relevancy and meaning to education. At this time, more than ever before in the history of education, there is a dire need to create "Schools for Children," to eliminate procrustean practices, to reexamine the changing values and conflicts evident in our existing culture, to transform our schools into mirrors and instruments which reflect our changing needs and values, and to foster constructive adaptation and acculturation. Our schools cannot continue to reflect the status "past"; they cannot continue to look backward. The impact of the present has been felt by all of us. We cannot continue to ignore it. The match must be made! This is our goal and our responsibility as professional educators.

It is time we ceased preparing rationales and lists of factors which serve to deter our efforts. We have the tools to promote change; we have adequate knowledge to move ahead and to prepare our children for a better future. If we are able to foster the processes of education, if we are able to provide our children with cognitive skills, if we are able to develop thinking individuals, we are insuring the best possible future for our children. These are our goals; we have but to undertake the task of implementation. The task is indeed ours, and the time for implementation is—*now*.

Bibliography

The following books and articles have been organized in order to provide for independent research into the Behavioral Outcomes Approach. The initial reading list is designed to provide both background and a general overview. The additional readings will provide for greater depth of understanding.

INITIAL READING LIST

Articles and Reports

Bruner, Jerome S., "Learning and Thinking," *Harvard Educational Review 29,* No. 3, 184-192, Summer 1959.

Kaya, Esin "A Curricular Sequence Based on Psychological Processes," *Exceptional Children,* April 1961.

Kaya, Esin, M. Gerhard, et al, "Developing a Theory of Educational Practice for the Elementary School," Project sponsored by the Fund for the Advancement of Education, June, 1967.

Kaya, Esin and May Walker "Evaluating Pupil Achievement in the Classroom: An Approach to Teacher In-Service Education," *Experimental Teaching Center,* N.Y. University, September 1961.

Russell, D. H. "Six Studies of Children's Understanding of Concepts," *Elementary School Journal* 63: 255-260, 1963.

Books

Ahmann, J. Stanley and Marvin D. Glock *Evaluating Pupil Growth.* Boston: Allyn and Bacon, 1963.

Association for Supervision and Curriculum Development, 1962 Yearbook *Perceiving, Behaving and Becoming.* Department of Curriculum Development of NEA, Washington, D.C., 1962.

Bloom, Benjamin S. (ed.) *Taxonomy of Education Objectives, The Classification of Educational Goals: Handbook I: Cognitive Domain.* New York: David McKay, 1956.

Bruner, Jerome S. *The Process of Education.* Cambridge: Harvard University Press, 1960.

Dewey, John *How We Think*. Boston: D.C. Heath, 1933.

Gallagher, James *Teaching the Gifted Child*. Boston: Allyn & Bacon, 1964.

Gerberich, J. Raymond *Specimen Objective Test Items: A Guide to Achievement Test Construction*. New York: Longmans, Green, 1956.

Kraniyik, Robert D. *Stimulating Creative Learning in the Elementary School*. Parker Publishing Company, Inc. 1969.

Krathwohl, D. R., B. S. Bloom, and B. B. Masia *A Taxonomy of Educational Objectives: Handbook II: The Affective Domain*. New York: David McKay Co., Inc., 1964.

Mager, Robert F. *Preparing Objectives for Programmed Instruction*. Fearon, 1962.

Massialas, Byron G. (ed.) *The Indiana Experiments in Inquiry: Social Studies*. Bulletin of the School of Education, Indiana University, Vol. 39, No. 3. May 1963.

Russell, D. H. *Children's Thinking*. Boston: Ginn & Company, 1956.

Schwab, Julius J. and Paul F. Brandwein *The Teaching of Science*. Cambridge: Harvard University Press, 1962.

Wertheimer, M. *Productive Thinking*. New York: Harper 1945.

ADDITIONAL READING LIST

Articles

Bingham, Alma and Doris May Lee "Intellectual Processes," *Review of Educational Research*, 29: 185-196, 1959.

"Curriculum Planning and Development" *Review of Educational Research*, Vol. 33: (entire issue) June 1963.

Elsner, E. W. "Knowledge, Knowing and the Visual Arts," *Harvard Educational Review*, 33: 208-11, Spring 1963.

Friedlander, Bernard Z. "A Psychologist's Second Thoughts on Concepts, Curiosity, and Discovery in Teaching and Learning," *Harvard Educational Review*, 35: 18-38, Winter 1965.

Guilford, J. P. "Three Faces of Intellect," *The American Psychologist*, 1959, 14, 469-479.

Suchman, R. "Inquiry Training in the Elementary School," *Science Teacher*, 27, 42-3.

Suchman, R. "Learning Through Inquiry," *NEA Journal*, 52, 31-2, 1963.

Tyler, R. W. "The Interrelationship of Knowledge," *National Elementary Principal*, 43: 13-21, February 1964.

Books

Adkins, Dorothy (Wood) *Test Construction: Development and Interpretation of Achievement Tests*, Ohio: Charles E. Merrill Books Inc., 1961.

Arnold, John "Education for Innovation." In S. Parnes and H. Harding (Eds.) *A Source Book for Creative Thinking.* New York: Charles Scribner Sons, 1962, 127-138.

Ausubel, D. P. *The Psychology of Meaningful Verbal Learning: An Introduction to School Learning.* New York: Grune and Stratton, 1963.

Berelson, B. and G. A. Steiner *Human Behavior: An Inventory of Scientific Findings.* New York: Harcourt, Brace and World, 1964.

Broudy, H. S., B. O. Smith, and J. R. Burnett *Democracy and Excellence in American Secondary Education.* Chicago: Rand, McNally and Company, 1964.

Bruner, J. S. *On Knowing.* Cambridge, Mass.: Harvard University Press, 1962.

Bruner, J. S. "The Conditions of Creativity." In H. Gruber and J. Terrell and M. Wertheimer (eds.) *Contemporary Approaches to Creative Thinking.* New York: Atherton Press, 1962, 1-30.

Bruner, J. S. *On Knowing: Essays For The Left Hand.* Cambridge: Harvard University Press, 1962.

Burton, William H., Ronald B. Kimball, and Richard L. Wing *Education for Effective Thinking.* New York: Appleton-Century-Crofts.

Cronbach, Lee J. *Essentials of Psychological Testing* (2nd ed.). New York: Harper, 1960.

Flavell, J. H. *The Development Psychology of Jean Piaget.* Princeton, New Jersey: D. Van Nostrand Co., Inc., 1963.

Getzels, J. W. and P. Jackson *Creativity and Intelligence.* New York: John Wiley Publishers, 1962.

Gruber, H. E., G. Ferrell, and M. Wertheimer *Contemporary Approaches to Creative Thinking.* New York: Atherton Press, 1963.

Hunt, J. McV. *Intelligence and Experience.* New York: Ronald Press, 1961.

Inhelder, B. and J. Piaget *The Growth of Logical Thinking.* New York: Basic Books, Inc., 1958.

Kingsley, Howard L. and Ralph Garry *The Nature and Condition of Learning* (2nd ed.). Englewood Cliffs, N. J., Prentice-Hall, 1957.

Kogan, Zuce "Methods of Furthering New Ideas." In S. Parnes and H. Harding (eds.) *A Source Book of Creative Thinking.* New York: Charles Scribner Sons, 1962, 269-276.

Miles, M. B. *Innovations in Education.* New York: Bureau of Publications, Teachers College, Columbia University, 1964.

National Society for the Study of Education, *Individualizing Instruction,* 61st Yearbook, Part I. Press, 1962.

National Society for the Study of Education, *Theories of Learning,* 63rd Yearbook, Part I. Chicago: University of Chicago Press, 1964.

New Jersey Secondary School Teachers' Association, *Critical Thinking,* 1963 Yearbook. The Association, Lester D. Beers, Treasurer, 1035 Kenyon Avenue, Plainfield, New Jersey.

Parnes, S. and H. Harding (eds.) *A Source Book of Creative Thinking.* New York: Charles Scribner, 1962.

Piaget, J. *The Construction of Reality in the Child.* New York: Basic Books, 1954.

Piaget, J. and B. Inhelder *The Growth of Logical Thinking from Childhood to Adolescence.* New York: Basic Books, 1958.

Project on Instruction, National Education Association, "Education in a Changing Society," *Schools for the 60's* New York: McGraw-Hill Book Company, 1963.

Spence, K. *Behavior Theory and Learning,* Prentice Hall, Englewood Cliffs, N.J., 1960.

Strayer, J. R. "History," *The Social Studies and the Social Sciences,* Turner, G. G. (ed), American Council of Learned Societies and the National Council for the Social Studies. New York: Harcourt, Brace and World, Inc. 1962.

Thorndike, Robert L. and Elizabeth Hagen *Measurement and Evaluation in Psychology and Education* 2nd (ed.). New York: John Wiley, 1961.

Torrance, E. P. *Guiding Creative Talent.* Englewood Cliffs, N. J.: Prentice-Hall Publishers, 1962.

Index

DATE DUE

APR 11 '79			
MAR 6 '81	MAR 6 '81		